POSTCARDS *from* COOKIE

ALSO BY CAROLINE CLARKE

*Take a Lesson: Today's Black Achievers on
How They Made It and What They Learned
Along the Way*

POSTCARDS *from* COOKIE

A MEMOIR *of* MOTHERHOOD, MIRACLES, *and a* WHOLE LOT *of* MAIL

CAROLINE CLARKE

HARPER

www.harpercollins.com

HarperCollins books may be purchased for educational, business, or sales promotional use. For information, please e-mail the Special Markets Department at SPsales@harpercollins.com.

FIRST EDITION

Designed by William Ruoto

Library of Congress Cataloging-in-Publication Data has been applied for.

ISBN: 978-0-06-210317-8

14 15 16 17 18 OV/RRD 10 9 8 7 6 5 4 3 2 1

For Veronica and Carter

Everything comes to us that belongs to us if we
create the capacity to receive it.

—TAGORE

> Mine is not a war story of endless effort. It is a
> story of ease and unearned blessings.
> —ORIAH MOUNTAIN DREAMER

AUTHOR'S NOTE

I grew up listening to my parents and their siblings recount old tales of their own growing-up years. It was always fascinating to hear multiple versions of the same incident told by people who were in exactly the same place at precisely the same time. The debates over whose version was the real one were lively and never ending. And so it goes with the truth; we each have one, each is distinct, and each is real—at least to us.

This is a true story, but it is only my truth. With very few exceptions names, dates, and locations are authentic, as are reproductions of correspondence and images, lyrics, and poems. The rest is drawn from memory—mine and a few generous others'.

Memory is a funny thing. It's a powerful and fallible source that, in the end, makes us who we are.

B.C.
(BEFORE COOKIE)

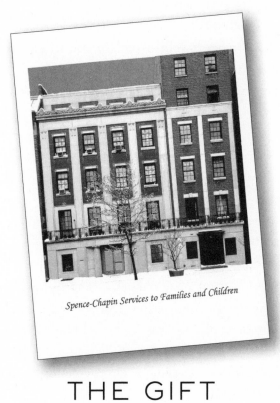

CHAPTER 1

Spence-Chapin Services to Families and Children

THE GIFT

$\mathcal{T}$he February sky is bright, but a rush of wind helps push open the door as I step into the lobby of Spence-Chapin Family Services, the adoption agency to which I essentially owe my life.

It's been thirty-seven years since my parents walked out of this very same building, on another cold winter's day, with me swaddled in a pile of pink blankets, newly their daughter at one month old.

I don't realize it now, as I step from the blustery midday light into Spence-Chapin's timeworn lobby, but my whole world is about to shift again.

I've returned to talk to Amy Burke, who happened to pick up the phone when I called. In response to my request for medical information, she's gone searching through my dusty adoption records and is prepared to share with me whatever the law allows, which I know isn't much.

I was born in an era when adoptions were shameful, secretive, and sealed. Whether you were giving up your baby or getting one—both daunting endeavors—you were urged to forget the whole process the moment it ended and just go live your life. That's exactly what we all did—my parents, me, and, I presume, my birth parents too. But here I am, back, perched in a beat-up pleather chair, waiting for Amy-the-social-worker to tell me what she's found.

I'm not an unhappy adult adoptee longing for clues to my past, dipping my toes into the searchable waters in hopes that a magical current will carry me "home." I already have a home and parents who have always loved me well and with abandon.

"You were given up at birth" is a tough notion to swallow when you're seven years old.

"You're the child we always wished for" made it go down a lot easier.

Knowing I was adopted—that I could have had some other life with some other family in some other place—only made me love and appreciate my parents more. They are not genetically mine, they were *made* mine by God, fate, the universe—take your pick. I've always known I am one lucky girl.

Now happily married with two children of my own, a career in journalism that I love, and too many blessings to count, I'm nonetheless anxious about a small list of health concerns including joint pain in my knees and hips that has been recurring for years. Tests for lupus, rheumatoid arthritis, multiple sclerosis, and assorted other genetically linked ailments repeatedly come up negative. The symptoms always subside but inevitably return, cuing deep self-doubt about the fortitude of my genetic makeup.

My misgivings peak every time a new specialist quizzes me about my parents' and grandparents' health. So does my frustration. Virtually every question they ask yields the same tired response: "I'm adopted. I don't know."

Worried that I might be passing health problems down to my seven-year-old daughter, Veronica, and my son Carter, four, I called Spence-Chapin hoping for a peek into my hidden medical past. Given that I know absolutely nothing about it, even the smallest disclosure would be compelling.

It isn't my first contact with the agency. Five years earlier, I had made a donation in honor of my parents on their fortieth wedding anniversary. It was 1997 and I was already full-grown and a mother myself, but my folks were as devoted to me as ever, and now to my husband and children too. I'd never be able to repay them for all they'd given me; the gift to the agency that gave us to each other was the least I could do.

No sooner did Spence-Chapin receive that check than they were ringing me up, the start of a courting ritual designed to draw me in as a regular donor and participant in their postadoption programs. Having simply been raised as my parents' child, not their *adopted* child, I knew nothing about such things, but I would soon learn that adoption and its potential aftermath had evolved a great deal.

Unlike three dozen years ago, when my parents left the agency with little more than a wave and a wish of good luck,

Spence-Chapin now hosted all sorts of support groups, counseling programs, and regular gatherings to celebrate adoption. It also helped facilitate searches. For adoptees like me, whose records were sealed with tomblike finality, there are national registries where matches can be made if both children and birth parents submit their information. There is also very limited nonidentifying information every adoptee can receive simply by requesting it. This generally includes medical information and skeletal facts, such as physical descriptions of birth parents, or their occupation at the time the child was born.

Initially none of it interested me and I might never have set foot back in Spence-Chapin's converted Upper East Side townhouse if not for my health concerns. My November call to the agency to ask what I had to do to obtain a medical history had been rote. Per simple instructions, I sent in a notarized request, and in mid-January Amy Burke called back with news.

Apparently my birth mother had lived under the agency's care for several months and, as a result, my records were more extensive than most. While information that could identify her or my birth father remained sealed, the agency was at liberty to share nonidentifying medical and personal details at its discretion—in other words, at Amy's discretion. But here's the catch: I have to go get them in person.

Amy cautioned me to make the appointment for a time when I'd be unencumbered afterward. I work. I have two kids. I'm never unencumbered.

"People are sometimes distracted after these meetings," she explained, her voice brimming with concern.

Even without identifying information, whatever is offered "could be a lot to take in," she warned.

Unfazed, I ignored her advice. What could she possibly tell

me that would throw my whole day? But now, sitting in the lobby of this place where my life essentially began, I feel uneasy. As I glance through a photo album of wide-eyed children with their gleeful new parents, unbidden tears suddenly blur the images, causing me to hastily put the book aside, wipe my eyes, and check my watch. It's time to get on with this and get back to work.

Before long I'm ushered into a small room with high ceilings, bare windows, linoleum floors, and two mismatched chairs, left over from another era, facing each other. I've never been in an interrogation room, but something about this place makes me think of one. Maybe it's the sparseness or utter chalk whiteness of it. Either way, I don't like it.

Amy, on the other hand, is a pleasant surprise. After two brief conversations on the phone, I wasn't sure what to expect. Prim and professional, her face melts into a warm smile when she reaches out to shake my hand. The fact that, like me, she's African American and maybe just a few years my senior, helps to put me at ease. This process feels so alien; she is at least somewhat familiar.

She sits, I sit, and mercifully, she seems ready to forgo the formalities.

"I'm sure you're eager to get right to it, so I won't delay," she says, tapping a small stapled stack of papers on her lap. But then the small talk begins.

"Just so you know, I'm a social worker here. I don't facilitate placements; I deal exclusively in what we call the postadoption field. I have both a bachelor's and a master's degree in social work and family counseling." She pauses, smiles expectantly, and when I don't so much as blink, she continues. "I just want to ask one more time if there's anything specific you were hoping to learn today or if you have any concerns or expectations I should be aware of before we start."

"Nope, I'm good," I say, attempting to seem relaxed and ready for anything, although I am suddenly decidedly not.

After our phone conversation a few days ago, I tried to imagine what might be revealed today. The worst possibilities—that my birth mother was raped or was a junkie or had abandoned me or all of the above—had already occurred to me long ago, so I felt fairly confident, prepared for anything.

Now, sitting across from Amy and her stapled stack, I'm no longer sure. Given her demeanor, she's either reading my mind or independently wondering the same thing. In an attempt to reassure us both, I start talking.

"I think I told you when we talked on the phone that I really only called because I want whatever health-related information you might have. This is not the launch of a larger search. I'm grateful for the family I have and know you can't give me any identifying information. That's not what I'm here for . . ."

My mouth is like a broken faucet; I can't shut it off. I hear my voice, taste the words, and know they are my own, yet they sound and feel disembodied and bizarre. Still, I go on.

". . . I'm just tired of not having any answers when doctors ask me about my medical history, so anything you can share with me in that regard will be helpful. But I'm realistic. I don't expect much. I don't expect anything, really. I just . . ."

. . . cannot stop yapping or moving my hands in a way that feels unnatural. Why am I so agitated and uptight? She's not likely to tell me anything I don't already know. Yet here she is with a pile of paper, not the one or two paragraphs I anticipated. She stares at me, thinking God-only-knows-what.

". . . I'm ready," I say, consciously pressing my mouth shut. She smiles politely, as if to say it's about time.

"Well, you'll be pleased to know—at least I hope you'll be

pleased—that I was actually able to gather quite a lot of information on your birth family from our records," she explains. "From it, I compiled this report." She lifts her stack, gives it a little shake, then puts it back down. "I'm going to read it to you, and then we can talk about it, if you'd like."

Finally, she peels back a blank cover sheet to reveal a full page of single-spaced type. I'm shocked to see how much she's written, and miffed that she won't simply hand it to me so I can read it myself, preferably alone back in my office. But I clasp my hands together and hold my tongue.

"I pulled together whatever I thought you might find of interest," she says, seeming oddly excited, as if she's about to give me a gift, or get one. "Of course, you'll get to take a copy home with you."

I like to think of myself as patient, but this preamble is killing me. Why does she insist on reading it aloud like some sort of twisted bedtime story? I imagine her beginning, "Once upon a time, there was a girl . . ." But where would she go from there? I had no idea. *Oh please*, I plead silently, *please start reading.*

"There's some health information here, which you asked for. But there's also quite a bit of what we call social history. That's nonidentifying information that describes your birth family at the time of your adoption. Feel free to stop me at any time if you have questions or if something is not clear."

Stop her? I almost gasp when she says it. How can I stop her when she has yet to begin? I lean forward in my seat hoping that my body language will speak volumes: *Start*, I silently command her with a small thrust of my chin. It works.

"Your birth mother, who was born in 1944, was a single, African American, Episcopalian woman. She was twenty years old at the time of your birth. According to the social record, she was born in the northeastern region of the United States and was raised on both the East and West coasts." The formality of her tone sets all the information at a strange distance. I struggle to draw it close, to be present and really listen, not just hear her.

"She was five foot three inches and 118 pounds, with large brown eyes, a small upturned nose, and a wide, large face with high cheekbones. Her social worker described her as extremely pretty."

It's the first description I've ever had, and it enables me to picture her: petite with big dark eyes in a moon-shaped face.

It's surprising to learn that she's four inches shorter than I am—I'd always imagined us as the same—and there are more revelations to come.

"Your birth mother was adopted." My brain jams. . . .

"She was three years old when her own mother died of tuberculosis. She told her social worker that she remembered going to the hospital to visit each day. She would stand on the lawn, her mother would appear at the window, and they would wave to one another," Amy reads.

I embellish the scene as Amy relays it and envision a tiny brown girl with chubby legs and a short dress, her braided hair tied with ribbons, standing alone on a vast lawn, waving up at the shrunken figure of her dying mother, sequestered and untouchable, in an asylum. Was the child even old enough to comprehend what was happening? Was she told that her mother might never come home, that they might be lost to each other forever? Her mother knew. I want to cry, but don't.

"Not long after her mother died, her father killed himself, leaving her an orphan. Her aunt—her mother's sister—and uncle adopted her."

Amy Burke has barely begun and already I'm struggling to keep up. I feel like that little girl she describes, unsure of what's occurring and unprepared for what's to come.

The report is dense with disjointed information including observations made by my birth mother's caseworker regarding her upbringing ("strict . . . privileged"), demeanor ("articulate and refined"), personality ("colorful . . . dramatic . . . and moody"), and popularity (as "a leading figure with the other residents"), as well as her relationship with my biological father (a "very bright" student with a "great deal of potential" who was nonetheless "too immature to assume responsibility" for the two of us). Her caseworker also divulged my birth mother's misgivings about relinquishing me.

Even given the peculiar setting and this graceless account, my birth mother begins to take on form and depth as never before. The many similarities between us are touching . . . and unnerving: she too was interested in music, loved to ice-skate, read, and dance, and she attended an all-women's college where she majored in English and dreamed of becoming a writer. Her plan, however, was to become an actress.

As ultraprofessional Amy reads her carefully compiled report, I feel increasingly anxious, off-kilter, pissed. I don't know what to feel. I don't want to feel any different from how I always have. I can't believe this is happening. I don't even understand exactly what is happening. Whatever it is, though, I'm hungry for more; at the same time, it's all too much.

I'm riveted by the passages about my birth mother's large nuclear family. She described her mother, the woman who raised her, as beautiful, forty-two years old, five foot seven inches tall, and 120 pounds with a light complexion and dark brown hair and eyes.

"Her mother attended business school after high school, worked as a secretary, and became a professional singer," Amy recounts.

I am five foot seven with a light complexion and dark brown hair and eyes. At twenty pounds more than she weighed, I'm still relatively thin. She must've been tiny. The report also made her—my grandmother!—sound like a bit of a shrew. She was insistent that her oldest child's predicament be dealt with in secrecy, never to be raised again, and distanced herself from the entire episode, never once seeing or calling to speak to her daughter during the months she was in Spence-Chapin's care.

Given the constrictions of the times, this may not have been that unusual. It was also typical of a certain kind of woman, and I know the type. My dad's sister, Beryl, was like this: well educated, well-bred, well coiffed and dressed, and utterly consumed by her social standing, as defined and reinforced by proper-ladies' organizations like The Junior League and its black counterpart, The Links. Witty and lovely to look at, Aunt Beryl was an absolute delight until she didn't get her way, and then, watch out. Beryl was an exceptional woman and a fabulous aunt, but she was also a mother, and not every woman should be.

I felt sorry for my birth mother. Her own biological mother died and her adopted mother may have loved her, but based on what I was hearing, she didn't love her well. I thought of my parents and felt a pang of intense gratitude for them, fused with guilt. What was I doing here? I hadn't even told them I'd contacted Spence-Chapin, much less come here today.

My birth mother's father adored her; she cast their relationship as "loving and close." The report put him at forty-five years old in 1964 and a trim 180 pounds at six foot one inch tall. It said he was a college-educated "show business professional" with a deep brown complexion, brown eyes, and black hair. *Maybe he managed his wife's singing career*, I thought. Described as "affectionate, playful, and fun," he sounded a lot like my own dad.

The family lived on the West Coast (Los Angeles, I presumed, given the show biz connection) but traveled often, not just throughout the States, but also around the world. When her parents were away (which my birth mother stated was often), the children were raised by "the household staff," said to include multiple nannies as well as a chauffeur.

She regaled her social worker with accounts of socializing "with both white and African American girls at boarding school" and being given an extravagant "coming-out party" that all of her friends attended. Clearly Amy Burke had updated the report's language. Nobody said "African American" in 1964. What were we then? Colored? Negro? What had my birth mother actually said? I wondered.

The report described the family's four other children at the time of my birth. There was a "brilliant and musically gifted" fifteen-year-old daughter; a son of around six, who was also adopted; and a set of twin girls, back then considered late-in-life babies, who were giddily celebrating their third Christmas as I was taking my first breath. It's clear that they lived well—extremely well.

Uneasy, I shift in my seat, clear my throat, and open my mouth to say something, but then reconsider.

Amy glances over at me, registers my need to speak, and rests the report in her lap. My face has always been an open book; poker is not my game.

"Are you all right?" she asks. "Do you want me to stop? You look as if you have a question."

"Yes, I have a question," I venture, still unsure of where I'm going. I have lots of questions. I'm starting to suspect that, at the tender age of twenty, my birth mother was already a better actress than anyone gave her credit for.

"Do you have any way of verifying this story? It sounds pretty far-fetched, don't you think? You're painting a picture of very serious wealth here. These are black people. In 1964. Maids, mansions, chauffeurs, prep schools, and debutante balls . . . what are the chances that this is all true?"

Here is where I become especially pleased that Amy is African American, because I can just be frank. "What black people do you know, especially in that era, who lived that well? There were a few handfuls, maybe. I mean, how many white people even lived like that back then? And, if they had all that money, why would I have been given up?" There it is, the crux of my distress.

"*We* didn't do that," I say, pointedly, "we" being the I'm-black-and-I'm-proud we, the Sister-Sledge-singing-*We-Are-Fa-mi-ly* we. "Black people usually kept their children within the family, especially if they could afford it, and if this is to be believed, they *clearly* could afford it. I mean, they had already done it! *They adopted* her, *their niece.*

"They had *babies* in the house when I was born—toddlers. They could have just acted like I was theirs too. I could've been raised as her sister. Isn't that what people did? Isn't that what anyone with the means would do rather than give a child away . . . to *strangers*?"

I'm too loud now and practically spitting my words, but I don't care.

"Black people still do this all the time: we raise cousins, nephews, and nieces as siblings all the time. We raise grandchildren as our own children every day. They didn't even have to raise me; they had a *staff* for that. Given your description of her life, wouldn't that have made more sense?"

My mind and my heart are both racing, and I want to grab Amy Burke by her nonresponsive face and squeeze, but truthfully she's not even the source of my swelling rage. I'm furious with myself for getting drawn into this story only to discover halfway through that it's false, pieced together by a bright young woman with a rich fantasy life who had nothing better to do while she waited for her baby to be born than to spin this very tall tale. My birth mother had obviously made a fool of her own social worker, and now, this Amy had bought into it too and wasted my time. I wanted to wake her up to the truth. Why couldn't she see how outlandish this sounded? Why couldn't she tell when she first read my file? What was the point of her having all those degrees? *What was wrong with her?*

"Everything I'm sharing with you is true," she says, eyeing me with a calm intensity that commands my attention, if not my trust. "Your birth mother spent many hours being interviewed by her social worker. She was assured that the information she shared would be kept confidential, and her background would have been thoroughly checked and verified before she was ever accepted into one of our mothers' homes. I understand why you feel the way you do, but . . ."

I stare back at her with my teeth clenched and lips sealed.

She looks away, frustrated, and then meets my gaze head-on before continuing. "Why don't I go on with my findings? Maybe you'll start to feel differently."

In spite of myself, I want to hear the rest. But I now question the veracity of every detail, and with each one, I grow more incredulous and more angry as well. In fact, I'm starting to fume. Why? Because they gave me away.

Amy waxes on about my birth father, conveying far less detail, and about my birth and adoption. Through it all, I don't say another word. I've shut down, stuck on the fact that, if what I'm hearing is true, a whole family—parents, sisters, a brother, even a dog—with the means to keep me opted out, threw me out, rejected me. My parents had made me feel cherished all my life, and now, for the first time, I felt unwanted. These people had abandoned me, and they had abandoned my birth mother too—at least while we were tethered to each other. I didn't want to know this. I don't want to know this. *What am I supposed to do with this?*

I'm too polite to get up and walk out and too upset to focus on the rest of Amy's incessant monologue. So I pretend to listen, all the while singing song after song in my head—an old self-soothing habit: L *is for the way you look at me,* O *is for . . .* —but every time I hear the word *birth mother* the music stops.

"Before leaving, your birth mother expressed the wish that you would lead a full and happy life," Amy reads. "Your birth mother was unable to say good-bye to her social worker, stating she 'hated good-byes.'"

The room is finally silent. She's done at last.

Abruptly I gather my bag and coat and stand to leave. As I reach the door, Amy jumps up and thrusts a fresh copy of her report at me, blank sheet on top.

"This is yours to keep," she offers. Apparently this is the gift she'd hoped to be presenting, but I haven't responded the way she'd expected, so she too now seems disappointed. "Feel free to call me if you want to talk more about it."

"Thanks," I say, curtly. Then, softening, "Really, thank

you." It's not her fault, I realize. It's not her fault that these people who could have kept me didn't.

The elevator reaches the lobby and I bolt out of it, past the receptionist and through the heavy doors that lead to the street. A deep, hungry gulp of cold air feels as jarring as if it were my first. It releases me from Amy Burke's strange hold and returns me to the world I know.

I move in quick, purposeful strides up East Ninety-fourth Street toward Madison Avenue where my car is parked and feel a warm rush of relief as I pull open the door and toss my coat, my bag, and the report onto the passenger seat. I climb in, close my eyes, and place both hands on the steering wheel, appreciating how solid it is, how dependable and familiar.

"Okay," I whisper to myself. "The car's still here, my life is still intact, nothing has changed."

But it's a lie, and I know it. I walked into Spence-Chapin seeking simple health information, hoping for clues to the source of joint pains that had an impact on my life but didn't fundamentally change it. Now I'd walked out with new knowledge beyond my wildest dreams—none of it quelling my health concerns—and more questions than I've ever had before. Questions require answers. The journalist in me always needs to know more.

I turn the ignition and let the car idle while I call my office to say I'm taking the rest of the day off. Then I call Leeba, our nanny, to let her know I'm coming home and I'll pick Carter up from his playdate on the way. She will have gotten Veronica off the school bus by the time we arrive.

"It's beautiful out," I say to her, my agenda hidden. "You and the kids should walk to the library later."

"No problem," Leeba says, cheerfully.

Some alone time will be key, time to reflect and hopefully calm down. Why am I so tense? It's a lousy feeling and I resent it. I resent the fact that oh-so-cautious Amy was dead-on with her warnings that I oh so flippantly ignored. The information she gave me has shaken me to my core. But it's also awakened something in me that I'm powerless to ignore.

In putting down my phone, I knock the report to the floor. I lean over to retrieve it and can't help myself once it's in my hands: I read it start to finish, surprised to note several details that had blown by me in that cold, stark room. At the time of my birth, my birth mother's dad was ill, with lung cancer. Although she had no family in New York, she had a godmother here. Also, she named me: Gretchen. I smile, delighted that she gave me a name, and that my parents gave me another.

I pull into the flow of traffic, drive two blocks, and stop at a light. My mind is cranking and my reporter skills are kicking in. Methodically, like puzzle pieces, bits of information are beginning to click into place.

I cannot stop thinking about this family—the patchwork of adopted and biological kids, their skinny, uptight mother and supersuccessful dad. I can't stop trying to picture this prominent black family. I know prominent black families. I married into one. My husband, Johnny, fit an enviable profile. The bright, hilarious middle son of black business icon Earl Graves Sr., he was halfway through his final year at Yale Law School when he proposed to me on a starlit carriage ride through the mountains of Vail, Colorado, on New Year's Eve. By then, I had my master's in journalism from Columbia and was cutting my teeth at a highly regarded media company that I knew would train me well for my desired career in magazines. A few years after we got married, when I was ready to change jobs, it seemed only logical that I would ply my trade within the Graves family firm, at the magazine *Black Enterprise*, the premier chronicler of African Americans in business.

I'm not a fledgling anymore; I'm a seasoned information hound, and this is the age of the Internet. How hard could it be to figure out who these people are? Given a few snippets of key information, a decent search engine, and enough time, everyone is findable. Not that it would even require much. With black folks, forget six degrees of separation; we're down to about two on a bad day.

As I turn east at Ninety-sixth Street, *Ebony* magazine springs to mind.

I'll search its archives, I decide, as famous faces of the era start scrolling through my head. Duke Ellington . . . Lena Horne . . . Ella Fitzgerald. *Ebony*, launched in the 1940s as the black answer to *Life* magazine, covered them all. It wouldn't be hard to figure out. The report said her father was tall (not Sammy Davis) and brown skinned (not Harry Belafonte), and his wife was black (not Sydney Poitier). Her mother was a singer. Maybe she was the big moneymaker and he managed her career. Dorothy Dandridge was married to that tap-dancing brother . . . what was his name? Nichols? Nicholas? But they only had one child, not five, and maybe that was before my time. Lena Horne only had one child too and her husband was white, so definitely not Lena. Too bad; Mommy *loved* Lena. . . .

Suddenly, I catch myself. *What am I doing?*

Seriously? Am I *seriously* entertaining being related to *any* of these people? These *stars*? I feel like a fool. Like a complete and utter ass. But as I drive toward home, I can't let it go: the glamorous mother, the musically gifted sister, the big gap between the first child—my birth mother—and the twins, who were so close in age to me, the father who was battling lung cancer when I was born. He was probably a smoker like my dad, although who wasn't in those days? Given the limited treatments back then he probably died. . . .

My mouth goes dry and tears flood my eyes as I hear a frantic voice rising. "Oh my God."

I pull the car screeching to the curb as I realize that the voice is mine. My head is shaking. "No!" I'm now yelling. "No-no-no!" I cup my hands over my mouth to stifle my cries as I struggle to fit the pieces together and, simultaneously, push them away.

I can't be right. This can't be true . . . this can't be happening.

Timolin. Timolin. Timolin. The name of my old college friend rings over and over again in my head. It's her family. I know this family.

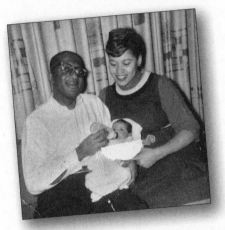

CHAPTER 2

LUCKY ME

$\mathscr{A}$ll adoptees are curious about their beginnings. Anyone who claims otherwise (as I have done many times) is lying.

How can you have no idea about the circumstances of your very existence—who you were born to and what made them decide to give you away—and not care? There's often concern for adoptees who dwell on that mystery. I'm more concerned about those who don't.

From the moment I was told I was adopted, I wondered about my birth mother and nursed a desire to know her. But it was something I kept in check, in part out of fear of what I might discover if I ever found her and in part out of fear of the wreck I might become if I searched and never found her—a possibility that was more likely than any other.

Shortly after we were married, Johnny, who at times seemed way more curious about my origins than I was, discovered a group called ALMA, the Adoptees Liberty Movement Association. Pitching it as a support group for adoptees, he encouraged me to check it out.

"It might be interesting," he said. "It can't hurt."

Being adopted wasn't something I churned over. It was a simple fact, like my gender or shoe size, although it was, without question, more interesting. Sharing the news routinely sparked intrigue and speculation about my mysterious origins. So it was with Johnny, and touched by his effort, I agreed to let him drop me off at an ALMA meeting held in a church in Midtown one Saturday.

It turns out ALMA is a support group for searchers, including birth parents. The first thing I spotted when I walked in was a woman wearing a gigantic button bearing a description of her son who had blue eyes, red hair, and a birthmark behind his left ear. His birth date indicated he'd be thirty-two, and given the wear and tear on that pin, she'd been looking for a long while. Twenty-seven at the time, all I could think was, I don't ever want my mission in life to be that.

In the 1980s, when surprise reunions were the big ratings-grabber on television talk shows, I had a virulent reaction to them. In my mind, the only thing worse than being ambushed on national television by a birth parent would be doing the ambushing. Most upsetting to me was that these spectacles gave adoption a bad name, painting adoptees as broken people who couldn't find peace until they found their birth parents. That wasn't me, and it wasn't any of the adopted people I knew. I believed I was exactly where I belonged. Was my family perfect? Far from it. Did they drive me mad at times? Absolutely, but no more than any family where adoption wasn't in play. We were close. We had our share of upsets, but our foundation was sure. So searching for anything more than I had wasn't a priority. I was curious, but my happiness—my sense of wholeness—didn't hinge upon having that curiosity satisfied.

What made me least inclined to search, though, was my fear of hurting my parents. From the time I was very small, they loved to spin this tale about my grandparents—all dead by the time I was born—picking me out from among all the babies in heaven and sending me down to them, "special delivery on God's most special day." Cloying as it was, I embraced it, clinging to that myth as to a lifeline in a storm at sea. It brought my unknowable grandparents to life and made me a vital part of a loving continuum of family ties. That heaven-sent story informed my entire belief system of life and death, of here and the hereafter, of destiny and self-determination. Even today, long since I've left childhood behind along with so many of its attendant fantasies and lies, I still believe it. Why would I discard something so beautiful? I held tight to it even when everything else I believed to be true fell apart.

$\mathcal{I}$ was nearly eight years old when Mommy sat me down in our living room one day to have "a talk." It was an otherwise typical day. I had gone to the Glenns' house after school and was having a ball with Janice, who was my age, and Jerome and Serona, who were younger. Mildred Glenn was the kind of extraordinary woman who takes in children even though she already has her hands full with her own: in her case, Janice and older sister Joyce. There were the foster kids Jerome and

Serona, and the occasional strays, and the children of mothers like mine who paid Mrs. Glenn to look after their kids until they arrived home from work each day.

Unlike my family's house, which was only-child quiet, the Glenn home was always full of kids and clamor and Mrs. Glenn's great southern cooking. After-school snack meant fried chicken lifted, still crackling, from a cast-iron skillet. Her juicy hamburgers were served on gooey white Wonder Bread, and she made crisp, hot french fries from potatoes that she actually sliced right in front of us. In our house, where convenience was key and cost was less of an issue, fries came frozen in a plastic bag, burgers in proper buns were picked up at McDonald's, and fried chicken arrived in a cardboard bucket with a cartoon-colonel's picture on it. Mommy cooked too, but not like Mrs. Glenn.

Although I wouldn't have minded a little sister, I liked not having siblings. There was no one to compete for my parents' attention or pocket change, no one to rat me out, steal my toys, or kick me when I was down. But it could occasionally be lonely, so I reveled in the after-school playtime at the Glenns', and it seemed that no matter when Mommy showed up to retrieve me, we were in the midst of one game or another that I didn't want to end.

On this particular fall day, Mommy's refusal to extend my visit prompted me to spin out like a speeding car on black ice. As we walked home, I was reckless and out of control.

"You're so mean," I cried. "I hate you!"

It was full-tilt tantrum time. I was usually polite and eager to please. Mommy beamed with pride whenever someone said, "Caroline doesn't seem like an only child," their tone implying that she possessed the secret to raising a pleasant, unspoiled youngster, even though the odds were apparently against it. Still, every child loses it at some point; today was my day.

As I stomped up our block two paces in front of her, I was bristling with a mixture of righteous indignation and fast-brewing confusion. Why wasn't she saying anything? Was she even still back there? I didn't dare turn to check.

"I wish you weren't my mother," I pressed on, emboldened by her silence. "You're probably not my real mother. My *real* mother would have let me stay and have fun."

With every step, I half expected her to grab my collar, yank me back, and yell me into a state of sobbing submission. I was raised better, I knew better; but I had lost my mind, and maybe she had too, because there was no snatch-back. She didn't jump in my face and give me "the look"—her brown eyes wide and bright teeth bared in that way that made me nearly pee myself—and that I frankly knew I deserved. Inexplicably, she did nothing.

By the time we reached our house, I was as spent and anxious as she was mute. It occurred to me that her wrath was going to be so outsize she was waiting until we were inside. Mommy had class; she might give you "the look" or a discreet pinch in public, but she did not go off in the street. As I watched her close the front door behind us, leaving the sun outside, I had the sinking feeling that I might never see Janice Glenn—or daylight—again.

I braced myself for the explosion, but it didn't come. Instead Mommy sat down on the couch and motioned for me to sit beside her. Her demeanor was gentle, solicitous even, when she put her arm around my narrow shoulders, pulled me close, and said, "Sugar, I have something to tell you. You are adopted."

Three words—just three—and my whole world came

crashing in on itself. The tears sprang to my eyes before the words had even finished tumbling from her mouth.

I thought back to just a few months earlier when I went for a checkup and my pediatrician, Dr. Carter, tapped my knee with that little mallet. I was ready for it, fully expecting it, and determined not to respond. During the entire walk to her office, I had pictured myself sitting on her examination table, on top of the crunchy white paper, my bent legs hanging over the side, frozen, while she tapped and tapped, baffled by my complete lack of reflexes. I was sure it was a simple test of wills, and I was going to win. But no sooner had her mallet touched my skin than my foot jerked upward. Try as I might I couldn't control it, couldn't slow the processes in my brain enough to prevent the inevitable from happening. And so it was now.

I heard the word *adopted* and suddenly my face was drenched and I felt as if I were alone on a train that was hurtling out of a station, down a steep incline, into the dark, with no brakes, no driver, and no other passengers, destination unknown. It was terrifying.

Adopted. I wasn't even entirely sure what it meant, but my gut told me it meant I wasn't hers. She wasn't mine. The most basic things I thought to be true about myself were suddenly, irrevocably, not.

Mommy was explaining how much I was wanted and loved and longed for as my head spun with questions, sorrow, regret, and the hope that I'd wake up and find this was all an awful dream. *How could this be? Why had I said the hateful, crazy things I'd said to her? If only I wasn't such a brat, if only I'd been able to play longer at Janice's house, none of this would be happening.*

Mommy was going on about how she and Daddy came

to find me. She wasn't able to bear children, so they went to Spence-Chapin, an agency in Manhattan where some of their friends had adopted. They wanted a girl and were well into the process when they ran into their social worker at a memorial service for three civil rights workers who'd been murdered in the South.

James Chaney, Andrew Goodman, and Michael Schwerner were young and determined when they showed up in a small Mississippi town to help register blacks to vote in the summer of 1964. Freedom Summer it was called, with all the optimism and naïveté of the small army of volunteers of which they were a part. But the three young men—Chaney was black, the other two were Jewish, and all were barely old enough to vote themselves—were intercepted by members of the Ku Klux Klan who beat and then shot them, slaughtering all three.

My parents didn't know these young men, but when they heard about a planned memorial service in Manhattan, they went. Whenever he told the story, Daddy, who had taken a bus from New York to Washington, D.C., the previous summer to stand in the baking sun on the National Mall as Martin Luther King Jr. delivered his I Have a Dream speech, insisted, "If those boys could go to Mississippi for us, the least we could do was go to that service for them."

My parents didn't know that their Spence-Chapin social worker was a close friend of the Schwerners. After the service, when she spotted Mommy and Daddy in the crowd outside the Ethical Culture Center, she went over to greet them. They explained why they'd come, and invited her to join them for coffee at a nearby shop. She did, and after they said their good-byes, Mommy said she and Daddy looked at each other and just knew that this woman was going to find them the best baby she could.

"And she did," said Mommy, looking straight into my eyes.

I didn't understand everything she was saying. It was a lot to follow, too much to take in, but then she said, "She found us you, a healthy baby girl born on Christmas Day.

"The best Christmas present we ever got," she added, as she had many times before, when my assumption was that they "got" me out of her womb, not from some social worker with a link to a principled and idealistic kid who was killed by the KKK. Only now she was explaining that they hadn't actually gotten me on Christmas at all. It wasn't until a full month later, on January 29, that I came home with them to our semi-attached three-bedroom house in the Bronx. I started to cry again, devastated and grateful all at once.

"Your mother loved you very much," Mommy was saying as she hugged me to her chest and rubbed my back.

I stopped crying and pulled away to look at her, dumb-founded. My "*mother*"? Her words hit me like a brick, toppling my reality once and for all. *I was not born into this family. I am not who I thought I was. My mother gave me away. My* other *mother.*

"Do you know her?" I asked, gripped by the possibility and simultaneously afraid to know more, overwhelmed by raw curiosity and grief, unable to organize my reeling thoughts.

Mommy's eyes widened in pained surprise, but she rallied quickly.

"No, sugar," she said gently, proceeding to share everything she knew about my birth mother, which wasn't much, and she knew even less about my birth father. I listened, intent on every word.

"She was young. She was a college student. So was your father. She was from out west, I think. Lots of families sent girls who got pregnant to other cities to have their babies. This way, no one at home would know what happened. Their reputations would be protected."

Mommy didn't have to explain beyond that. Just shy of eight, I already knew what the world thought of girls who got pregnant before marriage, and I knew it had been even worse back when I was born.

"We never met her. It wasn't allowed. But we were told she was a wonderful person—smart and kind—and I know she loved you very much because she wouldn't sign the papers letting you go until she was certain that they'd found just the right family for you. Only when she was sure of that did she let you go."

As I heard those words, the cynic in me was born. *She loved me so much, she gave me away.* As a child who was told I was loved every day by people who were there to show and say it, I silently wondered, *What kind of love is that?*

Then another thought flashed into my head.

"She was black," Mommy continued, as if reading my mind. "Your parents and grandparents were all black and they all went to college. They told us that your mother's mother was half American Indian, so you are part American Indian."

She said this as if it should be a point of great pride—black people love to claim they have some Native American blood. Or perhaps she thought it would help explain a few things, like my long, "good" hair and the fact that I could stroll through almost any of New York's countless ethnic neighborhoods— Dominican, Puerto Rican, Indian, Pakistani, Ethiopian, Egyptian, Brazilian, you name it—and, like a chameleon, blend in.

What I didn't resemble at all was my parents, and I knew it. Even when I was very small, I would search our faces for some similarity, and I always came up wanting. But my folks looked so different from each other, I had convinced myself that it was possible to mix the two—Mommy's cherubic roundness with Daddy's lean frame, her café-au-lait complexion with his dark chocolate—and get caramel-colored, oval-faced, skinny me.

Now it made sense, even if it made me uneasy. But I was black: knowing that for certain was a big deal. I was raised on black music, black poetry, taglines like black-is-beautiful, and Golden Legacy comic books, which brilliantly depicted the lives of famous trailblazers in black history. My heroes and heroines were black. My aunts and uncles were black. Most important, my parents were black. So it was a critical detail that we still had that in common, and it gave me something to hang onto—a fundamental piece of my identity to carry over the threshold from not knowing I was adopted to knowing, from having a solid sense of who I was to suddenly being deeply unsure.

It would take years to fully work through, but it only took an instant to accept. Children are amazing in that way. They adapt and move on.

As Mommy hugged me for the umpteenth time, she said that if I ever wanted to talk about my feelings or learn more about my background, she and Daddy would be there for me.

"Just remember how much we love you, how much we wanted you, and how happy we are that you're our daughter," she said. These were things I had always known, and in her way, she was insisting—perhaps she even believed—that nothing had changed. I smiled, weakly, to reassure her. But I knew it wasn't true.

We rarely talked about my being adopted after that day, which is not to say that it wasn't frequently on my mind. Although my parents left the door open for discussion, they almost never brought it up. Mommy had shared all they knew about my beginnings, and I accepted the fact that any other information was locked away in a dusty file in some courthouse basement, unavailable to anyone, least of all to me. What I did have, though, was enough.

Through every bump in the road that I dragged them across—adolescent insolence, teenage rebellion, bad grades, horny boyfriends, even an overnight stay in a Savannah, Georgia, jail cell for shoplifting—my parents were, as Mommy had promised, always there for me. And despite my occasional lapses in judgment and behavior, I wanted nothing more than to live up to that ideal of being their "greatest Christmas present ever."

Consequently I didn't ask about my biological parents. I almost never even thought of a father figure other than my dad. Adopted children—including boys—rarely do. I assumed he was long gone before I arrived. It was possible that he never even knew my birth mother was pregnant. But *she* knew, and I couldn't shake thoughts of her, the young mystery woman who carried me, gave birth to me, then gave me away.

From the moment I learned she existed, there was so much more I longed to know. What did she look like? How old was she? What did she do? Did she like to sing, as I did? Did she like to dance and skate? Was she lighthearted and fun, or solitary and dull? Did she have a big family? Live in a nice place? Did she think of me? Miss me? Did she regret giving me up, or giving birth to me at all?

I looked for her on the street, on buses and planes, in magazine ads and on television every Saturday morning. Was that her in the striped bell-bottoms and red platform shoes doing the bump by the *Soul Train* scramble board? Or maybe that was her, swaying in the sequined tube top, her baby hair slicked down around her temples, the rest pulled up into a towering cone-shaped bun.

When Irene Cara starred in the movie *Sparkle*, I was sure we were related. In fact, I'd first spotted the actress on *The Electric Company*, captivated by the fact that we had the same complexion and similar hair. Too young to be my mother, maybe she was a cousin.

My folks were older than those of my peers by about ten years, which automatically made them less cool than the parents of most of my neighborhood friends. It didn't help that they were stricter, better educated, more exacting in their standards, and thoroughly involved in my life. They were teachers, for God's sake. Nothing's less cool to a kid than that. My birth mother became their opposite, a composite of the mom I wanted to someday be and everything Mommy wasn't: young, funny, hip, permissive.

When I thought of her, cried for her, longed for her, I hid and kept it to myself. I imagined us literally bumping into each other on the sidewalk one day, each instantly recognizing the other. I secretly nursed a deep curiosity that triggered vibrant fantasies of kind, gorgeous women living ultracool lives marked by success, glamour, and at least one day a year, regret.

It was impossible not to indulge in a tiny, private pity party on my birthday. She had to remember; how could you give birth at 3:40 P.M., smack in the middle of Christmas Day, and forget? My secret hope was that each year she endured an entire season of remembering. That for every wreath she hung and Salvation Army Santa she saw and Christmas carol she heard being piped through a department store, there was a pang of sorrow, of heartache, of longing, of whatever I felt at any given moment in reverse—and multiplied by infinity. I didn't want her to suffer (at least, not much); I just wanted her to care.

At some point after my parents and I opened our presents by

our twinkling, artificial tree each year, I would steal up to my room, and as Nat King Cole's "The Christmas Song" played on the stereo downstairs, I'd allow myself to imagine for a moment some other life in some other place as I quietly sang another heart-rending song of his written by Charlie Chaplin called "Smile." Music was my balm for every hurt. People could fail you, but music never did. My dad taught me that.

My father never played an instrument or sang a note beyond goofing around, but he was passionate about music, and he'd passed his passion on to me. Nat, or "the King," as Daddy called him, was one of my father's favorites on a short list that included Billie (Holiday), Ella (Fitzgerald), Duke (Ellington), Miles (Davis), Jimmy (Lunceford), and a few others whom I came to love too. "Listen to his diction," Daddy would say, closing his eyes to savor Cole's rare elegance as he mouthed each masterfully formed syllable in sync with his idol. "Do you hear that, Lumpty? How he enunciates every word? Nobody else does that. Nobody."

It was true. Cole had a lush, distinctive sound that was captivating, and I came to know every lyric, every velvety voiced inflection and nuance in the accompaniments to nearly every one of his most famous songs and a few of the lesser ones too.

In junior high and high school, when no one else was home, I'd perform in our living room, singing into my hairbrush or the little microphone I'd detach from Daddy's cassette tape recorder. Cranking up the volume on his prized Fisher stereo, I'd imagine myself singing backup for Marvin Gaye, Minnie Riperton, Angela Bofill, and Phyllis Hyman; playing percussion for Stevie Wonder and horns with Earth, Wind & Fire; and singing in duet with Nat King Cole, on a big stage in a huge concert hall to an audience of one: my birth mother. It was a pitiful bit of private theater, performed far more frequently than I should ever admit.

There were times I was angry with my birth mother and times I felt sorry for her. There were stretches of time when I didn't think of her at all. But she always reentered my thoughts eventually, and always with the hope that one day the mystery of who she was and why she left me would be solved.

I didn't want to search for her. I just wanted to magically discover her. A fan of fairy tales as a young girl, long past the age when I shouldn't have been, I believed one day we'd joyfully reunite and live happily ever after.

In high school I moved on from reading stories to writing my own, pouring my heart out to her in poems that both bemoaned her loss and cursed her for not being there for me. Those were the bitter years when I stopped romanticizing her existence, accepting the likelihood that she'd been a down-on-her-luck teenage mother who'd become an out-of-luck woman with too many kids in a too-small apartment marking time in a dull life. So bleak was the fate I imagined for her, I sometimes felt guilty for having been spared.

During my college years, I let her go. Finally, it seemed, the grieving was over. I barely even thought of her on my birthday anymore. I'd begun to have my own life, and she wasn't a part of it. As I became more independent from the parents who raised me, who loved me not just unconditionally but well, I also let go of the parents I'd never known and whatever desire I had to meet them. It's the truest expression there is: life goes on.

Then one Thursday in February 2002, my life turned inside out again, just as it had when Mommy told me I was adopted almost thirty years earlier. As I slowly metabolize the Spence report, it dawns on me: I *know* my birth family.

CHAPTER 3

TELLING

$\mathcal{T}$here are moments in life that you envision. Winning the lottery; meeting the love of your life; cradling your newborn child for the first time; and, if you're adopted, discovering your birth parents. I had occasionally dared to imagine this moment. I had never imagined it would be like this.

As I finally steer my car toward home, I feel shaken, disoriented. A tangle of potent conflicting feelings—gratitude and terror, wonder and disbelief, elation and anxiety—wage battle within me. The fundamental normalcy of my life has been jarred loose, and my need to maintain it kicks in. For even as I struggle to process not only who my birth mother is, but also that I've known her family most of my days, my children still need tending, dinner still has to be made, my regular life is calling.

I retrieve Carter from his friend's house, and we arrive home to find Nica already there, bursting with an account of her busy day in second grade. After the kids devour their pizza bagels and juice, I kiss them good-bye, and hand in hand with Leeba, they stroll off toward the children's library around the corner as I head outside to my home office, a small room off our detached garage.

Once inside, I lose it, sobbing as if I've lost something precious and irreplaceable, instead of having been handed the key that unlocks my hidden past. Hunched over my desk, I cry with abandon, the way folks do in churches when they believe they've been touched by the Holy Ghost. I know there are people who don't believe in luck or fate, karma or destiny, Jesus, Allah, God, or a Higher Power of any kind. I don't know how they get through the day. I believe in it all, so my response isn't merely emotional, it's spiritual. A miracle: that's what this is.

The phone rings, nudging me to compose myself. It's Johnny, calling to talk to the kids. He's in Nashville on business and is surprised to find me home so early. He doesn't even know I contacted Spence-Chapin. As with my parents, I hadn't bothered to tell him, assuming so little would come of it there was no point. Now, there is so much I want to say, but I'm too overcome. Besides, this is not something to discuss over the phone. So I beg off quickly and promise to call back when the kids return.

Having to keep the news from Johnny makes me yearn to talk to someone. I dial Charise, who lives just up the street. Charise; her husband, Michael; and their children are bosom buddies with me and mine. Our two families, each with two kids, run between our two houses all day every day, sharing meals, opinions, secrets, and advice, watching movies together, taking trips together, making memories we'll never forget.

"Are you busy?" I ask as soon as she says hi. "Can I come over?" Despite trying not to, I sound anxious.

"Sure," she says. "Is everything okay?"

"I just want to run something by you."

When I arrive, she gives me a hug that I realize I need badly. We sit facing each other at her kitchen counter, each with a fresh mug of tea. She looks at me expectantly and waits. Charise is a social worker, as skilled and compassionate as they come. Enormous patience is one of her gifts.

"I had an interesting day," I start, not sure about where or how to begin. "I haven't told anyone. It's so bizarre." I veer off, wondering if I should sleep on it and let Johnny be the first to know. But there's no way I can wait. I'm ready to burst.

She furrows her brow but says nothing.

"I found out today who my birth mother is."

Charise's eyes grow wide. "You *what*?"

"It turns out I know her family. I've been friends with her sister for twenty years."

I retell the whole story as Charise listens with stunned attentiveness. She is an adoptive mother herself, so I know my news will have its own complicated significance for her, but I can't not share it, and it quickly becomes clear that she is the perfect person to tell. Seamlessly fusing her natural instincts with her professional training, she asks questions that help me dissect all of the information as well as start the process of discerning my feelings, intentions, and hopes.

Through our conversation, I realize I need to call my friend Timmie to get information, but I can't reveal to her what's happened until after I talk to the woman I believe is my mother,

her sister. I've no idea how to proceed from there, but at least I'm clear about that much.

Charise also helps me deal with the eventuality of telling my parents. *How will they take all of this?* Just thinking about it makes me queasy. *What if they think I went looking for her? What if they feel hurt or threatened?* I need to find a way to avoid this at all costs. *And what will Johnny think?*

Johnny and I first met as children in Sag Harbor, a summer enclave for our families. He is the only person who ever admitted to me that he believed I was adopted the moment he first saw me and my parents together. He claimed it was actually his mother who pointed out the glaring dissimilarity between us and said, "She must be adopted." It had never occurred to me that anyone would make that sort of leap when simply seeing my family.

Charise knew all too well the fun Johnny had with the few facts about me we knew for sure. Whenever someone would comment on my having a Christmas birthday, he'd balk: "Look, I'm sure she was born sometime in late December, but *Christmas day?* Give me a break. What better way to get a poor little baby a home than to say she was born on Christmas? People eat that stuff up—*her* parents did!" He'd said it so often, on occasion, I wondered myself.

After talking myself dry at Charise's, I walk home, feed and bathe my children, read stories, tuck them in, sing, say prayers, and kiss them good night. Moving through our bedtime rituals, I'm completely distracted and almost light-headed with exhaustion. I can't wait to fall into bed and sleep. But once there, without Johnny to talk to, to hold and soothe me, I feel jittery and wide awake. So I read the report over and over, eventually falling asleep with the light on and my hand still clutching it. Practically memorized, it plays through the night, a sound track for new dreams.

I awake with a plan that I put into action as soon as the kids are off to school. Alone in my home office, I dial Timolin's phone number. She answers on the second ring.

"Timmie, it's me," I say, sure she'll recognize my voice. "What's going on?"

"Honey! Oh, I'm so glad it's you," she exclaims, causing me to smile.

Timmie is one of the few people I know who use pet names almost all the time. In college, she worked hard to fit in, but she'd grown up with a level of privilege that put her a cut above even the so-called privileged kids, and it was impossible to hide. She dressed better than the rest of us, her cinder-block dorm room was beautifully appointed, and she and her twin sister drove twin BMWs—new ones. From our very first meeting, when I was a high school senior checking out Smith College (my first choice), and the four other options in Massachusetts's Pioneer Valley, Timmie was kind, caring, and eager to please, but something about her manner could at times seem affected. She had a sort of golden Hollywood vibe that was out of sync with our age group and environs. She was the only person who could greet me by saying, "That dress is *just darling*. You look *absolutely adorable*," and be serious. She was the only person I knew who even would.

Timmie was two years ahead of me at Amherst College, where our boyfriends introduced us. Everyone knew her because, thanks to her late father, she had a famous name. She also had a much older sister who was adopted, a brother who was adopted, and two biological sisters, including her twin—just as the Spence-Chapin report described. Their mother, whom I'd met, also mirrored the report's description, physically and otherwise.

Over the phone, I only half-listen as Timmie recounts entertaining stories from her mother's annual holiday visit. I am sure of it: Timmie's family is my biological family.

It hit me like a bolt of electricity as I drove away from Spence-Chapin the day before. As Tim prattles on about the latest in her life, I am drawn back to the scene, still vivid in my mind: sitting in my car, curbside, rereading the report; gripped by emotion, trying to make sense of it all; checking each word on the page against each fact in my head as the truth emerged and became undeniably clear. My initial reaction had been to question it, even push it away. Things like this didn't happen in real life, at least not to me. Reeling from the sheer idea of it, I panicked at first, thinking, What if I'm wrong? Then I remembered: Amy Burke. Desperate for confirmation, I picked up the phone and called her.

"Hello, Spence-Chapin."

"Yes, hello. Amy?"

"Yes . . ."

"Amy, this is Caroline Clarke."

"Oh, yes. Is everything all right?"

"Listen, I know you can't give me identifying information and I don't want to put you in a compromising position, so I'm just going to tell you a story and you can tell me if it makes sense or not. Okay?" My heart was pounding.

"I'll try," she said, cautiously.

"I've had a friend for twenty years. Her name is Timolin Cole, and she has a twin sister named Casey; they're three years older than me. She has a deceased brother, Kelly, who was adopted, and another biological sister, who is the singer Natalie Cole. Her oldest sister was also adopted. Her mother, Maria, had been a singer but gave up singing to travel with her father, who died of lung cancer when she was very young. Timolin's father was Nat King Cole." Now my voice was shaking.

"Is this just an outrageous set of coincidences, or do I now know who my birth mother is?"

"I'm sorry," I heard her say. She didn't even pause to think about it. My heart sank. "I can't tell you any more than I already have. It's policy. I hope you understand."

I instantly regretted calling her. Of course she couldn't tell me. She'd probably told me too much already. She was probably regretful as well.

"I understand," I said, my tone flat and beaten. "Thank you anyway."

"You're welcome."

I was about to press end when I heard her say, "I would just encourage you to follow up on whatever you may be feeling. Good-bye."

She hung up before I could respond. I stared at the phone: ". . . follow up on whatever you may be feeling . . ." My heart picked up speed, pounding so hard it reverberated throughout my whole body as I allowed myself to fully take it in. *Nat King Cole is my grandfather. My girlfriend Timolin is my aunt. I am her sister Carole's daughter.*

"Hon, did you hear me? Are you there?" The slight agitation in Timmie's childlike voice jars me back to the present.

"Yes, I'm here," I say, embarrassed and now uneasy. *How will I do this?*

We catch each other up on our kids (her sons Julian and Justin are similar in age to my children), husbands, and parents. Timmie always carefully guarded her privacy, but after I married Johnny, she became much more open, frequently confiding details of her family's complicated ongoing saga. She also expressed great curiosity about my in-laws, seemingly eager to compare notes on how wealthy parents managed their relationships—and money—with their adult children.

Her mother, Maria, routinely wielded access to her children's inheritance from their father as both carrot and stick, sparking resentment and major family discord. Timmie appeared to have more success in managing her relationship with Maria than any of her siblings, but the strain associated with the effort was often apparent.

I ask about her twin, Casey, who is still recovering from the sudden death of her husband, Kevin, a few years earlier. I also inquire about her famous sister Natalie who, I saw on television, had recently remarried. Then I try to sound casual as I ask, "How about your other sister? What's her name again? Have you seen her lately?"

"Who, Cookie, I mean, Carole? I haven't seen her, but we talk. She's fine." Timmie changes the subject as I fixate on the name: Carole. So like mine. Carole Cole. Initials CC, just like me.

In our twenty years of friendship, all I knew about Carole, who Timmie always referred to as Cookie (Natalie was called Sweetie; their family was big on nicknames), was that she ran King Cole Productions, the family firm that oversaw the rights to Nat's music. I never asked about Carole because she and Timmie were not close. Casey and Timmie were a pair; Carole and Natalie were a pair; Kelly bounced between them, plaything-little-brother to one set, admired big brother to the other. They were all devastated when, in 1995 at the age of thirty-six, he died of AIDS.

Back when their father passed away, the twins were barely three. Maria remarried and moved the family east to her home state, Massachusetts, where, by then, Natalie was in college. Natalie would never live at home again, and Carole, at twenty-four, was already out on her own. So it wasn't merely the gap in the girls' ages that divided them. Carole and her baby sisters had grown up in distinct times, distinct places, and distinct families in a sense. The clan rarely came together even now, and when they did, according to Timmie, their interactions were strained. It was a family completely unlike my own.

If it feels odd to suddenly bring Carole up, Timmie seems none the wiser, and she doesn't hesitate to give me Carole's phone number after I mention that I need subjects for a *Black Enterprise* article on women who run their family businesses.

"I want to be able to give the writer a few leads," I tell her. "It's best not to tip your sister off so she won't be disappointed if it doesn't pan out," I advise. "I'll call you first if the writer's going to pursue her," I promise.

Why all the lies? Why not just say, "Guess what? You're my aunt!" Because it's odd, and awkward, and there is every possibility that Timmie, who is eighteen years Carole's junior, has no idea that her big sister was pregnant at nineteen and gave a child away. After all, secrecy wasn't merely the standard for adoption back then; it was the whole point.

I also knew enough about Maria Cole to know that she guarded her image, her money, and her family's privacy with fierceness in the extreme. Between the few family secrets Timmie shared with me through the years and what the Spence report revealed, I expect that Maria never told a soul—not even her other children—about her first child's regrettable slip and I am not about to begin a relationship with my birth mother by outing her.

Our conversation winds down naturally, as talks between old friends do, as if nothing has changed, as if I have not even a hunch that we are related, that given a small twist of fate, we might have been raised side by side under the same roof as a family.

*J*ohnny arrives home from Nashville, but it's hours before I get him alone. Finally, once the kids are asleep and we're in bed, I pour my heart out, telling him all about my appointment at Spence-Chapin and what I'd been told. It's one of the few times in his life when he listens without interrupting. Then I hand him the report so he can take it all in himself.

He hugs me tightly after he reads it, and still, he appears at a loss for what to say. "How do you feel?" he asks, tentatively.

"There's more," I reply.

"What do you mean, 'There's more'?"

"I know who she is."

"Who, your mother?" His eyes are wide with amazement.

I nod and say, "I figured it out. You can too, just think about it."

"Think about *what*?" he says, impatient already.

"Think about what the report says. Think about the details about the family." I repeat the few facts given about my birth mother's father, his profession, his children, his illness.

Johnny nails it on the first guess: "Nat King Cole." He was a favorite of my in-laws too. Their first dance as newlyweds was to his tender ballad "When I Fall in Love."

Grinning, I nod, amused by the look of utter astonishment on his face. Telling Johnny is fun.

"Nat King Cole was your *father*?"

"No," I say, exasperated. "He was *her* father, my . . ." I can't say it, can't claim it. It feels too strange, presumptuous, unreal. Johnny finishes for me.

". . . grandfather. He's your grandfather! So, who's your mother? Natalie? But she's not adopted."

We talk for an hour as I clarify everything I know so far. Johnny asks more questions than I can answer, making me realize that there is still so much I don't yet know.

I ask him not to tell anyone, not even his parents. He agrees to keep my confidence, but I know the clock is ticking on his ability to do so. He probably realizes this himself as he begins a steady campaign of nudging me to take the next steps, starting with telling my parents. Nothing else can happen until I do. But just the thought of it makes my stomach churn.

My folks had been flattered by my donation to Spence-Chapin in their honor a few years before, but they'd also seemed mystified by it.

"What in the world made you do that?" I recalled Mommy asking. "We don't have any connection there—I mean, not in so many years."

It wasn't Mommy's way to go on at length, but she was clearly thrown by my having reached out to the agency. So I am justifiably worried about how they will respond to my news, and I promise myself that if they are the least bit disappointed, anxious, or ambivalent about it, I'll just stick my report in a drawer and leave the whole thing alone.

A week's worth of Johnny's rock-solid assurances that my parents will be fine eventually wins me over. He even questions whether they might have known some or all of the truth from the start. I'm confident that they didn't and that the report will hold as many surprises for them as for me. I call their house on a Saturday morning and say I want to stop by to talk.

"Sure," says Mommy, unfazed as always.

We sit down in their dining room, at the same mahogany table where we'd eaten together; played Candy Land, Battleship, and Boggle together; watched TV together; and decoded my toughest homework assignments together. Daddy's music plays in the background—Tony Bennett, Patti Austen and James Ingram—filling the space with a familiar aura that wraps around me like a blanket.

Their harvest gold rotary wall phone sits on a corner of the table, its tangle of curly wire wrapped tightly around it, as if to contain it from jumping up to overtake its touch-tone replacement and regain its rightful place. Given my parents' distaste for change and for disposing of things that are "perfectly good" even if completely outmoded, I know that this phone will probably sit there for the next month before one of them quietly spirits it away to a donation bin, or I do. They will never simply throw it out.

Even with their new phone and answering machine, Mommy still refuses to get call-waiting, insisting that it's "just rude" to interrupt one call to answer another.

"If someone wants to talk to me, they'll call back," she says when I complain that theirs is the only number in America that still triggers a busy signal. "If they don't, it wasn't important to begin with."

I scan the living room with its decades-old Roche Bobois furniture in late 1960s earth tones. An abacus I made in eighth grade shop class hangs on a wall beneath a West African mask. The house has barely changed since I moved out a dozen years ago. They have barely changed. With a pang I think, *Please don't let this change us.*

I start out by telling them that I'd gone back to Spence-Chapin seeking health information, nothing more. I'd been stunned when this social worker presented me with seven pages of details about my birth family and I thought they might be interested in hearing it. They are surprised, and delighted.

So, I start reading aloud, just as Amy did. No sooner do I begin than Mommy starts interjecting with lively comments.

"I didn't know she was Episcopalian like us," she says. "Isn't that something, Bob? . . . Yes, I remember that. I knew she was short. . . . What? She was adopted? No one ever told us that."

She goes on like this throughout. Daddy dabs at his eyes and leans over and kisses me when I reach the part about my birth. When I read, "On January 29, 1965, you began living with your parents . . ." he jumps out of his chair and starts cheering like he's at a Knicks game. He runs over and hugs Mommy, saying, "That's you and me, Vera Clarkeee. They're talking about our family!"

She giggles and blushes while scolding him. "Come on, Robbie. Stop it. Let her finish."

One more paragraph and I am done. I look up and am relieved: they are both grinning.

"So, what do you think?" I ask, knowing they think I'm finished when I've barely begun.

"It just confirms what we always knew," says Daddy, with a proud pout. "You come from good stock, and you were always loved. But nobody loves you as much as we do. Right, Vera Clarke?" He jumps up and hugs her again.

"Right," she says, blowing me a kiss across the table. "I think it's wonderful, sugar. I'm so happy you have this. Now you know so much more about where you come from, and so do we." She gives Daddy's hand a little squeeze.

"There's more," I say. The words are out of my mouth before I think. Everything is going so well, I might as well keep it going.

"More?" Mommy asks. Daddy searches my face for clues. Suddenly sober, he sits back down. "What else?"

"I know the family, and so do you, sort of."

"*What?*" Mommy exclaims, snapping that *t* at the end especially hard. "We *know* them? Who is it?"

Daddy looks stricken. This news definitely shifts the mood. Nervous, but still excited, I forge on.

"You can figure it out. Think about the family described in the report. That's how I figured it out. Her father was in show business, obviously very successful. He was tall, thin, brown skinned, and he was sick when I was born, with lung cancer."

Mommy is not even trying to guess. She just keeps repeating, like a bad owl impression, "Who? Who?" But Daddy is silently folding the details over in his mind as he narrows his eyes and intently studies my face.

"Come on, Daddy," I urge him. "Think about it. You *know* this."

Mommy turns to him, her tolerance for this game running thin. Her tone is almost accusatory when she asks, "You *know*, Bob? Who is it?" Daddy still says nothing.

"They had several children," I repeat, "including twins, close to my age . . . show business . . . he's one of your favorites, Daddy . . . he died right after I was born . . . cancer."

Daddy's eyes spring wide. "Not . . ."

"Who?" says Mommy, growing shrill. "Who is it?"

We ignore her. My eyes are locked with Daddy's. I am nodding my head, trying to will him to say it.

"King Cole?" he mouths, his voice barely a whisper.

"What?" Mommy shrieks, leaning in to hear him more clearly. "Who did you say?"

Daddy is smiling now but his eyes are wet. "Nat King Cole?" he repeats, audibly this time. I nod as Mommy sinks back into her chair, dumbfounded.

"My birth mother is Timolin's sister, Carole, Nat King Cole's oldest child."

Daddy takes off his glasses and wipes his eyes with a paper napkin. The older he gets, the more sentimental he's become. It started about ten years ago, around the time Johnny and I got married. Mommy and I kept warning Daddy to steel himself against crying as he walked me down the aisle. As my wedding day approached, it looked like a lost cause. He was apt to weep at anything, from sappy telephone company commercials to the mere sight of me brushing my teeth. Mommy would look at him and just shake her head. But when the big day arrived, he was as dashing and composed as could be.

The main aisle in Manhattan's storied Riverside Church is long enough to land a small plane, but we were both smiling and calm when the organ trumpeted our entrance and three hundred people turned to face us. My arm resting safely in his, we chatted with each other all the way up that aisle, laughing when the train of my billowy ivory gown was stepped on, stopping us dead in our tracks—twice—even as everyone else including Johnny gasped. But as we neared the altar, we heard sobbing. Not just delicate sniffling, but full-out bawling. It was Mommy, in pieces, soaking the top of her burgundy velvet dress.

Now they have reverted to their usual roles. He is emotional and she is solid as a rock. Together they strike the perfect balance, and despite the shock, they seem to be enjoying this moment of discovery. If they feel threatened or concerned, it doesn't show. I am flooded with gratitude, and relief.

Daddy leaves the house for a while, claiming he needs a smoke. We know that's code for I've-reached-my-limit-and-I-have-to-get-out-of-here-for-a-spell. While he's gone, I ask Mommy what she thinks I should do now.

"Write to her," she says. "I'm sure she'll be happy to hear from you. Or maybe you can call Timolin and get her phone number." I don't tell her that I already have it.

"If I called her, what would I say?" I am totally stumped by that part. Ever the pragmatist, Mommy doesn't see it as a big deal.

"You just say, 'Hi, I'm Caroline Clarke, I was born on Christmas day in Lenox Hill Hospital and I think I'm your daughter.'"

I shake my head and laugh out loud. That's my mom: clear-eyed, unsentimental, and guileless. She has never been the type who says what you want to hear or couches things in fluff and possibility. It is an aggravating quality, frankly, and was especially so when I was younger. But I have come to appreciate it in adulthood. There is a certain comfort in knowing that you never have to second-guess what she says. At the same time, I can't imagine calling my birth mother out of the clear blue and nailing her with a line that direct.

I'll have to think it over and come up with a plan that makes sense. But now, thanks to my ever-lovin' parents, I am free to move forward.

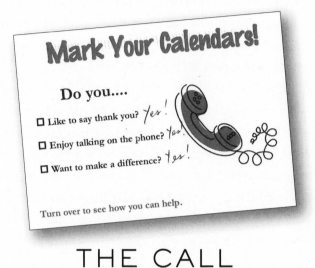

CHAPTER 4

THE CALL

I can think of lots of reasons not to make this call: I should be working. I'm on deadline. I'm not ready.

It's March 18, 2002. I've been staring at the scrap of paper with her number on it for weeks, trying to figure out what to say, how to say it, and whether or not I really want to open this colossal can of worms at all. She gave me life, then gave me away. I thought that was all there was supposed to be, but here I am, preparing to phone my birthmother at her office.

Needing the comfort (and guidance and crutch) of words on a page, I scripted and rescripted myself the way a girl does in junior high school the first time she's going to call a boy. In recent weeks, I had dialed her number twice. The first time I hung up before the phone even rang, the second time I hung up just as someone answered. I had delayed this third attempt, repeatedly.

Now, as I lift the receiver, I note the time. It's 4:06 eastern standard time; still lunchtime on the left coast. She's probably not even there, a notion that strikes me as somewhat appealing.

Finally I dial, fine with the potential futility of it.

Calling at one o'clock on a weekday makes perfect sense. It's like wading into the pool instead of diving. I never dive in. I always do the toe test first. I dip one foot in, then the other. I acclimate, then walk in up to my knees, then my hips, keeping my hands above the water. Gingerly, I splash my upper body and wait until the goose bumps recede before gliding in up to my neck. Once there, I finally let myself go until, voilà, I'm fully under. It's a process. I'm deliberate, practical. I'm also, generally, scared.

I punch in each digit, feeling pleased and message-ready. My foot's in the pool and the water feels fine.

One ring. I tuck the receiver into my neck, pick up my cream soda, and take a long sip. Another ring and then a female voice.

"KCP. Hello?" Young, breathy, a college intern maybe.

"Hi, may I speak with Carole, please?" I sound downright breezy.

I lean back in my chair, purse my lips over my straw, and hear the same voice say, "Speaking."

I sit up, swallow, and freeze. All sound, all movement, my breath, my heart, the revolving planet, and time itself seem to stall for a moment, waiting for me to process her one simple word, and I am having major trouble doing it.

I'm underwater, gripped by panic.

Think, I tell myself. *Breathe.* Oh God. *Speaking? No, no, no, no, no! This is not how it's supposed to happen* . . . and yet, it's happening. I'm in it, already way over my head, which is now screeching, *Find the script,* as my hands and eyes desperately dart about in search of it. *My script! Where did I put my script?*

It suddenly occurs to me that I could hang up. *Had I said my name?* I could hang up right now and she'd never know. . . .

"Hello?" That voice again, traveling across the distance, sounding unsure but richer suddenly, more seasoned, and slightly impatient.

It's her. I'm now fully focused on that single incredible fact.

I take a breath, simultaneously (miraculously) recovering the script from beneath a pile on my desk.

"Hi," I say, reaching for that breezy tone again to no avail. "This is sort of an odd call to make but . . ." I am ad-libbing, trying to buy time enough to calm myself and quickly scan the script.

The opening, which had seemed so right—simple and direct, per Mommy's advice—during practice readings (yes, practice readings), suddenly sounds implausible. But it's all I have. So I start reading, the way a child recites an oral report in class for the first time, nervously, too quickly, almost mechanically.

"My name is Caroline Clarke. I was born on Christmas Day in 1964 in Lenox Hill Hospital in New York City and I was adopted through the Spence-Chapin agency by a wonderful family."

I load the sentence with everything she needs to know to immediately realize what is happening. There's no way to ease what I know will be a blow, welcome or not. So I just go for it, blurting out my bio in one slightly shaky breath.

I hear myself, feel the weight of the phone in my hand, see

the late afternoon sun dance across my desk, but I feel so odd—almost disembodied—as I hear myself go off script to say, "I've had a great life, a happy life, and I don't need anything from you but . . ." *But what?* I have no idea, so I resume reading.

"If none of this means anything to you, or if you don't want me to continue, I'll . . ."

I'll just hang up and not bother you again. That's what my script says. The words, in my own scrawl, are right there in full view. I have carefully thought them through and am prepared to give her an out before I am even in. To spare her the cruelty—and me the humiliation—of her rejecting me outright, I am going to hold the exit door open for us both.

If none of this means anything to you . . . take care and just forget I ever called. If none of this means anything to you . . . I'll just slip back into my normal, busy life, a life without you, the way I've lived it for thirty-seven years. No biggie. No problem. Done.

That's what I am about to say, braced, I believe, to accept the consequences, the resulting anguish and regret, then move on. Or so I imagine. But before I can finish reading that last line, she interrupts.

"This means *everything* to me," she says.

Hot tears flood my eyes and I am on my feet. The room is suddenly too warm, too close, airless. I want to run. Dance. Scream a hymn of hallelujahs. Instead, I stand there, paralyzed. Relieved with a capital R, thrilled, and terrified.

My birth mother has said what I would have dreamed she'd say if I'd dared to dream of this moment at all. What now?

My life, my whole life, has been so solid, so predictable and sure. It's hard to explain, but from the moment I knew I was adopted, I understood that I had sidestepped some alternative fate that could easily have not been so rosy. I believed God had given me the wonderful family and life I was meant to have, even though I had done nothing to deserve them. In return, I owed my best effort. So I was a big dreamer whose dreams developed into detailed plans that I sketched out in notebooks and journals and letters to God, refined to a T over the years. The degrees, the jobs, the marriage, the kids were all part of The Plan, as I came to think of it.

This was *not* in The Plan. But here I am, and she is still talking.

As if for the first time, I hear that raspy, childish quality in her voice again. By my calculations, she is fifty-six or fifty-seven, but she sounds like a girl of twelve who chain-smokes.

"I definitely want you to continue," she says. "But can you hold on for a minute?"

"Sure," I reply, reflexively. But as the line goes dead, panic threatens. *What if she doesn't come back? What if she's having second thoughts? What if she just doesn't have the heart to let me down?*

This is bizarre. I've placed a call more than thirty years in the making, and after a few minutes, I'm on hold. "Just rude," I hear Mommy's routine admonishment of call-waiting in my mind. I almost laugh, but it's all I can do just to breathe.

Didn't I set out to control this crazy little endeavor from the start, with my careful timing and meticulously crafted script? Well, now the unscripted part of the conversation is about to begin and I'm a tense, pacing mess.

"Hi." She is back, and breathless. She laughs a little laugh. "I'm sorry, I was on the other line with my friend Ann, and I had to explain to her that I had to go because my . . . well, my *daughter* was calling." Muted alarm bells go off in my head the moment she says it: *my daughter.* The little laugh again. "How *are* you?"

I sit, but my legs keep pulsing. Every nerve and muscle in my body is on fire.

"I'm fine," I manage. "How are you?"

She lets out another small rumble of a laugh. We both know it's a silly question, leading us each to lie.

"Well, I'm fine too," she says softly, before taking a breath so deep I hear it across three thousand miles. Then she exclaims, "I'm better than fine. I mean, my God, this really is . . . incredible, isn't it?" She takes another deep breath as I hold mine.

What do you say during a call that you know will change your life forever? Where do you begin? And where do you go from there? You just start talking, as we did for more than two hours. We began by covering the basics. That I'd grown up in the Bronx without siblings in a large, close-knit extended family. That I'd been healthy and happy, had wanted for nothing, and was fine with being an only child. That my parents, both educators, were demanding on the academic front but extraordinarily affectionate, attentive, and kind, and they couldn't have loved me more.

"Bless them," she says, softly. "They sound perfect."

For someone who was caught completely off guard, she rises to the occasion as if she's been expecting it all her life. We quickly discover we have a lot more in common than the report had even implied. We both love all types of music and poetry and sweets, although not chocolate especially. While in high school, she had written an entire musical; I wrote music in high school too. One of my songs was performed at my high school graduation. We both work from home offices that are attached to our garages. We are avid readers and share similar opinions about certain novels. She is thrilled that I'm a writer: something she dabbles at and admires.

"You're so courageous to have called me," she says. "You have no idea what this moment means. I am so proud of you, I'm in absolute awe of you."

I feel myself shrinking under the glare of her spotlight. She is so eager to give me credit—far more than I deserve.

She's also anxious to give depth and detail to the skeletal outline Amy Burke so carefully compiled. The report had been mostly accurate, but as I'd suspected when hearing it that first time, Carole had purposely misled her Spence-Chapin overseers about certain things. She was born in West Medford, Massachusetts, to Babe and Kenny Lane. Baptized Carol, without the *e*, which she added much later, she was originally Carol Lane. As she says it out loud the similarity in our names—Carol Lane, Caroline—makes us pause in a moment of silent wonder.

"Now, is it Carolyn with a *y* or . . ."

"No, it's Caroline, *i-n-e.*'

"People must make that mistake a lot," she says.

"They do, but I don't mind."

"Where did you get your name?" Her speech is slow and easy, her voice is light and melodic. She seems excited, and a bit shy. I feel that way too, but I'm also tightly guarded. I can't— won't—give myself over to her, at least not yet.

"From my grandmother," I answer. "My father's mother."

Something in her tone sounded hopeful, like perhaps she thought I was somehow named for her. *How could I have been? I want to say. My parents didn't know who you were. Until a month ago, none of us knew your name, or almost anything else about you. How could we? You weren't here.*

Instead I explain, "Drusilla Caroline was her name. My dad always said he didn't have the heart to stick me with Drusilla, so he went with Caroline Veronica. Veronica is for my mother's mother, Eliza Veronica."

As I finish the sentence, my mouth goes dry. ". . . *My moth-*

er's mother." Does it hurt her to hear me say that? I don't mean to be insensitive, but what else could I say? *My mother is my mother and she is not you. My mother—Mommy—the woman who bathed me and fed me and taught me to walk, talk, and read; who kissed all my hurts and bought my first box of Kotex, packed me off to summer camp and choir rehearsal and college and sat bawling in the first pew of Riverside Church on my wedding day; the doting grandmother to my children and only mother I have ever known—named me for her mother.*

"Wow," she says. "It's a lovely name."

"Caro was my mother's name," she offers, adding, "my real mother. You know, I was adopted too."

"Yes, I know."

"She died when I was very small and I was raised by her sister, Maria. Did you know that too?"

"Yes," I answer as Timmie's face flashes through my mind. How to tell her about Timmie? This is not in my script.

"*C-a-r-o.*" She spells it out. "She was always called Babe, because she was the baby of three girls. Maria, who raised me, was the middle child and Charlotte was the oldest. But my mother's name was Caro." That little laugh again. "Caro—Carole—Caroline: that is amazing."

Uh-maaaaaaaaay-zing, is how she says it, and she is right. The fact that our three generations of names are graduated versions of each other's is indeed amazing.

"Caro," I echo her. "I've never heard that name before. It isn't short for something? It's not a nickname?"

"No, but we're into nicknames. My family always called me Cookie; Natalie is called Sweetie; Mother's older sister, Charlotte, who helped raise us, is Aunt Baba. Do you have a nickname? Are you ever called Caro or Carol or . . ."

"No," I say, flinching again at the suggestion that our names are connected by anything more than coincidence. "Not really. I had a friend who used to call me Clarkee, for my last name, because it has an *e* at the end. And my father calls me Lumps, for lumps of sugar." An actual lump rises in my throat at the mention of my father. *My father who adores me. My father who was my first best friend. My father who has never not been there for me no matter when or why I called. My father whom you've never met and who came so undone when I told him about you that he had to leave the house.*

This conversation is excruciating. It's like the pain inflicted by a desperately needed massage, both agonizing and merciful.

She lets out a long sigh and another small laugh. She sounds wistful, melancholy when she repeats, "Lumps of sugar . . . I love that."

Cookie. I like it. Of course, I knew from Timmie that that's what her family called her. Maybe it solves the problem of what I will call her. Any iteration of *mother* is out of the question.

We quickly discover that there are lots more "synchronicities," as she delights in calling them, between us. In addition to the fact that we are both adopted, both of our spouses are named John. (She refers to hers as her "man," as he is not technically her husband, although they've been living together for more than twenty years.)

"I don't believe in marriage," she says, "at least, not in the conventional sense. It's a jive legal arrangement that has nothing to do with what it should really all be about, which is a spiritual connection and commitment between two equally consenting human beings. Add to that the fact that historically, in virtually every culture on the planet, the institution of marriage has been oppressive to women . . ."

I stay silent as my parents' traditional values, including a healthy disdain for "shacking up," flash neon in my mind. They are about to celebrate their forty-fourth wedding anniversary. What, I wonder, would she think of that? Would she think that was "jive" too? *And what would they think of her?*

"I believe in the commitment," she goes on. "I mean, look at how long my John and I have been together. I certainly *feel* married, for better or worse." She laughs, and I hear the discomfort in it. *She's nervous,* I realize, *fretting about the impression she's making.* I understand. "Listen to me, going on. Of course, it's totally cool that you're married, as long as you're happy." She hesitates for a moment then adds, "Are you?"

"I am," I reply, stifling a giggle at her passionate speech against the "jive"(*did she really say that?*) institution of marriage and in defense of her man, John.

We were both baptized and raised Episcopalian, and although she'd attended Catholic schools, she veered off as an adult to explore Buddhism and various less ritualistic and less constrictive approaches to Christianity. Ultimately she settled into a sort of spiritual fusion philosophy that didn't include churchgoing, but in which she stays obviously and actively centered on living a life built upon her core beliefs in tolerance, fairness, generosity, gratitude, and eating organic food. She hates conventional medicine (and, it occurs to me, maybe convention of any kind); loves Frida Kahlo, Yoko Ono, and Deepak Chopra; and believes wholeheartedly in the value of psychotherapy. She subscribes to devotionals I am familiar with, such as the *Daily Word*, and her conversation is peppered with references to prayer, the universe, and "all that's divine." She alternates fluidly between references to God and Goddess, as I try hard not to roll my eyes. *She is so California.*

Despite the fantastic trappings, she describes her childhood more in terms of what it lacked. She and Natalie, "Sweetie," were inseparable playmates and best friends, but it sounds as if she spent lots of time missing their parents, who were so often away. Yet no matter the distance, Maria controlled the household, issuing edicts from each port and pit stop on everything from menus to outings and bedtimes. Her strict instructions were dutifully carried out by her childless older sister, the girls' Aunt Baba, who was paid to oversee the rest of the staff and her exuberant nieces.

I get the sense that Cookie never stopped longing for her own birth mother, about whom she knows very little, and maybe longing for Maria too. She makes it clear that their relationship is still a troubled one and implies that though their difficulties may have predated my conception, whatever transpired between them as a result of it made things worse.

"Mother wanted to send me to a place for incarcerated girls when she found out I was pregnant. She wanted me punished. Our family attorney, Leo Branton, talked her out of it because of whatever ramifications that might have had for Dad and the rest of us if the press got a hold of it."

Her tone has taken on darker hues, its edges singed with bitterness. "Leo was known in Hollywood as the black Perry Mason, but he lived under Mother's thumb. He was Kelly's godfather, but I didn't trust him. He's the one who found Spence-Chapin and made all the necessary arrangements for me to hide out at a home for wayward girls like me. It was called Washington Square Home for Friendless Girls. Can you believe that?" Her laugh this time is more of a growl. "I don't know about the others, but I lived there under a false name. I was called Carroll Gale, after my Jewish godmother, Auntie Ada, one of the only people I knew in New York. Lord knows why, but I borrowed a new spelling for my first name from the actress Diahann Carroll."

She confirms the report's assertion that Maria never called or visited, but her father did, offering comfort and reassurances.

"He told me I'd never have to give up a child again," she says, softening. "I don't think Mother ever knew he came.

"He must have been ill by then," she muses. "I was so caught up in my own shame and mess that I didn't notice, but I want to say it was November and so there must have been signs I missed. No one ever mentioned that he was sick. Even when I called home the day after you were born, nobody said a word.

"About a week later, I was folding clothes in my room back at Washington Square when I heard some announcer-man on the radio say, 'Nat King Cole is in the hospital, gravely ill with cancer.' He might have even said the word *dying.* I thought it must be a mistake. I ran downstairs to Mrs. Marvin's office. Kate Marvin was the sort of den mother who ran the home. She was a good and brave and wise soul, and I adored her. She was equally stunned when I told her what I'd heard. She shut her door, handed me her phone, and allowed me to dial home. Someone—Aunt Baba, probably—answered and told me it was true.

"I was in a state. You were in some sort of temporary care. The powers that be wouldn't tell me exactly where and they wouldn't let me see you. For days they had been pressuring me to sign the papers and let you go. They wanted me to sign before I was even discharged from the hospital, but I kept stalling. I was trying to figure out how to keep you. I had talked to Auntie Ada about it, and she said she would help us. But then, this news about Dad . . ."

Her voice trails off. Thinking of my own father and how

dear he is to me, I couldn't imagine, even as she described it, how desperate she must have felt, and how alone.

"Had I not heard Dad was so ill I really don't think I would've signed those papers," she continues. "I would have run away with you or figured out a way to stay in New York. I would have fought for you, and for us. It's all such a fog now, but I remember sitting at a desk, and being handed a pen, and hurriedly signing my real name. Some people were standing nearby—a lawyer, a social worker, I don't know who—telling me what a wonderful life you were going to have with your new family, and I would have too now, all because this was the right thing to do and it was really all for the best. . . . I wanted to scream and cry and to stop them, but I don't think I said a single word. . . . I sat there, quiet and broken and done. I flew home that same day."

Carole described the aftermath as a blur. She arrived home to find her mother bereft and their household in chaos. When she saw her father, shrunken and weak, she barely knew him. He died just five weeks later. She attempted to be a stabilizing force, especially for the babies, Timmie and Casey, while their mother grieved. But it wasn't long before she returned to her passion for acting. Ten months after I was born, she became the first African American woman signed to a contract with Columbia Pictures' new artist development program.

In 1967, she made her Broadway debut opposite John Forsythe in *Weekend*, a Gore Vidal play. By then, she'd begun shifting away from Maria's reach, forging a life that was decidedly at odds with her mother's expectations and that bore little resemblance to the one she'd known. When she eloped with an eccentric artist who called himself Charlie Nothing, an appalled Maria quickly had the marriage annulled.

"How could she do that if you were over twenty-one?" I asked.

"Maria could do anything," was her grim response.

If her father, Nat, couldn't have predicted the path her life would take, he was right about one thing; she never did give up another child. Her two sons, Sage and Harleigh, were born five and six years after me, respectively. She wasn't married to the boys' father and didn't stay in their relationship for long. In 1969, she moved her young family to Europe for a film role. Harleigh was actually born there in 1970. When she packed up and returned to the States shortly after, it was with her little boys and little else. She settled in New York, and rarely had contact with their father after that.

"Have you heard of Westbeth?" she asked me. I had; it was a housing complex in Greenwich Village well known in New York as a low-cost haven for artists. "That's where we lived. God, we loved it there."

Her sons attended preschool with the children of a few of her black actress friends, way uptown in Harlem, while she continued to try to make it as an actress in film and theater. "Those were hard but great years," she says. "The guys were a part of all these terrific communities, living in the Village and going to this little experimental school in the basement of Church of the Master."

Jolted, I nearly drop the phone. Church of the Master stood on the corner of Morningside Avenue and West 122nd Street. That's the block that Aunt Vonnie, Mommy's youngest sister, lived on, in the house where they grew up. I tell Carole this, and she gasps.

In 1974, she appeared in the New York Shakespeare Festival's production of *Pericles*, and the following year she starred in a groundbreaking production at the Public Theater called *Black Picture Show*. Around that time, she was also in the original version of the film *The Taking of Pelham One Two Three*, which starred Walter Matthau. When she mentions it, I don't react, having never heard of the movie about the hijacking of a New York City subway train.

"It's a great film," she says with pride. "I think you'd like it. Isn't that station in the Bronx? I remember shooting there. I'm almost sure it was the Bronx." She sounds excited at the mere thought.

"It is," I say, equally enthralled. "Pelham Parkway is actually very close to where I grew up."

As I listen to her talk, it occurs to me that during those years when I imagined bumping into her on the bus or the street, I might have actually walked right past her en route to or from Aunt Vonnie's house, which we visited often. Mommy was always dragging me to one cultural event or another. *What if I had seen her in a show?*

At first, it sounds as if Carole was in fact that glamorous figure I dreamed up as a child. But as she continues to tell her story, that bubble quickly deflates.

She allows that her work often received critical acclaim, but there wasn't enough of it, and her life as a single mother was neither condoned nor in any way supported by Maria. She struggled financially and became increasingly frustrated by the quality and dearth of roles she was offered. Her talent and unique pedigree as the child of a world-famous celebrity aside, she was a black actress, and neither Broadway nor Hollywood had much to offer her.

In the mid-1970s, she moved back to Los Angeles, where she starred as Ellie, the title character's daughter in *Grady*, a short-lived spin-off of the hit sitcom *Sanford and Son*. My ears perk up when I hear this. I loved *Sanford and Son* and was sure I had watched *Grady*, although I can't envision it, or her, at the moment. She describes *Grady* as the *Cosby Show* of its day, built upon the life of a middle-class black family whose head, her husband, played by Joe Morton, was a college professor.

"My dad was a college professor," I interject. "He's retired now."

"That's amazing," she responds, noting that "America wasn't ready to celebrate black folks in such a positive light in those days." *Grady* was canceled after a few weeks, and her disillusionment with acting hit bottom.

By then her sons were attending Highland Hall, a Waldorf school, where she met and hooked up with John, a young widower whose son, Seth, was a classmate of Harleigh's. I know a bit about the Waldorf philosophy of education. It's very child- and art-centered, nurturing, intimate, and slightly counterculture. It is certainly nothing like the conventional New York City public education I had.

"John and the boys have always known about you."

When she says it, I feel a surge of affection for her, and for them as well. I always wanted a sister—I cling to my girlfriends for dear life—but I had never truly imagined having siblings of any kind. To hear that her sons had grown up with an awareness of me as their missing sister was bittersweet. I wonder about the burden that this might have been for them, but I am overjoyed that I have been more than a mere memory for her . . . apparently, much more.

Throughout the years, she told everyone who mattered to her about the daughter she had to give away. (Meanwhile my parents rarely told anyone I was adopted, not because it was a secret but because to them it was simply irrelevant.) She is clear that the experience damaged her in ways that she is still realizing. Her mother was sure the scandal an unwed pregnancy might cause would ruin her revered husband's career and convinced Carole of it, sealing both of our fates. As it turned out, Nat died so soon after my birth—mere weeks—there was no career to ruin or protect. Carole came to understand that too late. My new life had begun by then, and there was no going back.

Understanding the proximity of these two pivotal events in Carole's life—my birth and her dad's death—offers a new and devastating twist to our emerging story. I feel like I did when I first learned she was an orphan: sad for her, even sorry for her, and incredibly lucky by comparison.

Through our meandering conversation, murky pieces of my past are taking shape. It was true what Mommy always told me, that my birth mother wouldn't sign the papers relinquishing me until she was sure I'd been found a good home. I had always doubted this, convinced it was simply what you were supposed to tell an adopted child. But Carole also reveals details of my first days that Mommy never knew: she held me, sang to me, nursed me, and bonded with me in the hospital despite being warned repeatedly to do none of it. I always wondered about this and had come to believe that I probably hadn't been held or touched or even looked at by my birth mother because it would have been too painful, or that she wasn't even offered the option of interacting with me, that it was against some ironclad rules. Hearing her describe our brief time together makes something that had hardened in me long ago go soft.

"The guys have always known to give me my space around Christmas," she says. "As you can imagine, it's never been an easy time for me."

It's an avalanche of information—facts, feelings, and images fall in on me, around me, over me. It is overwhelming, dreamlike, intense, good—wonderful even—but also stressful and frightening, and I'm not sure why.

My long-ago prayers that she would grieve and agonize over my loss have been answered but I now regret each one; she has suffered plenty—too much, in fact.

When I tell her that I'm an editor at *Black Enterprise* and that I just published a book, her response is over the moon: "What a powerful woman you are! You are beyond the beyond," she cries. "You are totally amazing!" There it is again: uh-maaaay-zing.

She's deeply relieved to learn I'm not a Republican (she had wrongly assumed that my three-piece-suit-wearing, American-dream-grabbing, ultra-enterprising father-in-law, Earl Graves, was one and that, by extension, so were Johnny and I) and delighted, if a bit thrown, to realize she is a grandmother twice over.

"Oh my." She sighs. "Veronica and Carter," she repeats, her voice revealing traces of joy and tears. She declares their names, their ages, their very being, "Divine!"

"Any pets? Dogs?" she asks.

"No." I laugh.

"Do you like to travel?"

"I do," I reply, again not elaborating. She confesses a fear of flying, and my heart sinks because I went from wanting to get my own pilot's license to developing a fear of flying as an adult that I am in a constant state of battling. I love to travel, but getting there is not half the fun; in fact, when flying is required, it's agony. Needless to say, the events of 9/11 didn't help. While I white-knuckle it through several trips a year for both work and pleasure, Carole admits she hasn't left Los Angeles in two decades. *A hell of a thing to inherit*, I think, wondering what else her DNA has stamped on me.

"Do you like postcards?" she asks.

"Postcards?" Did I hear her right?

"Yes, postcards. I adore them. I always have. Daddy and Mother always sent us postcards when they traveled, so I guess that's how it started for me. I collect them."

"Oh," I mutter, thinking, *How strange.*

"How did you find me?"

I feel a heavy weight descend just as another lifts. It is a loaded story and I'm not sure how it will make her feel. Timmie's image floats into my mind as I consider the fact that when this conversation is over there will still be another one left to have, with her. Honestly, after going through the telling of this story of discovery with Johnny, my parents, his parents, and just a few close friends, I'm tapped out.

"It's pretty incredible," I start off, telling Carole how I'd called Spence-Chapin to get health information, how Amy Burke went into my file and called me in to read her report to me in person, all seven pages of it.

"Am I to understand they have a *report* on me, and some secret fucking file?" Her tone has shifted dramatically. She is outraged, horrified, and I am caught totally off guard by her response. Mommy and Daddy never curse, insisting that profanity is the bastion of those who lack an expansive enough vocabulary. When pushed to the absolute limit, one of them might exclaim, "Dammit!" Carole clearly resides in a different camp.

She is still going off, reacting as if I'd announced she was on J. Edgar Hoover's infamous blacklist. "Do you have that file?" she demands to know. "Can we get it?"

Now I am starting to feel bad; she is genuinely upset.

"No, the file is sealed," I say, hoping this might actually reassure her. "New York law doesn't allow adoptees access. I don't think you could get into it either. But the report I have is pretty detailed. I can send it to you. I was told there was more information than usual, because you'd been at the maternity home for a good while."

"Was I?" She sounds as if she'd been knocked out and is struggling to regain her sense of time and place. "I honestly don't remember how long I was there. Washington Square Home . . . it was a brownstone. The playwright Lillian Hellman lived next door. I don't think we ever saw her, but we knew she lived there. There were several of us living together, sharing our same secret shame. We exchanged letters for a few months, or maybe it was years. I still have them somewhere. . . ."

"You saved them?" I ask, thrilled that there might be some tangible record of that time, as well as by the fact that this is something else we have in common. I save personal letters too—almost every single one I've received since I was a child.

"Yes," she replies. "I guess I wanted to remember, even though I was—we were all—instructed to forget. I suppose my saving those things was a small, silent act of rebellion. There were a lot of those." She continues to sound wistful and far-away as she peels back the years.

"So much could have been so different. My godmother, Aunt Ada, and her husband, Uncle Jackie, would have adopted you, but Mother wouldn't allow it."

"Mother" always sounded so odd—formal and rigid—to me, and when Carole says it, it makes me squirm. In addition to forcing her to give me up, what else had Maria done to her?

"Speaking of Mother, I think you may know one of my sisters. Didn't you go to Northfield Mount Herman?"

I hadn't mentioned my connection to Timolin yet, had I? "You mean Timmie?" I ask, incredulous.

"Yes, Timmie," she blurts out. "My God, you do know her!"

"I do, but I didn't go to Northfield. We met in college. I was at Smith and she was at Amherst; they're just eight miles apart. Our boyfriends were best friends."

"That was her boyfriend Kelby?"

"Yes, my boyfriend's name was Don. Timmie and I met through them, and we've been friends ever since. That's how I found you. It's how I knew who you were. I recognized the family in the report as Timmie's family. I got your number from her."

"Shit! Timmie gave you my number?" Now it is she who is shocked. "She knew you were going to call me?"

"Not exactly." I describe how I'd duped Tim and why.

She lets out a sigh that ends in a low, rumbling laugh. "Well, look at you. Aren't you clever?"

It sounds like a compliment, but I can't be sure. I had shamelessly lied and manipulated an old friend to get her number—way to make a lovely first impression. What, I wonder, does she really think of me so far?

"Some years ago, Timmie mentioned that she thought she might know my daughter," she says. "I don't know why I thought the connection was through Northfield. Maybe she said you'd met at school and I just assumed—"

"Timmie knew? Wait . . . What?" Tim knew I was her niece? *For how long?* Since I was sixteen? Or eighteen? Or twenty-five? We'd been friends for twenty years and she had never said a word to me. I struggle to imagine the conversation in which Tim told her sister that she thought she knew her long-lost daughter. Where was the follow-up to that? I ask myself. Wasn't there a natural next step, offering to bring us together, or to have a similar talk with me? Anything?

Here I thought I was being so cool with Tim. Looks like she wasn't taken after all; I was.

"Tim knew," I repeat, still disbelieving. "She *knew*?"

"Yes, my darling, she knew. And so did Mother." The imperious-sounding Mother again, Carole's tone thick with distrust and disdain as she says it. She waits for me to comment, but I say nothing.

I vividly remember meeting the elegant, charming, and imposing Maria Cole when I was a college freshman. Timmie and her twin sister, Casey, who went to Brown, were taking their boyfriends to Boston to see Natalie in concert; Luther Vandross was opening for her. This was a can't-miss show. Natalie was a star; she earned even Daddy's respect by scatting "in the same vicinity as Ella Fitzgerald." For Daddy, there was no higher praise. Meanwhile, Luther's *Never Too Much* album was a huge hit, and his star was on the rise.

So when Timmie invited me and my boyfriend Don to go, we jumped at the chance, sneaking behind my parents' overprotective backs to do it. They knew I was going to the concert with Timmie and staying at her mother's home, but if they'd known Don was going they would've put a stop-check on my Smith tuition and dragged my sixteen-year-old behind back home.

It was the first time I met Casey. The guys stayed with Don's brother, Roland, who was a sophomore at Harvard, and the girls stayed at Maria's luxurious apartment atop the Ritz-Carlton Copley Square. With its grand proportions and gorgeous layout, it was photo-shoot-ready and unlike any home I had ever seen. Every piece of furniture, artwork, and memorabilia was absolutely pristine and all the more impressive because I knew it wasn't even her primary home. The room I stayed in had custom-made French draperies on the windows that matched the coverlets and upholstered headboards of its twin beds. The carpet was so plush my feet sank into it and left their imprint. Sleeping there, I felt like a princess.

When I met her the morning after the concert, I was quite dazzled. She was the personification of the same elegant note that played throughout her home's decor: perfectly turned out, with her dark hair parted in the center and pulled into a tight bun at the nape of her neck. Her makeup was spare but impeccable. Likewise, her clothes and jewelry were exquisite but not overdone. Mommy had taught me about quality, and this was quality of the highest order. But what struck me most was her kindness, and seemingly genuine interest. I was taken aback and deeply flattered as she peppered me with questions about my background.

"Tim tells me you were born on Christmas. Isn't that something? Actually Christmas day?"

"Yes, the twenty-fifth."

"Well, I certainly hope you weren't cheated."

"Oh no, my family always made sure I got double gifts, and they always reserve a special part of the day for birthday cake and a champagne toast. People think it's terrible to have a Christmas birthday, but it's actually great! School's closed, no one has to work, everything's beautiful, everyone's happy. I love it."

She smiled, broadly. "That's just darling, isn't it, Tim?" she remarked, locking eyes with her daughter for an instant, then looking back at me. I was utterly charmed by her.

"And were you born in the Bronx?"

"No, I was born in Manhattan."

"Really? Where? There are so many excellent hospitals in New York."

"I was born in Lenox Hill."

"I see. And how old are you now? Tim says you're young for college."

"I'm sixteen, I'll be seventeen this year."

"Well, your parents must be quite proud. You were adopted, is that right?"

"Yes."

"As an infant?"

"Yes."

"How lovely for your family. They must have been thrilled. You know, we have two adopted children, a son and a daughter." I nodded. "And what do your parents do?"

"My father is a chemistry professor, my mom's a reading teacher."

It almost had the feel of an interview, and I beamed my way through it, answering all of her questions with gusto and the utmost respect. Tim sat nearby, grinning and listening and watching us converse.

Had Maria Cole been so curious about me because she believed even then that I might very well be her granddaughter? Had Tim tipped her off, having suspected it from the moment she first learned that I was a Christmas baby, adopted in New York? Mine was a unique backstory. Wouldn't I have been as recognizable to her as her family ultimately was to me twenty-one years later? Did she have some sixth sense or note some family resemblance that she rushed to mention to her mom? Had she invited me to Boston for that reason? Had they conspired to keep this secret, or had Tim yearned to tell me but been threatened with disinheritance—Maria was good for that—if she did?

"We have to remember something." Carole's voice cuts into my thoughts. "Tim and my mother had this information and they could have done something and they didn't. We will have to deal with them at some point."

I had expected to stun her with my Timolin connection, and here I am the one reeling from this revelation.

I'm completely unnerved, and more upset for Carole than I am for myself. Timmie is my friend, but she is Carole's *sister*. How could she believe she might know her *sister's child*, intimate as much, and then do *nothing*? What was the point of Tim's even telling Carole? To assure her that I was alive? Healthy? Happy? *What?* I wanted to give Timmie the benefit of the doubt, but I was suddenly overflowing with doubt. Major, deep-down doubt.

I tell Carole the story of the night I spent at the Ritz. Although she remains silent, I can almost hear her struggling to process the fact that her mother and sister met me when I was sweet sixteen, still a child in many ways, and they'd done nothing to reunite us. It's a bitter pill to swallow.

"After Timmie told me she thought she knew you, I asked her to arrange a meeting, or to at least see if you would be interested in meeting me," she says. "She told me that you were happy and had no interest in finding your birth parents."

I feel stung, and suddenly guilty. "I guess that was true," I say, as a passing conversation between Timmie and me floats to my mind, with her asking if I would ever want to search for my birth parents and me replying with conviction that I wouldn't. Was that conversation real or imagined? I wasn't sure. But when anyone asked me that question, as close friends did on occasion, that was my standard answer. Of course, if she'd told me that she thought she knew my birth mother, or that she suspected that her own sister might be my birth mother, my answer would have been entirely different. I was sure of it. But she hadn't.

"Well, let's put that aside for now," Carole says wearily. Abruptly shifting gears, she continues. "You know, I named you when you were born." There is such tenderness in her voice. I try to steel myself against it. "I called you Gretchen."

"Yes, I know," I say, well aware of the name she'd given me before giving me away. The instant I read it in the report, I envisioned a middle-aged barmaid in Nazi Germany; my only reference for such a thing sprang from the classic sitcom *Hogan's Heroes*. She was blond and thick—thick braids, thick accent, thick-waisted, thickheaded, and thick-skinned—unlike me in every way. "Why Gretchen?" I pry, sullenly.

The laugh, now growing familiar, is, I realize, often an expression of nervousness, not amusement. "I take it you don't like it," she says.

"It's not my favorite," I reply, putting it mildly.

"I hear that," she says, sounding more like my daughter than my mother. "I found it in a little pamphlet that was put out by some milk company. When I lived at Washington Square, things for expectant mothers would arrive in the mail. You know, samples and brochures, which, of course, they would keep from us for obvious reasons. But I found this little booklet and stashed it away. It listed tons of names and the meaning of each one. Gretchen meant 'little pearl.' I guess I was drawn more to that than to the name itself. I thought of you that way, as this tiny little pearl swimming along in the sea of me."

Tears sting and threaten but I refuse to yield. I am clinging with all my might to my composure, my safe distance, my life as I know it.

"I suppose I could have just named you Pearl, but Gretchen . . . well . . . I didn't know anyone else named Gretchen, so I chose that. I have thought of you as Gretchen ever since. And I have prayed for you, prayed that you would have a wonderful family and a whole and happy life, ever since."

"Oh," is all I can choke out as I struggle not to let my emotions spill. But in that moment, I stop fighting and begin to give myself over to her—her voice, her words, her laugh, her tenderness and warmth, and her magnetic pull, which I am powerless and, finally, unwilling to resist.

She wanted me, I now know. Moreover, she still wants me.

I picture a pearl, shimmering and smooth, and am reminded of something I read once about the pearl being the only precious stone that is rendered through pain, suffering, and, finally, death.

CHAPTER 5

MIXED-UP

$\mathscr{A}$lmost twenty years after I had been told I was adopted, the second shoe dropped. "What are you?" is an odd and annoying question to be asked, one that you never get used to, no matter how often it's posed.

It was reassuring as a child to have a straight answer—black—and I never questioned it, even if I was frequently put in the position of explaining, defending, insisting upon it to those who refused to believe that my ethnic origins were that simple, or that at all. Native Spanish-speaking people often addressed me in Spanish, assuming I was fluent, and that it was my native tongue too. I had roughly the same experience with people of various other ethnic origins who would eye me with curiosity and then ask: "Where are you from?"

"New York," I'd say, knowing what they wanted but determined to make them work for it.

"No, where are your parents from?"

"Harlem and the Bronx."

"Originally!"

"Oh! They're from the West Indies."

"From India?"

"No, the *West* Indies. You know, the Caribbean. Barbados and Grenada."

"So, you're Indian?"

"I'm black. I'm a black West Indian."

"Black? No, but what are you, *really?*"

Perhaps that's why, when I learned I was adopted, it was one of the first questions that jumped to my mind: What was I, really?

Mommy's declaration that day that "your parents were both black" shored me up. It was the glue that held me together, that linked me to both my destined family and my biological one. It was the critical detail that enabled me, at eight years old, to hold on to my definition of myself.

Decades later, grown and thriving and newlywed, I discovered that this detail—stated with such certainty by my mom and then perpetuated—was a lie. My beloved aunt, Yvonne, Mommy's baby sister, was the one to break the news. It was as close as I have ever come to hearing a deathbed confession.

Aunt Vonnie was my hero and champion. A big woman (at six feet tall) with a big heart, she had always been a people magnet, joyfully presiding over big meals at her big kitchen table, her laughter providing as much sustenance as her always delicious food. For as long as I could remember, she had been in my corner, lavishing praise on me and urging me to pursue my own dreams and define myself by my own standards. As wonderful as my parents were, their expectations could sometimes be confining. They didn't shove me toward a particular profession, but they didn't allow for much veering from the tried-and-true either. Doctor, lawyer, teacher—any of these would do. Engineer, scientist, architect: fine. But musician, writer, artist of any kind? Too risky, too flimsy, unwise. My folks appreciated and encouraged my creativity, but only as long as my grades were top-drawer.

My exuberant and more free-spirited Aunt Vonnie took a broader view. With a wink that simultaneously said, "Don't take it all so seriously," and "I'll be there to catch you if you fall," she nudged me to break free of convention and do my own thing. We shared a love for writing that she never pursued, taking the more prudent course of becoming a teacher while stuffing personal file drawers with poems, short stories, and essays that only she would ever read.

When I auditioned for Music and Art High School (my pick) and also took the test for the Bronx High School of Science (per my parents), it was Aunt Vonnie who had my back. I wanted to pursue music, specifically composition. Although I auditioned as a singer, I knew I was strictly chorus material. In fact, in junior high I was in every singing group I could join, which, between church and school, meant six, total. But I wrote songs on our secondhand piano at home, hoping one day to become a jingle writer, or—when I really dared to dream big—a popular songwriter. My parents didn't discourage it as a hobby, but as a career? They wouldn't hear of it.

When I was accepted at both schools we went to battle and Aunt Vonnie argued with my folks on my behalf. I strained to listen from the front parlor of her Harlem brownstone as the adults sat around the large oak table in her kitchen debating my future. I knew, having fought myself blue at home, that Mommy's and Daddy's minds were sealed. But if anyone had the power to change things, it was my magnificent aunt.

"At some point we have to trust our children and let them do what they want," Aunt Vonnie said, in her best let's-be-rational tone. I could practically hear Mommy's eyes roll. "It's not as if there's a bad option here. Science is a great school, but so is Music and Art. In fact, it's a fantastic school, and she's talented. We know she's smart, but she deserves to develop her creative side too. This is just high school. What's the worst that can happen?"

Daddy didn't miss a beat. "I'll tell you what can happen," he snapped. "Unemployment can happen, that's what. There's a whole lot of fully developed creativity and great talent living at the Y!"

"And waiting tables," Mommy threw in, "living hand to mouth!"

"Oh please," Aunt Vonnie said, slapping the table with a heavy hand and bursting out laughing. "You *must* be joking. This is Caroline we're talking about. That will *never* happen."

"You got that right," said Daddy. "Do you know why? Because she's going to Bronx High School of Science. Then college. Then graduate school. That's why. You want your boys to go to Music and Art or Ringling Brothers or Timbuktu when the time comes, that's your decision. But this is *our* child we're talking about and it's *our* decision."

Case closed, I thought, as my waning hope turned to vapor. *Bronx Science, here I come.*

Even though her passionate advocacy on my behalf made no impact on my parents, it sealed our bond forever. From then on, I went to her with questions and concerns that I would never take to Mommy, who was older, more conservative, and less empathetic than her baby sister. When I cried to Aunt Vonnie over having a curfew three hours earlier than any of my friends, she seemed as outraged as I was, and soon thereafter, I got a slight reprieve. I shared my writing with her, and her encouragement became key, as did her approval, her joyful outlook on life, and her unerring confidence in me. When it was clear that I was in love with Johnny and in it for the long haul, it was Aunt Vonnie who pulled Mommy aside and advised her to stop resisting the relationship or risk alienating me.

Of course, it was easy for Aunt Vonnie to say, since she loved Johnny from the start. She was charmed by his quick intelligence and wicked sense of humor. It didn't hurt that she was a natural defender of the underdog, and in my house, at least with Mommy, that's what Johnny was. Daddy was Canada: he remained neutral.

During our summer getaways in Sag Harbor Mommy had observed Johnny's wisecracking adolescence with a seasoned schoolteacher's decided lack of amusement, and she was even less impressed with him as an adult. He clearly stood apart from the previous boyfriend or two who showed up regularly bearing flowers and plenty of yes-ma'ams and eager-to-please grins. She loved those guys.

Johnny didn't kiss up to anybody, and if he sensed you didn't like him and he hadn't given you ample reason, he was apt to go the other way entirely, not being rude exactly, but not making any attempt to win you over either. My suggestion that this might not be the best approach with my mom, given that he loved and wanted to marry me, was met with only mild improvements in his attitude and deportment. She was equally stubborn. But she ultimately took her sister's counsel to heart and stopped scowling when Johnny came around. Eventually she grew to love him too.

By the time we got married—six years after our first date— Aunt Vonnie wasn't able to dance at our wedding. Suffering from sarcoidosis, an incurable respiratory disease, she went everywhere with a portable oxygen tank by then. A year later, she rarely went out at all.

When she was in her midfifties, a wife and the mother of two young men, the disease had robbed her of the teaching career she excelled at and a future she deserved. Hospital stays no longer gave her much physical relief, and the disease began robbing her of her buoyant spirit as well. With a relentless and cruel disregard for all of her hopes and plans, it was stealing her life away, bit by bit. Mindful of ebbing time, I went to see her every chance I got, and more than once she asked me, her eyes desperate and pleading, to help her die. I would cast my gaze downward and shake my head or, behaving as if I hadn't heard her, I'd attempt some cheery change of subject. She'd turn away from me then, disappointed and still longing for death.

One hot stunner of a day in June 1993, I stopped by her house on my way home from work. When I entered her room, it was clear that Aunt Vonnie was having a rough time. She was sitting on the edge of her bed by an open window, her head sunk low between her broad shoulders, which were sloped heavily forward. Her chest rose visibly, shuddered, and fell with each breath as she adjusted the small plastic claw that was now always in her nose, attached to a long narrow tube that laced around her neck and traveled the short distance to a large stationary oxygen tank.

She had just taken her medication and was waiting for it to kick in when I breezed through the doorway, smiling and bearing orange tulips.

"Hey," I chirped, attempting my best Florence Nightingale.

Cut the bullshit, her eyes seemed to say as they shifted to meet mine. Even on her worst day, she didn't say it aloud, but I wouldn't have blamed her if she did.

How I missed the bright greetings I used to get, the countless times she'd see me and sing out, "Hey, Carolynee-binnee," arms flung open wide. "Give me a hug and a kiss and a squeeze, if you please!" Now she could barely muster a smile.

I dropped the flowers into a vase, tossing their limp predecessors into the trash before leaning in to kiss her and hold her close for a moment. "How's today?" I asked, softly, as if I couldn't tell.

She shrugged and slowly shook her head. I hadn't seen her this low in a long time, and I knew better than to launch into some sunny monologue to try to lift her. Instead I grabbed a book from a side table and sat down beside her.

"Let's read," I offered, opening her dog-eared copy of *Collected Poems of Edna St. Vincent Millay* to its marked page. "The Unexplorer," I read. " 'There was a road ran past our house, too lovely to explore. I asked my mother once—she said, "That if you followed where it led . . ." ' "

"Stop," Aunt Vonnie's husky voice broke in. I looked at her and waited. "Did your mother . . ."—she paused for breath— "ever tell you . . ."—breathe—"about your . . ."—breathe— "about the girl . . ."—breathe—"who had you?"

She was agitated, her eyes were wild with worry, as if a terrible crisis loomed. I closed the book and laid it down.

"You mean my birth mother?"

She nodded. Now I took a deep breath.

Aunt Vonnie and I had never discussed my being adopted or anything related to it. We had talked about countless silly, deep, and intimate things over the years, but never this. Why now, I wondered, and where was this headed?

"She told me some things," I said, trying to keep my tone light.

"Did she tell you that . . ."—she struggled—"the girl was white?" Her voice was trembling, her eyes dug into mine.

Whatever I might have been expecting, this wasn't it, and her words shattered the tension I'd started to feel. For the first time, I thought Aunt Vonnie was talking out of her head. Maybe it was the medication. Or delirium brought on by oxygen deprivation. Maybe she was losing her mind. The most important thing was to calm her down.

"Yes," I said, as if her news made perfect sense and I'd known it to be true all my life. I took her hand in mine. "She told me."

Aunt Vonnie brightened instantly. "She did?" I nodded as the lines in her brow vanished, she sank back onto a pile of pillows and even offered up a faint smile. "Oh good, that's good," she said, as if to herself. I returned to reading aloud, and in minutes, she was asleep.

When I got home to Johnny, I told him how upset I was by her condition that day, but I didn't mention what she'd said. Why would I, when it obviously wasn't true?

A few weeks went by with me trying not to think about it, not to entertain the possibility that my parents had lied, but I couldn't shake it. The question nagged at me until one day when our paths crossed on another visit to Aunt Vonnie's. Having left the room to give Mommy some time alone with her baby sister, Daddy and I were walking down the stairs and I blurted out, "Was my birth mother white?"

I was two steps behind him, unable to see his face, but I could tell by the way he paused for an instant, then sped to almost running, that I had clipped a nerve. He didn't respond, so I pressed on.

"Aunt Vonnie told me that the woman who gave birth to me is white. Is that true?" I pulled on his shoulder slightly, forcing him to stop and face me. His body turned, but his eyes stayed glued to the front door. He looked desperate to get out of the house.

"Come on, Lumps," he said, patting himself down in search of his pack of cigarettes, still not meeting my gaze. "I have to go get my fix. That's a question for your mom, anyway," he added as he bolted for the street. Before he even reached the door, he had grabbed a cigarette from his breast pocket, put it in his mouth, and lit it—sacrilege in this house where his sister-in-law lay gasping for air.

I struggled against a slightly sick feeling rising from my gut. Glancing around the room at the framed sepia portraits lining the parlor walls I walked over to more closely examine one of my favorites. In it Mommy was just three, standing beside her older brother, Phil, who wore a sailor suit and a sweet smile. In a short dress and ankle socks, she stood at solemn-faced attention, her chin-length hair brushed into its best attempt at ringlets. She looked both angelic and slightly afraid.

"Where does the time go?" Mommy asked from over my shoulder. I was so engrossed I hadn't heard her enter the room. Before I could respond, she was out the door.

I was on her heels as she joined my dad on the sidewalk. Mommy turned to face me and reached out to brush a stray hair from my eyes then she looked me over once, in that way that only mothers do, and smiled approvingly.

"So," she said, "how was your day?"

Daddy was puffing away, his eyes darting in every direction except mine. He spoke before I did.

"Caroline has something to ask you, Vera," he said as Mommy looked at him, puzzled no doubt by his agitated tone. He finally turned toward me. "Go ahead, Lumps. Ask."

Mommy smiled innocently and said, "What is it, sugar?"

I spit it out: "Was my birth mother white?"

"What?" She clipped the *t* sharply, as she did whenever she was outraged. "Of course not. You know she's black—black and American Indian, I mean, Native American. What in the world would make you think she was white?" She actually looked amused.

Relief spread through me as we both laughed. "I was over here one day, and Aunt Vonnie must have taken some new medicine," I explained, feeling like a fool for ever doubting Mommy. "She was really upset and she told me that my birth mother was white. I just acted like it was no big deal, like I knew already and she calmed down. I thought it was ridiculous—that it was probably the medication talking—but she was so uptight about it that I just had to ask."

As the words left my mouth, I sensed a subtle change in Mommy's demeanor.

"Well, it's not true," she said. "Your mother was definitely black." Before I could exhale she added, "It's your father. He was white."

"My father was white?" I didn't even like the taste of the words in my mouth.

"Yes," Mommy said calmly as Daddy flicked a spent cigarette toward the curb and dug into his pocket in search of another.

"But you told me he was black," I said, still not quite comprehending. "You always told me they were both black, that all my grandparents were black. You lied to me?"

Mommy took my hands in hers and drew me near. "That's what we were told to do, and we thought it was best. Your mother was black, her parents were black, we are black, *you* are black. None of that has changed. And everything else we ever told you *is* true."

I pulled my hands away and stared at her. I wanted to scream, to cry, to run. I turned toward Daddy, seeking some sort of explanation or consolation. I wanted him to tell me this was all a bad joke. I wanted him to fix it. His face a twisted knot of despair, he looked away. Daddy had never been able to bear even the thought of me in pain. For as long as I could remember, whenever I was sick or injured, he seemed to suffer more than I did, and I was definitely hurting now.

The three of us stood there together but falling apart, our entire history and future, questionable. I was crushed. She had lied to me. *They* had lied to me.

"Caroline, these are different times," Mommy was saying, her tone pulsing with that totally self-assured, arrow-straight edge I knew so well. She wasn't apologizing; she saw no reason to. She was ever the master teacher, and this was yet another teachable moment.

"You were a child—*our child*—and we did what we thought was best for you at the time. It might be hard to understand, but it's true. You still are what you are and who you are."

"That's right," Daddy chimed in, suddenly buoyed by Mommy's aplomb, "and do you know who you are? You are *our* Caroline, that's who! No getting away from it, Lumpty. You will always be *our* Caroline."

I wanted to nail them with a red-hot stream of how-could-you-how-dare-you-how-can-I-ever-trust-you-again outrage. I wanted to go completely *off*. But I knew that like everything else that had driven me crazy through the years—their over-protectiveness and high standards, their constant tutoring and towering expectations—their decision to massage my truth was born of love. Whatever doubts this revelation sparked, there remained this one unshakeable truth: I was their everything.

Besides, what was the point of rehashing it all now? It was done. There was nothing left but for me to process this new piece of information and figure out how to fit it into the puzzle of my life, just as I'd had to do at age seven.

As much as I wanted to fight her on it, in my heart I believed Mommy was right. This news was rocking me at age twenty-seven; what would it have done to me back then? It would have made me feel like an oddball, different from my family and from everyone else I knew—black or white. It would have made my answer to that annoying question—what are you?—more complicated, less sure at a time when I desperately needed to feel sure about something. It would have torn me apart.

When I was growing up, my parents and I always had a diverse group of friends, but we had no biracial friends, or what would have been referred to back then as mulatto, half-breed, zebra, or worse. It was the 1970s, long before politically correct labels like "blended," "multiethnic," "biracial," or "mixed." There were three choices for race on applications: black, white, and the alien-sounding "other." You couldn't check two; you had to choose just one.

My parents carefully shaped my environment, leaving little to chance. We lived in a neighborhood of middle- and working-class strivers. Our house was sandwiched between the Millers, a retired Puerto Rican couple with three daughters, none of whom married a Puerto Rican, and Mrs. Williams, an Irish Catholic widow. It was a neighborhood teeming with first-generation immigrants whose English was heavily accented and who still addressed each other in their native tongues. The West Indian population, primarily from Jamaica, was increasing rapidly and would eventually dominate.

I attended public schools that were well integrated both racially and economically. We were a soup of black, Puerto Rican, Irish, Italian, Dominican, and Jewish kids who lived in the Eastchester Projects and in single- and two-family homes. I sensed that my parents could afford to live more lavishly, but they had come a mighty way from where they each started out and they were content with the life they'd made. My dad's brother, Uncle Buster, lived right around the corner, and although we usually drove, we could walk to his sister Iris's house too. That familial closeness was paramount to them and unattainable in the suburbs, which had lured many of their friends.

We loved our neighborhood with its German-Jewish bakery where thickly accented Rosie always stuck an extra rainbow-sprinkled cookie into the bag with my dad's rugelah. There was Nina's, the Italian restaurant where my parents let me dig out the soft, buttery center of the hot garlic bread always placed on the table in a basket, leaving them the ragged crusts (which they claimed were their favorite part). There was the Chinese laundry, which smelled strongly of starch and wrapped Daddy's folded Oxford shirts in crunchy brown paper tied with butcher string; Rexall Drugs, presided over by two WASPy-seeming pharmacists in white lab coats and wire-rimmed glasses; and Lipkind's Shoes, which was managed by a cheerful young black man who started out sweeping the place and eventually bought it. It was a world where racial harmony was the goal, and for the most part, we achieved it. But racial mixing? That was something else.

I'll never forget going to the wedding of one of my dad's nursing students, a Jewish girl who married a black guy, when I was about ten. I was mesmerized as the wedding party sang "Hava Nagila" and danced the hora, carrying the bride and groom around in chairs on their shoulders. The band played a lively mix of rhythm and blues and golden oldies while we ate baked chicken and butter cake. My dad gave me a dollar for successfully eating my chicken without ever touching it with my fingers. I loved weddings, and the entire day left a huge impression on me.

The next night at the dinner table, out of pure curiosity, I asked my parents how they would feel if I married a white man. There was the crash of silverware dropping onto plates as Daddy, who rarely yelled, exploded: "WHAT? Don't talk foolishness! You don't even know what you're saying! You'd better understand right now that I will *never* let that happen!"

I sat there, shaken and mute. Mommy, whose face could speak volumes even on the rare occasions when she said nothing, just stared at her plate. After a moment, Daddy picked up his fork and we all went back to eating, and that was the end of that.

A few years later, when I was in high school, Uncle Joey, one of Daddy's oldest friends, let it slip that before my father met Mommy, he had been married to a girl who was Jewish. One day while he was at work, as Uncle Joey told it, her family kidnapped her and sent her to live in Israel. They had been married for less than two weeks, and Daddy never saw or heard from her again. When I asked Mommy about it, she confirmed the story but knew no more of the details than I did.

Daddy never spoke of his first marriage, and even nosy me instinctively knew to leave it alone. But it forever changed how I viewed him; Daddy had been in love before, and married before . . . to a white woman. When I thought back to that dinner conversation, Daddy's reaction to my innocent query made more sense. But it was hard to imagine him as that man who had married outside our race, a race for which he constantly expressed outsize affection and pride.

Learning what little I did about Daddy's secret past made me yearn to know what else lay beneath life's neat, familiar surfaces. I believe it planted the seed that would grow me into a journalist, hungry to uncover the hidden details that tell the truest stories of who we really are. I knew my father as well as I knew anyone, but that disclosure altered how I saw him in the most subtle and significant ways.

Standing with my parents in front of Aunt Vonnie's house as my own covered-up history lay wide open, that sort of fine, irreversible shifting was in the air again as I struggled to make sense of it, and to keep things neat and contained. My racial identity; my trust in them; my sense of self, of cultural allegiance, and of belonging—everything felt up for grabs. What were my choices? Cling to it all or lose it all.

Half white. I was so proud and happy to be black, to be a part of the traditions—the music, art, dance, food, faith, drive—and rich history that my parents had worked so hard to instill in me. Many black folks were ashamed of our history of slavery and degradation; I saw any shame as lying squarely on the shoulders of the slave makers, not the enslaved. I never dwelled on the fact that my ancestors had been slaves; I reveled in the fact that they'd survived, endured, and risen to become what my family now was: educated, flourishing, triumphant. I had never seen myself as anything other than 100 percent black and—genetics be damned—I wasn't about to start now.

Of course I never anticipated my first phone call with Carole, or her asking me a question I'd never been asked before.

CHAPTER 6

PLANTED

$\mathcal{H}$ow do you feel about being biracial?"

Her question hovers between us for a moment, unexpected and bizarre. I've never been asked this because in the decade since I'd been told about my birth father, I had chosen to tell almost no one.

"I'm not," I reply automatically, instantly recognizing the need to clarify. "I've never considered myself biracial. I am black." I wait.

"Oh," she says. Her response is sandwiched between a few awkward moments. "I hear that . . . but you do know your father is white, don't you? Didn't your parents tell you?" Suddenly, she gasps. "Oh my God, is it possible that they didn't know?"

"They knew," I say, not enjoying this part of the conversation at all. "But I was raised believing you were both black. They thought that would be best, and it was . . . for me. I found out the truth when I was grown, but it didn't change how I see myself. I was raised in a black family and I love being black so . . . I'm black."

"I see," she says, not very convincingly. "I guess that makes sense. I always wondered about that."

"Why?" It sounds more like an accusation than a question. My guard, my back, my dander—they are all up. Of all the things to wonder about during thirty-seven years, two months, and nine days away from me, her daughter, she wondered about *that*?

"I'm just intrigued by the whole biracial reality," she explains. "I wondered if you were raised knowing that you were biracial, and if that was challenging for you. Have you seen the film *Secrets and Lies*?"

"I think so." Vaguely I remember the British movie about a black woman who has a tense, rather miserable time trying to reunite with her white birth mother. I must have seen it on television.

"It's brilliant. If you had, I'm sure you'd remember. You know, Sage and Harleigh are biracial, and we've talked a lot about how it's impacted them. They have some very strong feelings about it, and we don't always agree, but it always makes for interesting conversation. Like you, I think they think of themselves more as African American."

She's getting excited just talking about it; I'm quiet and tense, feeling defensive about her wanting me to identify as biracial. *Enough, already. Let's move on. I'm talking to you for the first time in my life and you want to talk about* Secrets and Lies? *With all the territory that lies uncharted between us, we have to go there? Now?* Maybe sensing my displeasure, she reels herself back in with a sigh.

"We don't have to get into it now. It's just that I always wondered how you'd be raised," she says. "Would they find a biracial couple to raise you? Would you be told the truth? Would it be difficult for you?"

"It wasn't hard," I assure her flatly. "It wasn't even an issue. It was great."

The laugh again, forced. "Well . . . I hear that and that *is* great. You are just divine. Your parents are divine. I'm in awe. But did you never feel a need to explore that other reality? I mean, here we are talking, which is so incredible. Aren't you at all curious about your father?"

"No." Somehow, through the silence, I can hear her shock. "I mean, I didn't even go searching for you, really," I try to explain. "This all just sort of happened."

"Yes, and thank Goddess it did!" *Goddess? At best she was quirky and colorful. At worst, she was just plain weird. Please, Lord, let it be the former.*

I realize I'm starting to feel overloaded. We're two hours into a conversation that's veered off into more directions than I can keep straight, and this is a road we just don't need to go down, at least not yet. *How about we just stay focused on us?*

"Your father was quite something," she continues. "His name was Stanley Goldberg. He was Jewish, obviously. I haven't seen him since before you were born, but I can try to find him, if you'd like."

Stanley Goldberg? She is just full of news. My parents, and the Spence-Chapin report, said he was Irish; the report had gone so far as to describe him as a White Anglo-Saxon Protestant. Interesting discrepancy. Before I can ask, she volunteers.

"I lied about your father to my social worker at Spence. I don't know . . . it just seemed less complicated that way."

My best friend from first grade pops into my head: Marilyn Klein. Hers was one of the few houses outside our family where my parents once let me have a sleepover. I remember well her cool rec room with its beaded curtains and peace sign decals and her mom, a petite go-getter who was head of our school PTA. But what I remember most was discovering at breakfast that not only was there no bacon on the menu, there was *never* bacon. This informed my concept of Judaism perhaps more than anything.

That their Sabbath was on Saturdays instead of Sundays was no biggie. Their primary religious symbol was a star instead of a cross? Fine. Men wore beanies—technically yarmulkes—to worship? Great. They worshipped God, but not Jesus? Got it. But no bacon or pork ribs, ever? No *ham*? Unthinkable.

My birth father was Jewish: surprising . . . but so is damn near everything else that has happened to me in the last month. I'm trying to stay with it, to take it day by day, to be open and willing and ready for anything but I am reaching my saturation point. At the same time, I don't want this once-in-a-lifetime first encounter to ever end. I decline her offer to seek him out.

"Mommy, come have dinner!" I look up and am startled to see Nica and Carter standing in the doorway. Hand in hand, they are clearly united in their determination for me to walk away from my office for the rest of the day. Food isn't all they're hungry for. They need my attention, and they aren't going to be satisfied until they get it.

So, with great reluctance, I tell Carole I have to go.

As the children entertain each other with knickknacks on my desk, she and I exchange addresses, e-mails, and phone numbers. I carefully record every digit, code, and character as

I feel myself already beginning to crave our next contact before our first has even ended. I make sure to get her fax number so I can send her the report.

Finally, there is nothing to do but say good-bye.

"I'm so thrilled that you called. What you've put on my plate is unpredictable and wonderful. This was a dream realized for me, and in spite of what I might have guessed about myself, I was ready." She pauses, and sensing what she's about to say, I panic. "I want you to know that I—"

"Great! So, I'll fax that report later tonight," I blurt, determined to drown her out. But I'd heard what she said, and lest I didn't, she says it again.

"I love you. I have always loved you." I am not ready to hear it and I'm certainly not prepared to say it in return. "I just want you to know what this call has meant to me. Bless you, my darling. Thank you. I salute all that you are, and I'll never, ever forget this miraculous day."

I had steeled myself for her possible rejection, but I understand at that moment, I am unprepared for her embrace. My family has always been demonstrative. So, not only am I open to love, I've been known to greedily seek it. But this is different. How can this woman love me? She doesn't even know me.

My life is already fine and good, blessed and full; *I don't need this.*

Some core piece of me had spent our entire conversation— and every moment since I first learned about her—fighting it, pushing against it, urging it away, but to no avail. Instantly there it was, that *need,* planted deep inside me, a tiny hole I had refused to acknowledge was there all along. As she places herself in it, the hole expands, and I am hungry for her as never before.

CHAPTER 7

HURDLES

*J*ust as the kids and I reach our back door, Johnny's car pulls into the driveway.

"Daddy's home!" Carter squeals, releasing me so he can run to his dad. Nica follows, and I seize the chance to flee to our bathroom, splash some water on my face, and grab a minute to think. As I dry off, I stare at my reflection in the mirror, wondering, as I have so many times before, if I resemble the woman whose words keep replaying in my mind.

"You did it," I say out loud to myself. "You called her. She's real."

I channel Donna Reed through our dinner, smiling and laughing and nodding on cue, but only pretending to follow the kids' and Johnny's chatter. I am still back in my office, fixated on the sound of her voice, the nuances in her many modes of laughter, the jumble of details about herself that she let fly, the fact that this is all really happening.

When we are done eating, in another attempt to grab some alone-time, I offer to clean up solo while Johnny and the kids head upstairs to play and get ready for bed. I clear the table and go about doing the dishes and wiping everything down, making extra-slow work of it as I try to summon each minute detail of our conversation into view.

We'd covered a lot of territory. She now knew where I lived and worked, where I'd grown up and gone to school, and that I was married with children—her grandchildren. She knew who my favorite authors were, what kind of music I listened to, that I loved to sing but no longer played the piano and clarinet, and that I never painted, sculpted, or drew, having a stunning lack of talent in the visual arts. She obviously revered art and artists of all kinds, and we had gotten into a mini-debate about whether or not I qualified as one. I held that, as a journalist, I was not an artist. She insisted that as a writer, I was a creator, and as such, I was indeed an artist. We ultimately agreed to disagree.

I knew the reciprocal facts about her life, but it was the broader impressions that captivated me most. She was suddenly alive, in every sense of the word. She was smart and creative. She was sensitive and caring and kind. She cursed! She was an actress, an artist, a feminine feminist/humanist and peacenik. She was a seeker, a prayer, a dog lover, and a garden dweller; she sounded like the type of woman who might name, talk to, and hug a tree.

I imagine her as a sort of new millennium hippie in a purple caftan, holding court while sipping organic root juice in the sultry Southern California sun. I was charmed by her youthfulness, her quirkiness and vulnerability. I can't say she was familiar, that she'd tapped into some long-buried memory of our brief time together, but instantly, I felt I knew her, and I wanted to know so much more.

I now understood that, contrary to assumptions and appearances, Carole didn't have an easy life. She was a woman's woman—a *real* woman—whose disappointments were many but whose hopes ran high.

She had a challenging and distant relationship with her mother and, to a lesser degree, Timmie and Casey. (*My mother worked hard and long to put a real space between her children*, she told me.) But Carole remained ironclad-close to Natalie and their combined three sons, all of whom, at thirtysomething, were still struggling to secure their footing in the world. Robbie, Natalie's son, and Harleigh were both musicians. Harleigh was divorced and living with Carole and her man, John. Sage, an artist who worked sporadically, mostly in transportation on film crews, was in a long, committed relationship with his college sweetheart, Jen, as well as the early, fragile stages of recovery and reestablishing himself in Los Angeles after years of living with Jen in Santa Cruz. Jen worked full-time as Carole's assistant. Carole, who clearly fretted over them all, kept apologizing for the chaotic state of her family while I kept insisting that there was no need for such apologies.

She noted that her brother, Kelly, had not had children, and all four of the Cole girls had borne boys—with one exception. "You," she said triumphantly, "are our only girl!" That fact made her downright giddy; it made me feel happy too. Why, I wasn't quite sure.

"Have you ever had therapy?" she asked.

I laughed. "Uh, no."

"Well, I've had plenty, and I'm a big believer. Wait until I tell Dr. Rowe about this miraculous call. I've been seeing Dr. Rowe for years; he's quite brilliant, and, of course, he knows all about you. You know, even if you have never talked to anyone professionally before, now might be a good time to start."

It was clear that she was a survivor but a fragile one. It was also clear that our call was the long-awaited answer to a decades-old prayer.

As promised, I fax the report to her before turning in. I expect to hear back from her quickly, even if it's just to confirm that she received it. It's all I can think about as I tell Johnny about the call in bed that night. He listens with rapt attention, happy for me and also relieved.

"It's wild how much you have in common," he says.

"I know." It is. He looks at me as if I have something hanging out of my nose. "What?" I ask, touching my face self-consciously.

"I don't know," he says. "Are you okay?"

"Sure," I answer, surprised. How could I not be?

"You cry over everything and you seem so . . . calm."

"Well, this is a first," I say, trying to make a joke out of his concern. "You hate when I cry." He keeps watching me, as if he expects me to fall apart at any second. I shrug and snuggle into the crook of his arm, partly so he can no longer see my face. Not having the emotional response he expected makes me feel uneasy.

"Maybe it's not really hitting me yet," I say, quietly.

"Maybe," he says. Pulling me closer, he kisses the top of my head and holds me tight. "Did you talk about meeting?"

I almost leap out of his arms. *Meeting? We had one call! She doesn't fly, I hate to fly. Meeting absolutely did not come up.*

"No," I say, struggling to be still and mask my outrage.

"Well, you know the Golf and Tennis Challenge is in California this year, so we're going to be out there in a few months anyway. You should let her know. If you don't meet her sooner, that'll be the perfect time—and the kids will be able to meet her then too. I don't know if your parents are coming this year, but if they're up for it, that could work out great."

He is talking about our company's annual golf outing, a social event one thousand people strong, including subscribers, corporate sponsors, scores of our colleagues, his entire family, and—usually—my parents. I couldn't think of a less ideal environment in which to meet my birth mother if I tried. Everything in me seizes as Johnny talks, but I remain quiet and still.

Black Enterprise, founded in 1970 as a monthly guide to success for African American strivers, has grown into a full-blown media company. As head of BE Unlimited, its events arm, the Challenge is on the top of Johnny's mind. A gifted manager who does everything way in advance and never leaves even the smallest detail to chance, he's already been working on it for months. Usually the event takes place in Miami over Labor Day weekend, but for the first time, it's being held in Palm Springs, which, he is quick to inform me, is less than a two-hour drive from Los Angeles. He continues talking, sifting through a range of potential logistical hurdles for which he then proposes multiple solutions, but I'm not listening. Johnny means well, and his penchant for meticulous planning and taking charge is among the traits I most appreciate about him (most of the time), but this isn't his to control. This is mine and Carole's alone. What, when, and how we proceed are for me and her to decide.

Satisfied by my silence that I am on board with his evolving plan, Johnny turns his attention to ESPN, and I relax, grateful to have him beside me, and quiet. Reflecting on the three thousand miles of distance between me and my birth mother, I am grateful for that too. It's a natural enforcer of time and patience. It will prevent us from moving too fast. If she lived driving distance away, I'd probably already be knocking on her door—or at least peeking through her window.

*N*othing awaits me the next morning—no fax, no e-mail, no call. I try to play it cool at first by taking into account the time difference and the fact that she had mentioned she wasn't a morning person. But every time the phone rings or the fax beckons I fly to them, only to have my heart sink when it's not her. Notoriously resistant to technology (I own a cell phone but don't know the number and rarely carry it; I reluctantly use e-mail but only for work), I charge my phone and keep it nearby. I also begin compulsively checking my e-mail every twenty minutes, at most.

After a few hopeless attempts to focus on work, I look for ways to kill time. I go food shopping, write in my journal, and call my parents to tell them that I'd reached out to Carole and all had gone well. They each get on an extension and listen attentively, saying very little.

I am careful not to gush, even though the longer I replay our conversation in my head, the more fantastic it all seems. I tell them they'd been right about almost everything: she never wanted to give me up; she is charming and smart. I pass on her thanks and blessings to them, and they seem touched and appreciative.

"Well," Mommy says, playing it straight as ever, "that all sounds very nice. We're glad you had a good talk." Daddy likens us to "two gloves coming together for the first time, cut from the same cloth, a matched set." I am moved by his sweet analogy, so much that I can't respond.

"So, what will you do now?" Mommy asks. Does she sound tense or am I projecting? I can't be sure. Either way, I make an effort to seem very blasé.

"Oh, I don't know," I say. "I'm sure we'll be in touch. We exchanged contact info. I'll probably write her and we'll just see where it goes."

Downplaying my hopes and expectations for the future, I tell them only what I think they want to hear. Am I protecting them, or myself, given that I still haven't heard from her?

When there is nothing from Carole by five that evening (two, her time), I am near desperate. *What if she had second thoughts? What if one call was enough for her?* By the time I go to bed, I am despondent, believing that, in spite of her enthusiasm, kindness, and seeming joy, she has decided against pursuing a relationship with me. Maybe that damn report had taken her over the edge. Or maybe it really is enough for her to know I've had a good life, and she's now willing to leave well enough alone.

But then, early one morning two days after our call, as I try to regain my equilibrium and get back to my pre-call life, I discover her e-mail while scouring my computer files for a work-related message I feared got deleted by accident. There she is, tucked between all the lewd, crude, and crazy junk-mail titles in my electronic trash.

Relieved and elated, I laugh out loud—at myself and how worried I've been, at technology and how confounding it can be, at God for displaying such a dark sense of humor, and at Fate for handing me a royal flush.

CHAPTER 8

WE BEGIN

Dearest Caroline,

I have no words to entirely express what a joy it was to speak to you today!

I so admire the courage you displayed by just picking up the phone and getting on with the impossible task of introducing yourself to me. I remain ever grateful for all that's Divine that managed to position me to be here at that moment to answer your call.

It's been a long journey for both of us since the blessed day of your birth. As much as I always believed this day would come, I am admittedly as grateful as I am bewildered and as thrilled as I am (slightly) terrified. Geez, one magic phone call has opened up so many doors and windows: past/present/future.

Thanks for faxing the report. After glancing through it, I promptly realized it was too much to deal with right away. I asked you to send it without being smart enough to think about the consequences. I guess it will take more than a NY minute to process.

Issues regarding my mother and Timolin's long-term knowledge of you present us with some additional questions. I have to remind myself that things happen when they are meant to happen. One step at a time, right?

For now, I send you thirty-seven years of love and blessings. Have a glorious Tuesday.

She'd e-mailed me right away, but because she is an unrecognized sender, her note automatically went to my junk mail folder while time ticked by and my worst fears took root. After reading (and rereading) her e-mail I'm over the moon. I write back right away; my fingers can't type fast enough.

Dear Cookie,

Your letter was lovely. Thank you for writing. . . .

I tend to be emotional and sentimental, but I am almost eerily calm. My husband is so excited for us, but he's been watchful, second-guessing my response. It's not that I'm not floored by all this, I am. But there is also a hint of, is that all there is? You live with this huge mystery all your life—it's always there. And then, in a flash, it's not. The BIG moment comes and then it's over. Mystery solved. Prayers answered. Life goes on.

Somehow, without knowing what it would be like, I thought it would be different—more dramatic maybe, more emotional, just . . . more. But please don't misunderstand. It's still more than enough to fill me up with joy and a certain peace.

It's occurred to me since we talked that we have approached this moment from drastically different vantage points. I realized only after I faxed you the report that it must stir up painful memories and complicated emotions. You have a truth to compare it to, and a trauma that you probably fought to lay aside years ago. I wouldn't have sent it to you so soon if I'd stopped to think about all of this. . . .

This is the longest e-mail I've ever written (by far!). I'm going to stop here although I could go on and on. Blessings right back. . . .

Less than an hour later I receive her long and light-as-air response. Typed in bold Kelly green print on a sky blue background, its subject line reads, "Tra-la-la."

Almost-instant gratification can be very rewarding, and it's as addictive as light, speed, and carbs—combined.

Darling Caroline,

Now check this out: In spite of myself, I have been stressing since I sent you my e-mail, wondering WHY, OH WHY I hadn't heard back from you! I was trying to be cool & created a few hundred scenarios as to why you hadn't responded yet. I managed to get paranoid a few times. I asked Sage & Jen if they thought I was overreacting & they of course told me to chill & be patient. Then I thought there was a remote possibility that you never even phucking received my e, so I considered faxing it but since I hadn't received it back saying it was undeliverable, I thought faxing it would come across as being too pushy, too anxious.

Obviously we were going through some changes! Ain't life just a scream & a gas?!

Needless to say, work has taken a back-back seat. I keep trying to be on top of my so-called work-game, but I'm feeling too giddy to focus.

I'm so glad that Johnny is pleased with our encounter. I totally understand how both your Johnny and mine are somewhat at a loss as they attempt to gauge our reactions. I suspect it's damn near impossible for anyone else to figure out what we're going through. That's part of our struggle as well. From what I hear from those who have been through a similar experience, each and every one is unique unto itself. If there is any commonality, "profound" would be the best word to describe it.

We are living proof that miracles happen. There is a blessing to the way we finally met. It feels . . . authentic! Perhaps this is like what Sage said (quoting someone neither of us can recall), "We're all spiritual beings having a human experience."

I send you big electronic hugs and I toast your entire being!

You're an angel!

Happy Spring!

I want to call her again right then and there, but it's only seven in the morning in New York, four in California, and I need to get my kids off to school and myself to work. Besides, I know if we get on the phone we'll be on for hours. When it comes to her, less is not more. I am already beginning to see what a drug Cookie will become. I can't get enough of her; I am addicted from the start. I don't want to just go about my routine. I want to learn more about her, hear her voice, mine her thoughts. All I want to do is be with her, even in this way, at this distance.

The new pattern of our days has begun with the new season. Without realizing it, in the wake of that first call, my life shifts completely. Forget my longtime refusal to become too technofied. Suddenly I am a slave to it all, checking my e-mail each morning before even brushing my teeth, racing to answer every call no matter the hour, nearly accosting the FedEx guy, and watching the clock for the mailman.

The giddy thrill of our budding relationship has all the earmarks of a new and promising love affair. I can't resist being drawn further and further into her sphere, and I don't try. She is my first thought every morning and my last at the end of each day.

Before, I'd awaken with the alarm at six, grab a little extra cuddle time with Johnny, hit the shower, dress, and attack the day, focused on the kids, work, my parents, my husband, and my home. Now I jump out of bed when the alarm goes off and head straight for the nearest computer. She rarely disappoints, having usually sent me a message in the twilight hours the night before. Each time her familiar e-mail handle (*johncarole: blessings*) appears, my stomach flutters uncontrollably. I often end up scrambling through the rest of my morning routine because I lingered too long, rereading her words, or taking time that I didn't have to respond.

Johnny's tolerance for the new distracted, e-mailing, moonstruck me quickly wanes. Normally dressed, having roused the kids by the time he left for work at seven, now I am often still sitting at his desk in my robe at that hour, gazing at the screen gooey-eyed or typing furiously.

"You can't keep doing this," he snaps one morning. Unlike me, he is never late—ever. "The kids are waiting for you. Enough!"

He's right, but I can't stop. To avoid arguing, I start reading her e-mails first thing every day, then I get the kids up and begin their routine, not writing my response until after he's gone. In order to accommodate the change, where I'd once taken the lead in readying the kids each morning, I let Leeba do it, racing downstairs at eight, just in time to walk Nica to the bus and drop Carter at preschool on my way to work. I rationalize that the kids won't care—they love Leeba—and Johnny, already gone by then, will never know.

My parents and the few friends whom I've told about Cookie have no idea of the intensity of my feelings toward her either. Like any junkie, I try to get my fixes in private, and when asked how things are going, I downplay, especially my growing need for her. I do this to protect what she and I have. I don't think anyone else will understand. How could they, when I'm not even sure I do?

Timmie, the connector between us, frequently crosses my mind, but I don't reach out to her. Lacking a sister myself, I revere that bond and leave it to them to work things through. Cookie believes Timmie and Maria knew the truth and kept us apart. I'm not sure what to believe. Their relationships are complicated, there's so much I don't know, and that's just as well. I want no part of it. So I stand aside, avoiding the issue with Cookie and avoiding Timmie altogether. It's not hard to do, as she doesn't contact me either.

Meanwhile Cookie and I often write each other more than once a day, especially when you factor in the steady stream of snail mail that begins flowing back and forth across the miles between us. She sends lots of little gifts, as if trying to play thirty-seven years of catch-up: CDs (many of her own King Cole Productions), palm-size books of jokes or poetry, flip books that when handled properly make little moving pictures, a "Joy of Cooking Cookie Kit" smaller than a deck of cards. Often, when I pull a note from its envelope, a little burst of confetti flies out—tiny metallic stars or colorful sequins that sparkle and shine and make me laugh.

The postcards are perhaps the biggest surprise. Cookie is a postcard fanatic (a "deltiologist," she happily shares with me). She sends reams of them. Johnny rolls his eyes every time an especially big bunch arrives. I just smile and croon, "Jealous?" In fact, he is, and he's admitted as much. Who wouldn't be? For the lavish attention, for its consistency, creativity, and cheer.

The little cards fall through our mail slot in bunches of three, six, a dozen or more, scattering across the hardwood floor of our center hall like pick-up sticks. I bend to gather them, bursting with anticipation, knowing that she'd neatly crammed more into each three-by-five-inch message box than most people do on a single-spaced full page.

She'd write original poems, riddles, haiku; she'd copy great quotations unearthed from books by Alice Walker or spotted on the bumper stickers of passing cars; she'd pen tiny novelettes to accompany mini black-and-white portraits of Frida Kahlo or Muddy Waters, characters carved out of vegetables, or two anonymous people on a train. Sometimes she'd adorn them with shimmering stickers or collectible stamps and they'd arrive addressed to "C. C. Writer" or "Silly G" (for Goose) or "See Sea." She is a marvel. I love them all and, apparently, so does my mailman, Kevin.

Red-haired and nosy, Kevin is a big friendly guy. He'll wave at you from halfway down the street or ring your doorbell to ask all about your vacation after you had your mail delivery interrupted. He's been known to pop in on longtime neighbors for a cup of tea in winter, or a cool drink in the heat of July. He isn't the guzzle-and-go type either; he'll sit and stay awhile.

In the age of catalog overkill and lots of junk mail, he must've been beside himself when he noticed the big uptick in my personal mail, and he made no secret of the fact that he was reading all that he could. Occasionally, tucked between our incoming bills and magazines, I find notes he wrote on scrap paper: "Wow! LOTS of PCs today!" "The monkey card's a riot!" "Read the one with the dancing flowers first!"

Given all this, I shouldn't have been so surprised when I answer the doorbell one day and find Kevin on my porch, beaming.

"Your mom is really something else," he says, handing me a stack of mail that he could have easily pushed through the slot instead. "I just love her!"

I stare at him, dumbfounded: *my mother*? Had he ever met my parents? He gestures excitedly at the pile of mail in my hands. The postcards on top finally clue me in: he means Cookie.

"How did you know who they were from?" I ask, slightly mortified.

"She always writes all those funny pet names in your address—To Daughtermine from Cookiema; To Little Pearl from See Sea. You must love that, huh? No matter how old you get, you're always Mommy's baby, right?"

I am mute, bewildered.

"Hey, don't be embarrassed. My wife is like that with my kids too. What's a mother for, am I right? And all these postcards! Geez, I just love it. She's got a Jimi Hendrix in there today—great shot," he gushes, his bright blue eyes popping out behind too-large glasses. "You gotta tell her I was a big Jimi fan too. Awesome guy. Me and her might've been at the same concert sometime. I'll bet we were."

Isn't it illegal to read other people's mail? Doesn't he have anything better to do? But I don't say anything, because he's a good guy, and deep down I understand: Kevin is smitten with Cookie too.

Of all the postcards, one, the first, which arrived in late March, took my breath away. No matter how many times I reread it, my reaction is the same. Like her it is uncommon—a six-by-six-inch square instead of the traditional, smaller rectangular size. With a silent nod to politics—the war in Afghanistan that we both bemoan—it is a black-and-white photograph of an armed Hekmatyar soldier guarding a beach just outside Kabul. The photo was taken in 1992.

Cookie has managed to fill nearly all the white space on the card. There is a quote from James Baldwin, a short poem by Sue De Kelver, and her succinct critique of a little-known book of haiku by Langston Hughes. But it is her note regarding the photo on the postcard itself that stops me cold:

> Is it that a picture is worth a thousand words or is it that sometimes words just get in the way? Donde está mi niña? A simple question in any language, yes? What does this simple question imply in the mouth of the man in this photo? In the mouth of a butterfly, a panda, or a woman named Alice? Donde está mi niña? A simple question. A loaded question. A political question? A silent question stuck inside one or ten zillion mouths for nearly as many years. . . .

Donde está mi niña? Where is my daughter? I envision my Nica and what life would have been like if I didn't know where she was . . . how she was . . . who she was. For the very first time, I put myself in Cookie's place, and it is like a kick in the gut that doubles me over with indescribable pain.

CHAPTER 9

OCTOBER 26
Did you ever see the
movie "EVE'S BAYOU"?
Did you ever dance the
WALTZ? Do you think
you're a Jackus Peterson?
Do you own a RED VELVET
DRESS? Do you ever want to
sing an aria in the
shower? Do you care if
your lipsticks contain
whale blubber? Do you own
a hairpin? Do you play
Monopoly? Do you play as
you play? Do you skip to
your lou? Do you like
hardboiled eggs? Do
you understand electricity?
Do you do you do you?

LITTLE C

William Claxton
The Eureka Brass Band, New Orleans, 1961
TASCHEN
JAZZ SEEN – WILLIAM CLAXTON

LITTLE C

$\mathscr{A}$s much as I revere words, I subscribe completely to the notion that a good picture is worth a thousand (at least) of them.
So to bolster the mostly written dialogue that had feverishly
begun between us, I start sending Cookie slews of pictures in
an effort to reproduce in living color all that she's missed.

I'm fearful at first of wearing out my welcome or coming
on too strong. But she seems so delighted by every new in-
sight, I am soon revealing myself in free fall. I send her images
of me as a baby in Africa, as kindergarten valedictorian, with
missing teeth in grade school, and with straightened hair in
high school. There I am in a bikini, as a bride, on a ski slope,
eight months' pregnant, with my parents, with my children as
toddlers and on their first days of school. You name it, I tell

it, show it, fax it, e- and snail-mail it. I believe that's what she wants because that's what I want from her.

As our weeks "together" become months and she sends precious few images in response, I come to realize we don't need or want the same things.

I want to know all about her life and for her to know all about mine. Despite her initial surge of seeming candor, she is generally less forthcoming than I am, and less inquisitive as well. Not that she even has a chance at being inquisitive. Without her requesting it, I'm so intent on sharing every detail about my life, that it takes a while for me to see that she really only wants to be assured of one thing: that I've been happy.

I wasn't raised in the lap of luxury that Cookie was as the daughter of an American treasure, but I always felt privileged and never wanted for anything.

My parents and I lived on a block of attached brick houses that each had three bedrooms, one and a half baths, and vaguely Tudor facades. Traffic on our street ran in only one direction, which made it perfect for bike riding, roller-skating, and playing tag until the streetlights came on. It also afforded us the occasional thrill of yelling "ONE WAY!" at carloads of outsiders who dared turn east onto a street that only ran west.

The neighborhood kids referred to Wilson Avenue as "the jungle" because of the way the large oaks, which stood in their rectangular patches of dirt carved into the sidewalk in front of each house, grew together to form a lush, green canopy over our narrow street in the summertime.

As the neighborhood declined in later years, those trees died one by one. My generation had moved on by then—off to college and marriage and early adulthood—and was replaced by other children who rarely came out to play. Although many of their friends and neighbors left for nicer neighborhoods, bigger homes, or warmer climates, my parents refused to move, even after they retired. Home was home. The house was paid for, and they were content.

I was the baby among a close-knit brood of cousins, doted upon by the grown-ups but sobered enough by the pecking order of kids not to become too spoiled. My cousins did their part to help shape me, for better or worse, and we had a ball in the process.

Like Cookie, both my parents were one of five children growing up, but any similarity in their upbringings probably stopped there. Mommy and Daddy were both raised by parents who had little education and were new to this country. My Caribbean-born grandparents worked hard to scale the bottom rungs of the American ladder of success, all so that their children could, with luck, easily reach the middle and, perhaps, rise even higher. For Cookie, who lived her young life at the top of that ladder, there was really nowhere to go but down.

My mother, Vera, had a wide-eyed, apple-cheeked, guileless loveliness that earned her the nickname Cherry, for her likeness to a cherub. She grew up steps from Morningside Park in Harlem, the second child of Grenadian immigrants who believed, as most West Indians did back then, that education and home ownership were the keys to success in any land—most of all, in their adopted one. My grandfather, Charles Greenidge, worked multiple jobs, from cook to cabdriver, to purchase two houses two doors apart from each other, and he vowed that all of his children would graduate from college. Three of the five did; Mommy was the first.

Like Cookie, Mommy was the oldest of four daughters; each was tall, bosomy, and opinionated. She never lacked for male attention, but at twenty-six—an advanced age for a 1957 bride—after much stalling, she chose to marry my father, a lanky, bespectacled Bajan (his parents were born in Barbados) boy from the South Bronx who made up for what he may have lacked in looks and athleticism with his keen intellect and wit.

When I was a preteen, just interested in boys myself, glancing through old albums filled with black-and-white photos of Mommy's doe-eyed face beside those of several dashing failed suitors, I could never help asking, "Why Daddy?"

Her smiling reply was always the same: "He was the smartest man I ever met, and he could always make me laugh." It seemed lame to me at the time, but I came to understand: Daddy was an absolute charmer.

Robert (Robbie to his pals) Clarke was seven years Mommy's senior. They met at City College, where she majored in education and he in chemistry. When he first entered City, it was highly competitive, all male, and completely free of charge, the last being the biggest draw, since he was the youngest in a large family rich in love, but lacking in funds. "The poor man's Harvard," it was called back then (especially by all the poor young men who matriculated there).

Daddy was always a scholar, taking to school and to every chance to learn with nerdish gusto. When he was drafted into the army, he was nearly as afraid of never getting a college degree as he was of being sent home in a flag–draped box. By the time Daddy did return from the Korean War, City had gone coed, "the launch of its long decline," in his only half-joking opinion. But he did get that degree, as well as a master's, and thanks to coeducation, he met his future wife there too.

Their courtship was a long and winding one. Mommy agreed to marry him but put it off for years, during which she launched her teaching career and traveled, once spending an entire summer touring Europe alone. Whenever she and her sisters would reminisce about those days, I'd struggle to envision this bold, romantic, free-spirited version of my mother and wonder where she'd gone.

What I had no trouble understanding was why Daddy had fallen in love with her. Older and more experienced than she was, he'd had his heart broken badly by his first wife. What he saw in Mommy back then that had never changed was that she was devoted and true, as loyal as they come. So, he patiently tolerated her need to explore, until one spring day in 1957 when he picked her up for a date, drove across the George Washington Bridge into New Jersey, and abruptly pulled onto the shoulder. Daddy's demands were simple: she could drive with him to Virginia, where they would marry that night, or he would U-turn back over the bridge and drop her off at her parents' home in Harlem for good.

After calling to check with her parents, who had long since given their blessing (Mommy was the quintessential good girl), my folks eloped. One month later, at my grandmother Eliza's insistence, they had a proper wedding in All Souls Church so the neighbors could see for themselves that Mommy wasn't pregnant and they had not eloped out of necessity. Ironically they would soon discover that Mommy couldn't get pregnant at all, a probable side effect of radiation treatments she'd received for a benign brain tumor in her early twenties. This would lead them to adopt me, the child of precisely the type of scandalous situation my grandmother was so anxious for my mother to avoid. By the time I came along, my parents had been married for seven years; Mommy was thirty-five and Daddy was forty-two.

My folks were a good match, sharing tropical roots and a set of solid values that held the closeness of family above all else. Together they bought a home and built dependable careers they loved—both in education. Eighteen months after bringing me home to Wilson Avenue, they rented out our house and moved to West Africa, where Daddy had a three-year fellowship teaching chemistry at the University of Liberia. It was heady stuff, and it was for them both a dream come true.

The self-proclaimed King of the Ticklers, Daddy was my favorite playmate when I was young. An uncompromising taskmaster when it came to academics, he was equally full of fun. On the first snowfall of each year, he'd fill our bathtub with pristine piles of freezing flakes and then drop me in, fully clothed. Or we'd have a snowball fight indoors, leaving Mommy to be the voice of reason, and the cleaner of our wet mess.

When he left for work each day, Daddy would kiss me and say, "See you in the funny papers," which I thought was hilarious. When I heard the rattle of his green Volkswagen Beetle pulling up in front of the house each evening, I'd be standing at the door before he could get his key in the lock. The moment it opened, I'd leap into his arms, which never failed to open and pull me close.

Unselfish to her core, while Daddy had most of the fun of raising me, Mommy did most of the work and endured the inevitable struggles of will that went with it. She taught me good manners and how to read, cook, and clean, and she insisted that I eat vegetables every day and liver (which I detested) once a week so I'd be healthy and strong.

Not much of a fashionista herself, she splurged on my wardrobe, shopping at Bloomingdale's even when I was quickly outgrowing my clothes, prompting her girlfriends to suggest that if she spent half the amount of time and money on herself that she did on me, she'd be a knockout. Even then, I knew that Mommy might have been more self-indulgent—because she loved clothes and had great taste—if she felt better about herself. She was overweight and had challenging proportions—long arms, a short neck, a large bust, and long, bowed legs. This was back when plus-size clothes were the fashion equivalent of Sasquatch: large, shapeless, and ugly. So shopping for herself was a discouraging chore, whereas shopping for me gave her pleasure.

She introduced me early to the finer things—nice restaurants, the theater, concerts, and summer productions in Central Park—though I usually went under protest. Unfazed by my sullen self, she'd drag me on cultural outings, yanking my hand the whole way. But I almost always came floating home afterward. *Bubbling Brown Sugar*, off-Broadway, Shakespeare in the Park, Dance Theatre of Harlem and Alvin Ailey, open-air jazz at Grant's Tomb, performances by the Negro Ensemble Company, elaborate church basement productions of Gilbert and Sullivan; I rarely admitted it, but I loved them all.

I was too self-involved to realize that my going with her on these outings wasn't merely for my benefit. Mommy didn't believe married women should go many places alone (and one should *never* venture into a liquor store or bar), and Daddy usually wasn't game to accompany her. So, I was often her date.

My folks were big believers in old-school rules, and they always seemed sure-footed, no matter how uneven the path. Children did not wear black. The proper underwear (slips and camisoles when called for) and no white pants, skirts, or shoes, except between Memorial Day and Labor Day, mattered. Honesty and eye contact mattered. Integrity and character mattered. Proper grammar and diction mattered. There was to be no calling grown-ups by their first names, even at their express invitation. Adults were not to be questioned. The elderly were to be revered. Reputation mattered *a lot*, and, as a girl, I was taught to take extra care with mine.

The seriousness with which Mommy would issue the exact same warnings her own mother laid down to her in the 1940s sent me and my friends into fits of laughter. "A man can lie down in the gutter for a week and get up and still be called Mister," she would say. "A woman spends a minute in the gutter and she's a tramp for life." Being a "good girl" mattered.

Good girls didn't call boys up, ask boys out, or make the first move of any kind—ever—according to Mommy. They didn't open their own doors, accept extravagant gifts, or respond to whistling or honking horns ("If he wants you, he can come to the door like a proper gentleman and ask for you," she would say). As for sex, there were no references to birds or bees; she had one direct message and it was repeated often enough: "Do not have sex until you're married."

I'd nod or give some other indication that yes, I understood, and of course, I would wait, but in my head I'd roll my eyes, suck my teeth, and think, *She is way out of touch with the times.* More to the point, she was way out of touch with me. At a time in my life that was complicated by feminism, television, and the sort of intense, totally over-the-top romantic love that a combination of raging teenage hormones and overprotective parenting only heightens, her perspective seemed absurd.

"Why should a man buy the cow when he can get the milk for free?" That was one of her favorites. Growing up in the Bronx as opposed to, say, on a farm, I could barely keep from laughing in her face every time she said it. But I did not— ever—laugh in her face.

"I am not your friend, I'm your mother," Mommy would snap whenever some ill-considered sassiness suggested that I'd gotten confused. I hated when she said that; I would have given anything to have a mom who was more like a friend. Cookie was that kind of mother to her sons, and I had no doubt she would have been that with me. While I might have enjoyed it as a girl, as a grown woman and mother myself, I had done what most of us do and become a younger version of my own mom. By the time Nica turned eight one month after Cookie and I first spoke, she had already heard me say more times than she probably cared to recall: "I am not your friend, I'm your mother!"

My parents were vigilant when it came to vetting my friends, and their radar was as sharp if you lived on Park Avenue as if you lived in public housing. So my friends spanned the range from those whose families were just getting by to those who had multiple homes and were legacy members of Jack and Jill (a black social group that my parents refused to join because they deemed it "too bourgeois." They did, however, allow me to attend all its parties).

Weekdays were devoted to schoolwork and music lessons. I was shuttled to choir rehearsal and Girls' Friendly Society meetings at church on Saturdays, and to Sunday school on Sundays followed by a quick weekly visit to Aunt Iris, the Clarke family matriarch.

Between my mother's and father's eight siblings and large circle of extended family and friends, I had a dependable clutch of aunts and uncles, both real and anointed, to help shape my ideals and aspirations. They represented a broad spectrum of hue, shape, and opinion. What they shared was a commonality of core values and absolute loyalty to one another.

My parents and their siblings never tired of each other, nor did I tire of them. Cookie loved to hear me reminisce about my clan's big dinners on holidays. Unlike her family, which she said was intentionally isolated by Maria, our family gathered often and those fetes weren't obligatory burdens but highly relished events.

Major holidays—even lesser ones like Mother's Day and Father's Day—usually found the Clarke tribe all pulled up to a long stretch of elaborately decorated card tables in Aunt Iris and Uncle Ralph's basement, laughing and teasing one another as we dug into endless helpings of food they'd taken days preparing. After dessert, we'd often pile in to watch grainy films and slide shows of past family gatherings, reveling in our closeness and aging images of good times.

We lit fireworks at a big cookout every Fourth of July and never passed up an occasion to make a champagne toast in which every person, down to the youngest speaking child, had to raise a glass and have a say. It was the grown-ups way of encouraging us to speak in public and get acquainted with alcohol in a setting that was safe.

Labor Day Weekend we all trekked out to Sag Harbor with dozens of other relatives and friends to live dormitory style for three days in the big house owned by my dad's Cave cousins. It was there that I met Johnny, the love of my life, when I was nine, though we didn't start dating until we were nearly out of college.

We were a family of traditions and routines, and I never grew bored with them. There was reading before bedtime, take-out food for dinner on Fridays, and travel every summer, often to Barbados, where Daddy would search out remote members of his family tree. Every weekend our house came alive with the music of Daddy's massive album collection. The years changed, but his tastes never did. Life on Wilson Avenue had a fabulous sound track.

When Daddy was happy, we'd scat along with Ella or Lindy Hop to Stevie's *You Are the Sunshine of My Life*, which was soon eclipsed by his *Isn't She Lovely*. Forever after, that was Daddy's song for me. I have shimmering memories of him deftly circling me around the coffee table and cruising through our kitchen as he taught me to waltz and two-step and Lindy. But there were cracks in the armor.

Even traditions happily celebrated can't stave off discontent. When Mommy was mad, she'd sing Billie's *God Bless the Child* at the top of her lungs as I clapped my hands over my ears and ran for cover. By the time I was a teenager, even their closed bedroom door could not keep hidden the discord that grew between them. Bitter arguments would often end with Mommy hissing, "I should have never let you force me to marry you."

"You got that right," Daddy would yell back as he bolted for the door, the street, his car, and on to who-knows-where to be with God-knows-whom.

While he sought physical escape through outside romance, she'd escape into a Harlequin romance. Though they were formulaic and far-fetched, she inhaled the cheap paperbacks in stacks while Daddy was out, often into the wee hours. I hated Daddy for breaking both of our hearts, and I hated those silly novels. But I was in awe of my parents' ability to carry on.

Mommy never spoke ill of Daddy in my presence; she became a giant to me in that way. At the same time, I resented her for tolerating his neglect, his dishonesty, and his splintered priorities. I wished she would force his hand. I wished she would value herself more. As much as I loved him, I wished she would leave him. I became convinced that I was the main reason they both endured the unhappy years of their union, and it wasn't merely because I was their child; it was because I was their *adopted* child.

They had pledged to give me what my birth mother presumably couldn't, and they weren't about to break that pledge. They never said as much, but I instinctively knew it, and even during the hours I spent alone wishing for a different reality, I was secretly, deeply, desperately grateful for the one I had.

By the time Cookie fell into our lives, Mommy and Daddy had long since rediscovered each other. They were like that old L.T.D. song *Back in Love Again*. Their life together wasn't perfect, but it was enduring. It's been said that only a few have a truly happy childhood. I was one who did.

CHAPTER 10

ROYALTY

*C*harmed. It's reasonable to assume that's what Cookie's life has been. But the more she dodges questions about it or—worse—goes dark and mum, the more I realize I have to tread lightly in my attempts to piece together her past.

I study her correspondence for clues. By May, she's sent enough postcards and letters that I have to empty a large double-wide file cabinet in my home office to make space for them. Our e-mails have their own fast-filling electronic file as well, and we talk on the phone at least once a week. So we've made a lot of headway filling each other in on the past thirty-seven years—the lost years, I call them—and things are generally going well. But after our weeks of thrilling at every new discovery and similarity, our differences are beginning to surface, and at times clash.

Primary among them: pacing.

"I'm moving slow in a fast time." It is Cookie's mantra, the default button she hits every time I try to delve beyond her comfort zone. At first I find it endearing—yet another synchronicity between us—until I realize "slow" is a relative term.

I have never thought of myself as someone who plows forward at warp speed. On the contrary, given my resistance to technology and my daily struggles to keep up with the demands of my life, I too always saw myself as moving a few paces behind most of the world's quick-step. But Cookie sees me as a race car—and she begins jamming on the brakes more and more.

After an initial attempt to please me at every turn, she's grown weary. Her desire to satisfy my bottomless curiosity proves no match for her resistance to revisiting a painful past. Despite her professed admiration for my so-called directness, she isn't used to being pelted with questions, and she isn't going to answer a damn thing until she's good and ready—which I soon come to understand might mean never. While I am instinctively sensitive to her feelings, and often consciously try to put myself in her place so I can better understand, her tendency to shut down at times is disappointing. It can also be infuriating.

Anything having to do with illness or death, or Maria, or her own birth parents makes her squirm. So do most questions directly rising out of Spence-Chapin's report, the faxed copy of which she put away and has still not been able to retrieve. I want to more fully comprehend why the report is so loaded for her when it had been such a godsend for me. I understand that it recalls a traumatic period in her life, but my very existence does that, and she'd mined many of the details from her own experience at Washington Square Home for me already. When I probe the subject, even gently, she goes mute.

The one topic she's eager to explore is the one I care least about: my birth father. She's irked by my lack of interest in him, but she doesn't push. I, on the other hand, continue to dig into holes she's filled with cement, hauling out the proverbial jackhammer when necessary.

"Tell me about Babe," I say on the phone one day, inquiring about her birth mother, whose life is a complete mystery and whose death when Cookie was barely four remains shrouded in tragedy.

"I wish I remembered her," she responds, quietly. "I really don't know much."

"Didn't Maria or your aunt, Baba, ever talk about her?"

"No," she says, her tone hardening defensively. "Mother never talked about her, and I think I knew not to ask."

"Why?"

Cookie takes a deep breath before answering. She is forcing herself to hang in there, but I can tell she wants none of this.

"Babe was their sister and she died very young. I'm sure I was reluctant because I assumed it would be painful for them. And remember, Maria was now my mother, so it was awkward—kind of like you asking Mommy about me." She always refers to Mommy like that. She never says "Vera" or "your mother."

"You have to understand too, it was a different time," she continues. "Adults back then didn't share things with children. Children really were—as the saying goes—expected to be seen and not heard."

"What about your birth father? Do you know any more about him? Do you even know how he died?"

"No."

"You never asked?" Cookie sighs heavily, my cue to let it go. But I just can't. "Aren't you even curious?" Another heavy sigh on her end.

"Of course," she says. This is followed by a request for me to hang on. A moment later she's back, claiming she has a business call on another line and has to go.

Cookie learned from the best how to turn her back on the past and keep moving. From the time she was a small child, Maria required it, just as she did immaculate grooming and impeccable manners. While that approach may have been a plus in Cookie's relationship with the woman who raised her, it wasn't helping our relationship at all. I desperately want to know her history. What did she long for? When was she happiest? Why did she make the drastic shift from how she was raised to how she'd chosen to live and raise her sons? She's had such an uncommon, rich, and winding life; how does she feel about it all?

In time I would learn that, even when she was an adult, Cookie's rare inquiries about her biological parents were summarily dismissed by Maria as well as by Aunt Baba, who did her younger sister's bidding with a level of obedience that bordered on the pathological. Mindful of Maria's edict to leave well enough alone, Cookie has never gone back to her West Medford, Massachusetts, birthplace, even though she believes some of her biological father's family is still there. She has no recollection of the New England town or her early years as the doted-upon only child of Caro ("Babe") and Kenny Lane. Undeterred, I resort to good old-fashioned research. But despite my persistent attempts to find records or anecdotes that might flesh her parents out, Babe remains a one-dimensional figure, defined by birth and loss and nothing more, and Kenny Lane eludes me entirely. Only this much is clear: a tragic shadow, stretching back three generations, hangs over our family.

Babe, Maria, and Baba were the children of Mingo Hawkins, a Boston mail carrier; and his wife, Caro, a native of Paget Parish, Bermuda. In 1924, Caro died giving birth to Babe, leaving her three small daughters motherless. At the tender age of twenty-four, Babe succumbed to TB, leaving Cookie an orphan. Less than two decades later, Cookie would be forced to relinquish her only daughter—leaving me. Perhaps because of Cookie's steadfast prayers, my children and I were spared a similar fate; and now she and I had gotten each other back too.

While I found little documentation on the family Cookie lost, there was plenty on the one she gained, and gradually Cookie's riveting story took shape. The Cole family was large, and Nat made the name famous, but Cookie was shaped by more of a Hawkins sensibility.

The Hawkinses were an impressive clan. Just two generations removed from slavery, they'd emigrated from North Carolina to Massachusetts and transformed themselves through education and a driving ambition to achieve social standing and material success. Mingo Hawkins's position as a U.S. postal worker was emblematic of their progress; it afforded his family financial security and respect. After his wife Caro died, Mingo remarried, but his new spouse proved a tough fit with his daughters. Maria deemed her stepmother to be cruel, and she never minced words about it, flatly telling her own children, "I hated her."

Mingo ultimately turned to his childless sister, Charlotte Hawkins Brown, for help raising his girls. As founder of the venerable Palmer Memorial Institute and a popular speaker on education, race relations, and other social issues, Brown was the family's first celebrity of sorts. As soon as the girls were old enough, they were sent to live with her on Palmer's sprawling campus in Sedalia, North Carolina, where they would be educated both scholastically and in the social graces.

As steeped as my parents were in black history, I grew up with only a vague awareness of Palmer Memorial and the accomplished Charlotte Hawkins Brown. I was intrigued to learn that Palmer Memorial Institute was *the* prep school for America's black elite in the first half of the twentieth century. Everything about the place was a direct reflection of Brown's ironclad beliefs, her exacting standards, and her lofty aspirations for her people. Much of her vision was inspired by Booker T. Washington's perspective on how to uplift the race as well as by the widely published philosophies of another giant of that era, W. E. B. Du Bois.

Brown herself epitomized Du Bois's "talented tenth." A standout student and church orator from a tender age, she aspired to greatness early and worked doggedly to achieve it. A few lucky strokes of fate didn't hurt. A wealthy Boston board of education trustee, Alice Freeman Palmer, spotted Brown reading Virgil in a Cambridge park one day and was so moved by the image of this studious young Negro girl that she wrote about it in a local paper. The story goes that Brown saw Palmer's column and wrote to her, explaining that she was the girl in the park, and that she hoped to train as a teacher and eventually open her own school. Palmer responded by taking Brown under her wing, underwriting the cost of her education, and becoming her mentor.

Palmer went on to become the first female president of Wellesley College and Brown's primary benefactor as she pursued her lofty dreams. Not surprisingly, after Palmer died,

Brown named her school in her mentor's honor. Among the many unexpected gifts Cookie sent me was a collection, edited by Harvard professor Henry Louis Gates Jr., of Brown's only two published works, a novelette entitled *Mammy* and a book of etiquette for young black men and women called *The Correct Thing to Do—to Say—to Wear*. It was accompanied by a handmade postcard featuring Cookie's own ink portrait of her formidable great-aunt.

Mammy, the story of a tragically devoted black servant who was ultimately abandoned by the white family she served all her life, was thought to have been based on one of Brown's ancestors. *The Correct Thing to Do—to Say—to Wear*, published in 1941, embodied all that Brown was about. A granddaughter of slaves, Brown attributed her own success to the two-pronged powers of education and being an exemplar of the social graces. It was that formula she sought to replicate in all of Palmer's students, her nieces primary among them.

Several passages in the book stopped me short, but none so much as Brown's dedication, "To the youth of America, in memory of my mother, Caroline Frances Willis." *Caroline?* I ran my index finger across the name I shared with two forebears: Daddy's mother, Drusilla Caroline Clarke; and Cookie's great-grandmother, Caroline Willis Hawkins.

Cookie inscribed the book, "For my C, with love."

Aunt Lala, as Brown was affectionately called by her trio of nieces (Baba, Maria, and Babe), lived in Canary Cottage, a pale yellow two-story house surrounded by a white picket fence and said to be as charming as its name. Imperious and unyielding in her demands, she ruled supreme over the girls' lives, cutting them no slack in her expectation that they become the quintessential Palmerites: disciplined, devout, impeccably groomed, polished, polite, and, of course, academically accomplished. For the most part, the girls complied.

But despite years of classical voice and piano training, Aunt Lala couldn't distract middle child Maria from her love of popular music. When Maria returned to Boston in 1938 to attend a clerical college by day, she ended up singing in a jazz band at night. Before long, she was singing in New York full-time, using a stage name so she wouldn't embarrass her highbrow family.

Maria married Spurgeon Ellington, a Tuskegee airman from Winston-Salem, in 1943. By then her little sister, Babe, was married as well. In short order, Babe became a mother and Maria a widow when her husband was killed during a training flight after the war. Maria continued to pursue her musical career, performing with Duke Ellington (no relation to her late husband) before striking out on her own in 1946. She was working as the opening act for the Mills Brothers at New York City's Club Zanzibar when in walked tall, dark, and famous Nat King Cole.

Three years into his recording contract with fledgling Capitol Records, Nat's star was on a steep incline. His lush voice and distinctive way with a lyric had already won him legions of fans, but what earned the undying respect of fellow musicians was his genius as a jazz pianist.

One of five children of Edward Coles, a southern Baptist preacher in Chicago, and his wife, Pelina, Nat hit the road performing while he was still in high school and would soon drop the "s" from his surname. Nathanial Adams Cole was charming and kind but neither well-educated nor well-bred by Hawkins family standards, which meant that, except for music, he and Maria had little in common. By her own measure, they were opposite types from different sides of the tracks. Born in Montgomery, Alabama, he was at heart a country boy, laid-back, fun loving, and nonconfrontational. Although she might have been hard-pressed to admit it, Maria, who took great pride in her mother's Bermudian heritage, was much like her prep-school-founder aunt, Lala—driven, high-minded, and controlling.

One other key distinction between the lovebirds: Nat was married—to a chorus girl named Nadine Robinson. She was several years his senior and he would soon leave her for Maria.

Not surprisingly, Aunt Lala was displeased and disapproved of the relationship. The Coles loved Nadine and were less than thrilled as well. But with the exception of Nat's preacher father, who did not condone divorce, everyone attended Maria and Nat's lavish wedding at Harlem's renowned Abyssinian Baptist Church on Easter Sunday 1948. The fete took place just six days after his divorce was finalized.

Life magazine covered the extravaganza, which attracted thousands of Harlem revelers as well as celebrity guests like the jazz singer Sarah Vaughn and Mr. and Mrs. Bill "Bojangles" Robinson. Adam Clayton Powell Jr., who was accompanied by his famous wife, Hazel Scott, officiated.

Life claimed that the reception, at which "600 guests plowed happily through 75 pounds of coleslaw, 18 turkeys, 20 hams, 18 rib roasts of beef and 197 bottles of champagne and whiskey," cost the groom a stunning twenty-five thousand dollars.

Among the article's several photos is one of Nat kissing the bride's three-year-old niece, their adorable "flower girl, Cookie Lane." Of course, Cookie was familiar with the photos, but being just three at the time, she could remember little about the actual day.

One year after Maria and Nat wed, Babe lay dying in a tuberculosis asylum in Boston. The only vivid memory Cookie retained of her mother was the one recounted in my Spence-Chapin report, of her being taken to stand on a grassy hill outside that large brick building where she could look up at Babe standing in a window, and wave.

Babe died on May 7, 1949—the day before Mother's Day—and a battle over Cookie ensued. Contrary to the Spence-Chapin report's chronology, Cookie's father predeceased Babe, and it's unclear how he died. Cookie's Washington Square Home assertion that it was suicide was erroneous. "I don't know why I said that," she later told me. "I made it up."

After Babe died, Nat immediately stepped in to adopt Cookie, but Aunt Lala, who was already caring for her great-niece at Canary Cottage, proposed to raise the little girl herself. Maria was loath to oppose her aunt's will (and to take on motherhood so soon after marrying), but Nat wasn't having it. The newlyweds and Aunt Lala, then in her early sixties, all petitioned the courts; Aunt Lala lost.

Although Cookie remembers Aunt Lala and speaks of her with affection, she never volunteers an opinion on the outcome of her adoption case. She seems to view the past through a wall that she perceives to be impermeable. Her one takeaway about her adoption came directly from Maria: "Mother made it clear that it was Dad who wanted to adopt me, not her," Cookie tells me. "It was his idea, he insisted, he wanted me."

She says it matter-of-factly, without a trace of the visceral outrage it triggers in me. My parents had taken such pains to reassure me of how loved and longed-for I was. How could Maria have said something so cruel?

Cookie moved across the country to live in Los Angeles with her aunt and uncle. The glamorous couple whose big wedding she was in a year earlier were suddenly her new mom and dad. She was four years old, too young to appreciate the depths of her loss or the dramatic shift in her fate.

By then her new father's career was like a fully fueled rocket already in midcountdown. The release of "Nature Boy" the year before had made Nat the first colored radio star. Maria put her own career aside to travel with him and involve herself in every aspect of his life, from upgrading his skin care regimen and wardrobe to influencing his choice of music, managers, and band members.

She placed herself squarely between Nat and anyone who might sap his attention or finances, including his own family, to whom he had once been close. Her involvement earned her few friends and plenty of detractors—on both the professional and the personal fronts—but she was unmoved, determined to give her new husband the polish and sophisticated image she believed would help take him over the top. In her own way, she went about Palmerizing him.

The 1950s were the Cole family's heyday as Nat released one huge hit after another (including "Mona Lisa," "Unforgettable," "Smile," and "A Blossom Fell"). Natalie, a little ham they nicknamed Sweetie (in part as a match to Cookie), was born about a year after her big sister was adopted, and helped put the shine on a golden era for the family. They famously desegregated Los Angeles's Hancock Park, moving into a sixty-eight-hundred-square-foot ivy-covered English Tudor despite angry protests, death threats, and a widely publicized incident during which the word *nigger* was seared into their front lawn. Perhaps most painful to Nat was the fatal poisoning of his beloved boxer, Mister Cole, for which no suspect was ever caught.

Despite the devastating affronts to his family, Nat made it clear they were staying put. So Maria outfitted the twenty-room house on Muirfield Road, and her children, to the nines, making sure every detail was top-drawer and beyond reproach.

When they were in town, Nat and Maria frequently hosted lavish parties in their guesthouse, referred to by their little girls as the playhouse. The adults would revel on the main floor with its spacious living room and grand piano, and the children would hold court upstairs, where they had their own soda fountain and endless sources of entertainment, from a massive train set to exquisite dolls and elaborate dollhouses. According to *Ebony*, once Maria tricked it out, "the playhouse" cost more than the family home.

When I mention it to Cookie (who was tickled by all my research), she explodes in laughter, unable to contain the happy memories it triggers. "Sweetie and I *loved* that playhouse, especially the soda fountain. We had the *best* times in there. We would par-tay!"

The Cole family fortune continued to swell as Nat scored massive hits in Spanish and Portuguese, becoming an international sensation as well as a sought-after star for television appearances and movie roles. Nat's appeal was sweeping the world as he and Maria traveled to perform throughout Europe and Latin America. In 1956, he became the first black man to host his own nationally broadcast television show, on NBC no less. That same year, Maria made an attempt to revive her own singing career, performing live at Ciro's in Hollywood and appearing solo on the cover of *Jet*. She and Nat also recorded a few songs together, although none scored big.

At the height of his career, Nat made about three million dollars a year, so there was no shortage of material comforts, fancy parties, or famous friends. There were also tax issues, which the Coles would blame on faulty advice.

As the girls got older, they occasionally accompanied their parents on the road. Cookie recalled loving these trips and being especially fond of Monte Carlo and Saint-Tropez. But mostly Nat and Maria were away while their daughters were at home, tended by Maria's well-trained staff of nannies and maids along with dutiful Aunt Baba. Postcards, many of which Cookie saved, kept them connected.

In 1959, Maria and Nat adopted a son, whom they named Nat Kelly Cole. Kelly's adoption, like most other major Cole family events, was featured on the cover of *Ebony* magazine. Cookie adored Kelly, they were close, and she was devastated, as they all were, by his death in 1995. They shared a passion for acting and also bonded over being adopted, even though their situations, given that Cookie was a blood relative, were markedly different.

Cookie said Nat was a huge practical joker and baseball fanatic (Casey was named after the famous Casey Stengel); he loved to get on the floor with his children and horse around, and he'd play piano and sing with them, especially the precocious Sweetie. Maria was the enforcer, insisting that everyone—Nat included—maintain a high level of class and composure at all times. No doubt she was clear that, as a black family, they had to appear twice as refined, twice as delightful, twice as well groomed, trained, and talented to be regarded as half as good—and half would never be good enough for her.

Press clips routinely referred to the family as Hollywood royalty, and Maria took the title seriously, assuming a level of arrogance and elitism that repelled many, especially in the black community. Although Nat contributed financially to the civil rights struggles of the day, he was frequently criticized for not being more fully immersed in them, and for continuing to perform in segregated clubs in the South. At the same time, given the Cole family's fame, wealth, and status, they were celebrated and sought after in both white and black Hollywood, occupying an enviable position that Maria guarded like a pit bull.

Just as Maria had been sent off to prep school as a child, when her own children came of age, they were sent away—to summer camps outside Chicago and Detroit, where they could get the exposure to a more down-to-earth existence Nat wanted them to have, and to exclusive New England boarding schools for the education Maria desired for them. By the time Tim and Casey turned one in September 1962, Natalie and Cookie were already living in the Northeast much of the time—Natalie at the Massachusetts prep school Northfield School for Girls, and Cookie at Cazenovia College, in upstate New York. But their parents' influence still loomed large, and both remained Daddy's girls. When the two schools had a conflicting parents' weekend requiring Maria and Nat to split up, Sweetie was miffed when their dad went to Cazenovia, and she got stuck with Maria.

By the time Cookie left for "Caz," as she called it, she was a petite, smart, and beautiful young sophisticate, with an emerging public profile of her own. In fact the previous year, she appeared, resplendent, on the cover of *Ebony* magazine. The occasion: her debut at the annual Los Angeles Links Cotillion.

There is a long, rich history of debutante balls in black culture, dating all the way back to the late 1800s. As in the white world, where they began as a way to introduce "proper" young ladies into society as candidates ripe for marriage, in the 1920s cotillions were mainly reserved for those with a certain social standing. They made a show of reinforcing class boundaries and establishing one's position within an elite community.

Into that tradition marched The Links, a social club founded by a small group of well-heeled, well-educated black women in Philadelphia in 1946. Their mission: to rally like-minded ladies around civic, educational, and cultural causes, raising funds, spreading awareness, and serving as a proud pillar of the race. The Links soon spread to other cities, where many hosted regional cotillions, elegant annual affairs that became aspirational events for prominent and wannabe prominent black families. The grandiose evening hasn't changed much through the decades. Built around the formal presentation of escorted debutantes—most often the daughters of doctors, lawyers, corporate executives, and successful entrepreneurs—in their virginal white finery, it also centers upon a precisely choreographed cotillionette waltz. However, The Links sought to go beyond mere appearances, highlighting young women's scholastic achievements and community service as well. From the start, they required their debs to perform a minimum number of hours of volunteer work. In the 1960s, when Cookie debuted, it was fifteen; today it's seventy-five.

The first Los Angeles Links Cotillion was held in 1952 at Ciro's Ballroom in Hollywood, because the city's more mainstream hotel ballrooms were not yet available for use by African Americans. Nonetheless it became the black social event of the year. A decade later, the extravagant fete featuring Cookie and twenty-seven other debutantes was held at the exclusive Beverly-Hilton Hotel. *Ebony* spent the entire day with Cookie, snapping pictures in her bedroom from the moment she woke up through the formal ball for five hundred that night. President John F. Kennedy, who was staying in the hotel, stopped by at Nat's request (Nat had performed at Kennedy's inauguration and at a Kennedy fund-raiser earlier that evening). In addition to photos of Cookie greeting the president and dancing the cotillionette waltz, *Ebony*'s February 1962 cover reveals the celebrated seventeen-year-old in a white princess-cut gown of imported silk faille descending the stairs as her father, gazing at her proudly in his cigarette-thin black tuxedo, holds her hand, which is enveloped past the elbow in a fine French kid glove. The cover line proclaims: "Carol 'Cookie' Cole Meets Society."

When I was a senior in high school, I begged my parents to let me participate in our church's annual cotillion. A few of my friends were set to be St. Luke's debutantes, and I was envious of the snow-white ball gowns, matching satin stilettos, and long white gloves they planned to wear, as well as the pageantry and excitement the night would hold. My parents bought me a pale beige gown and allowed me to attend as a guest, but they drew the line there, saying that the whole debutante concept was ridiculous and that a cotillion was nothing but a fancy party for status-obsessed phonies. Poring over the feature on Cookie, I doubt my parents would view her coming out differently, President Kennedy's presence be damned.

The *Ebony* article, which describes Cookie as "a refreshingly pleasant teenager," gushes that "even the most lavish production in neighboring Hollywood will never equal the star dust sprinkled excitement of Cookie's real life."

Just two years later, in the spring of 1964, Cookie was thirty-five hundred miles away preparing to graduate from Cazenovia College when she suspected she might be pregnant. Her "real life" had hit a snag, and this was one Cole family moment that *Ebony* would not be invited to capture.

CHAPTER 11

FAR AWAY

$\mathcal{C}$ookie never could remember exactly when or how she told her parents about her pregnancy. There were many things that, no matter how she tried, she simply could not recall. But we deduced that she had to have revealed it late in the summer of 1964, while she was working in summer stock theater in Warren, Ohio, because she was sent to Washington Square Home that fall.

Oddly enough, she recalled that summer as being a lot of fun. I couldn't imagine; I would have been stressed out of my mind. But then as now, it seemed, Cookie had the ability to block out whatever she just didn't want to face.

"I, at the very least, suspected I was pregnant by the time I graduated from Caz," she tells me on a late-night phone call. Interestingly, she vividly remembers her father coming to her graduation, then being upset when he discovered she hadn't packed a single thing. "I threw a few things in a bag and left the rest," she says. "I closed the door and walked away. I'm sure there was some deeper meaning in it—who knows. I was never good at good-byes." I had heard this before, in the report.

Cookie would have been nearly through her first trimester by then, but she wasn't showing and wasn't overly concerned. "I had a way of pushing things aside in hopes that they would just turn out fine somehow. I had my share of moments of being in a funk, but I just kept going day to day, rationalizing that all tragedy would be averted and happiness would reign in the end. Acting was a way to escape. My life that summer—so far away from everything and everyone I knew—was ideal for helping me to convince myself that my situation was somehow not really real."

She arrived in Warren in June, the day after her graduation, and moved into a rented room in the home of ninety-two-year-old Mrs. Abell, "just a doll" whose first name she's not sure she ever knew. Her job with the The Kenley Players at Packard Music Hall involved fourteen- to sixteen-hour workdays that were far more grunt than glamour. The latter was reserved for the show's marquee players, who happened to include some of the era's acting legends.

"I worked like a dog," she tells me, "but it was real, valuable theater experience. One week, I was Peggy Cass's dresser, since she needed help with quick changes. I also dressed Jane Morgan. Dressing the stars wasn't bad when they were patient. But if they were nervous and ungrateful, it could be really rough."

She groans with embarrassment recounting her wide variety of acting parts, from a Jewish girl in *Take Her, She's Mine* featuring Durward Kirby, to a walk-on in *Guys and Dolls* starring

Dan Dailey, to multiple parts—as a baseball player, reporter, and teenager—in *Damn Yankees* with Bert Parks. The comedian Paul Lynde, who went on to *Hollywood Squares* fame on television, was probably the most popular Kenley Player of all time.

"In *Teahouse of the August Moon,* I played a geisha girl and a Japanese peasant," Cookie says, laughing. "I even spoke Japanese in the show, which was really theater jibble-jabble. It was a riot."

But as the summer drew to a close, a riot of another kind had ensued on the West Coast. Five months' pregnant, Cookie must have finally told her mother about her predicament. All hell broke loose, and her banishment began.

Maria led Cookie to believe she'd dealt the family—and Maria in particular—a crushing blow. What she didn't let her daughter in on was the fact that there were other crises afoot at home in Hancock Park, and in the balance, Cookie's pregnancy may have been far from the worst of it. The Cole union was strained and had been for some time. It was rumored that getting pregnant with the twins was an attempt on Maria's part to keep Nat from straying romantically any further than he already had, despite her hovering. If so, it hadn't worked.

In addition to marital woes in the Cole house, there were professional worries too, thanks to a new "king" in town named Elvis, and a popular new sound called rock and roll. Nat's elegant melodic style was becoming elevator music for an emerging generation of beatniks and hippies. While groundbreaking and known for its top-flight guests including Ella Fitzgerald and Peggy Lee, his television show had lasted only a year. He pulled the plug on it after NBC wasn't able to secure a single national advertiser. The snub prompted his famous comment "Madison Avenue is afraid of the dark" and left him deeply disappointed and understandably bitter.

Despite his plum roles, such as playing W. C. Handy opposite Ruby Dee in *St. Louis Blues*, Nat's film career never quite jelled either. So, looking for new ways to bolster his success, he produced a live musical variety show called *Sights and Sounds*. While Maria stayed home with their babies, he hit the road with the cast of his show, including a nineteen-year-old Swedish dancer named Gunilla Hutton, with whom he fell in love.

Thousands of miles away in Manhattan, Cookie knew none of this, but Maria learned of Nat's affair and panicked, clinging for dear life to her husband, status, family, and dignity. Cookie's pregnancy was in some ways the manifestation of a harsh truth: no matter how hard Maria tried to prevent it or how obedient Cookie was in the face of her mother's wrath, their lives were about to change dramatically.

The most tragic testament to this was Nat's diagnosis of late-stage lung cancer, made in early December 1964, days after he recorded his final album, *L.O.V.E.* Believing cigarettes offered a sort of elixir for his voice, enhancing its richness and depth, Nat had long been a three-pack-a-day smoker. He grabbed his first smoke before getting out of bed each morning, stubbed out his last in a bedside ashtray each night, and was known to purposely smoke several cigarettes in succession just before recording. Shortly before such warnings went public, Nat Cole discovered firsthand what the medical establishment had been telling cigarette maker Philip Morris: the habit was deadly.

Holed up at the Washington Square Home under her assumed name, Cookie was lonely, afraid, and completely oblivious to the nightmare unfolding on Muirfield Road. But as the child of performers and an aspiring actress herself, she knew well how to put on a good face, and she did a flawless job of it. She was popular with the other girls and became especially close to the woman who ran the home, Katherine Marvin, who she said reminded her in both spunk and stature of the actress Katharine Hepburn.

Cookie struggles in vain to recall other details of her months sequestered in New York. She admits that every time she tries to read the Spence-Chapin report, hoping to jog her memory, she has to stop; it is still more than she can bear. But perhaps motivated by a desire to send me something priceless to commemorate our first Mother's Day, she digs out a packet of letters and artifacts she'd tucked away from that time, and sends them to me without warning.

On the night the package arrives, I rip open the large padded envelope to find a thick stack of decades-old documents wrapped in clear plastic and labeled WASHINGTON SQUARE HOME in bold black type. As I pull them from the envelope, I feel as if I am unlocking a long-buried hope chest.

I carefully untape the wrapping and lay seventeen pieces of yellowing correspondence out before me. One by one, I pick up each envelope and examine every inch. There are letters written on paper torn from legal pads; crisp, dark onionskin; and pastel stationery from "Mrs. M" and Cookie's Washington Square Home housemates, many of whom had names (and nicknames) that are nearly extinct: Barby for Barbara, Millie for Mildred, Mo for Maureen, and Carly for Carleen. Most of the paper has grown fragile with age, so I handle the letters gingerly, fearful that it might disintegrate and blow away, destroying the only connection I have to this strange other time, just before and after Cookie gave birth to me.

In addition to personal letters, there are a half-dozen original documents rendered buttery soft and slightly faded with time: Cookie's Lenox Hill Hospital bill; the Pet Milk Co.

("makers of America's first name in evaporated milk . . .") bro-
chure of 799 baby names from which she'd made her choice for
me; and a form used to complete my birth certificate. On it,
she'd filled in *Gretchen Tristene Gale* on the line beside "name
of child." She listed her own name as Carroll Gale, her address
as 65 East 82nd St. (Washington Square Home), and her age as
twenty. She left the spaces for her "color" and birthplace blank.
All questions pertaining to my father went unanswered as well.

I gingerly open a dilapidated marbleized notebook. Still
sporting its old Woolworth's price tag, it cost all of thirty-nine
cents. Inside are handwritten poems, apparently Cookie's own.
One is set to the tune of "Favorite Things" from *The Sound of
Music*: *We have big tummies and we wear tent dresses, These are the
factors that seat us on buses, When in a crowd we act dumb, shy or
coy, These are a few of our pre-natal joys.* In the margins she noted,
"Inmates Talent Show—Common Room, Friday." I imagine
them: a small chorus of outcast girls in homemade costumes
with protruding bellies, singing their hearts out, masking their
shame.

It's thrilling to touch things that Cookie touched back then.
I kept everything from the births of my own children—the
little hospital-issued knit caps that were placed on their heads
the moment they were born, the plastic ID bands we all wore
while there, and their first scrunch-faced photos, taken on the
days we were released to go home. I had none of this from my
own birth. My baby album overflows with pictures, but it begins when I'm one month old.

To see these things from Washington Square—and realize
that Cookie saved them in spite of the pain they caused her—
made my first days in the world come to life in a way that satisfied some deep, long-abandoned desire. They also made me

understand more fully how much I continued to mean to her all those years.

I feel a pang of kinship with these women who only knew Cookie during the time she was pregnant with me, and only during her last trimester at that. It is clear they looked up to her. I feel sorry for the losses they all endured, even as I read their news of engagements and weddings, new jobs and next steps. Their letters share a tone of happy optimism laced with shadowy, nagging doubts. I wonder how much of their chirpy correspondence was genuine and how much was a facade. I wonder what, if anything, Cookie wrote to them in response. I wonder what became of them.

Mrs. Marvin had apparently stayed in touch with Cookie the longest. Her Christmas cards were by Cartier, and most of her notes were written on cotton ecru stationery with a raised navy monogram from Tiffany; time had rendered them the texture of fine cashmere. The earliest was dated January 20, 1965, a few weeks after I was born:

Dearest Cookie,

I watched the clock the day you left trying to visualize your arrival and the many crises that awaited you. Your letter tells me you have risen to the needs in real form with maturity and dignity.

I know how you feel about Daddy; there is nothing more difficult than to see a loved one suffer and be unable to do a single thing to alleviate the condition. Taking charge of your little sisters is a good beginning.

Gretchen's new mother just finished her exams for her master's degree. They visit with her next Tuesday and the tentative plans are to take her home at the end of the week. They are very happy and I believe have a lovely home to offer her. Daddy is a college professor.

My love and prayers are with you.

Always,

Mrs. M.

When I speak to Cookie on the phone later that night, she tries hard to fill in the gaps, even though she sounds tense and weary. She admits that plowing through the documents jogged her memory but in ways that have left her exhausted and deeply unsettled.

"Washington Square was such an unnatural existence for me and all of my dorm mates," she tells me. "We were constantly encouraged to think that our months of pregnancy were just passing moments, meant to be quickly and cleanly forgotten. We were advised to make the best of it and then get on with life. The whole premise was just insane. If it hadn't been so deathly serious, it would really have been quite laughable."

Her voice drifts off, and I sense her yearning to escape this trying subject, but I want to get all I can from her now, as I know her willingness to dig around in this old memory box might not recur for a long time. "Did you make any lasting friendships there?"

"I adored Mrs. Marvin," Cookie says tenderly. "I should have kept in touch. But the home was just a way station, a place for us to receive the best care and produce the best babies that money could buy."

Suddenly she's brought up short. "I guess there was actually an exchange of money," she cries. "My God, what *do* adoption agencies charge? What *price* is put on a baby's precious head? I mean, I know some kind of fee is necessary but . . . never mind. I don't want to know what Mommy and Daddy paid for you. I don't want to know how the system worked."

I have no idea what the Spence-Chapin fee structure was back in 1964 or how much of my parents' savings was tapped to create our family, but what I know for sure is that no one paid a higher price for my adoption than Cookie.

CHAPTER 12

DA BLUES

*U*nearthing the Washington Square paraphernalia brings the days surrounding my birth rushing to the surface for Cookie. Whether she can't stop the deluge or doesn't want to for my benefit is unclear. All I know is that she allows her torrent of memories to flow, records them in a journal, and sends it to me. Finally, it explains so much.

> *I am trapped in that square circle of: Damned if you do. Damned if you don't. What can I do? Someone please, please help me. Tell me what I can do.*
>
> *So-called smart people said this would be easy. They had a laundry list of Don'ts: Don't look into her eyes. Don't hold her. Don't feed her. Let her go the moment she arrives. Don't-don't-*

don't do anything other than sign those papers and walk-skip-run away. You can do that, can't you?

Don't worry about it. Everything will be okay. It will be like nothing ever happened. Lucky-lucky-lucky you . . .

But there was a baby. There IS a baby. MY BABY! My little girl, no longer umbilical bound. She is freely free to be my own bright red baby yelling Herself purple in the blue Christmas air. Proclaiming Her identity. Her legitimacy. Her right to be. She will not be denied. My One. My First. My Only Daughter.

You see, we were intimates, She and I. Intimates! Mother and Child.

I did what I had to do: I held Her, fed her, caressed Her satin cheeks, stroked Her brand-new hair. She was all aglow with Light. We swam into each other's eyes. We understood that reflection, our connection. We knew The Story, a Christmas story like no other. A story full of silence, stillness without fanfare, family, friends or a father-husband. What would it take to keep you? To remain incognito? What's the real risk of exposure? Whose life is this, anyway?

On a snowy morning, the day after Christmas, I bawled like my baby. There was something and nothing I could say. I said all that I could think to articulate. I begged. I pleaded into a telephone wire in a hospital phone booth. I reversed the charges and placed a very long long-distance call from the maternity ward in New York's Lenox Hill Hospital to my parents' house on Muirfield Road: three thousand miles away in Los Angeles.

I sang my song. "You have to see her! She's so beautiful. She's a gift, a blessing, a Godsend!" With hope in my heart, I sang, "Can you, will you come and see Her? Can Mom come and see Her? Can Dad? When you see her, you will know . . ."

Did some disembodied, disengaged female voice cut off my happy tune?

"Now you be a good girl, Cookie. Don't create more problems. Do you hear me?" Defeated, I quietly hung up the phone.

I should have returned to that phone booth with my baby. I should have ripped that phone off the hook! I should have slammed that fucking folding door shut and blocked it with my feet, sealed it shut with all my might. I should have sat down on that little metal seat, my tiny newborn cradled in my arms and the mask of obstinate determination on my face. I should have stayed in that old, cold public phone booth for however long it would take for my so-called family and the so-called authorities to let me and my baby have each other forever. Oh YES! I should have made a scene, a public spectacle of myself. I should have been a woman warrior prepared to do battle to protect my child by any means necessary and at any cost.

Should of. Could of. Would of. But didn't. DID NOT. I did not have the power to stay in that phone booth. What did I do? What was my plan? Their plan: sign the release papers (is that what they were called?) before leaving the hospital.

I left Lenox Hill but I held out, held firm, said I needed time to THINK. The papers remained Unsigned. Where did they say they planned to take my baby? Was I allowed to visit?

I returned to Washington Square Home, the brownstone that I shared with X number of other single, somewhat shamefaced girlwomen, all of us indoctrinated to do what I was struggling NOT to do.

My thoughts were clouds of doubt and defiance. Did I make another round of phone calls "home"? Did I beg and plead and cry again? No one called me; that I know for sure. No one wanted to talk to me. No one came to see me. Even if they may have wanted to, no one came. After all, I was being punished. A kind of solitary confinement. No visitors allowed. Those were Maria's strict rules.

The Post Partum Blues was my new and old sad song. The blues is the bloos is the blooz. I couldn't see my baby. I couldn't see myself. I couldn't see for lookin'. I had the blues that only women know about. Blues that knock you to your knees.

All the female operatic voices chimed their aria of control: you need to, you MUST sign those papers! How can you possibly think you can raise this child? People will talk. What will you say? The newspapers will have a field day. This could RUIN your father's career!

Think about what a wonderful opportunity this is. Your . . . er, the . . . THAT child . . . will have the best life has to offer: a mother AND father that will give her everything her heart desires. What can YOU give her? Nothing. Not a thing. You have absolutely nothing to give her. Just think about it. You can get on with your life. You're young. When you're more mature and married, you can . . . you will . . . have OTHER babies. Don't. Don't you dare deprive this child of a happy life! Don't do that.

I held out. I couldn't didn't wouldn't sign.

But one stinging, sunny, still January morning, I had the radio on while I was making my bed. Whatever song was playing was interrupted with some newsperson droning, "Nat King Cole: hospitalized . . . sick . . . dying . . ."

I thought I couldn't have heard what I thought I heard and being anonymous and stupidly incognito, I couldn't openly, immediately react. After all, I was Carroll Gale, not Carole Cole. I had to put on an act until I spoke with Mrs. M in her private office, behind closed doors.

She was incredulous as she aimed to calm me down. Wouldn't they? Yes, of course. Someone would have called her, or me.

Mrs. M offered me her phone. "You must call home, dear." I asked her to stay near me as I dialed.

That same voice I tried communicating with from the phone booth answered, only this time the tone was strained, uneasy: "The press leaked the news before your mother could prepare her statement. You must come home sooner than planned.

"Have you signed the papers yet? Sign them. Come home. Your father is . . . yes, yes, he's in the hospital. Mister Driver Man will pick you up from LAX. Have you lost any weight yet? We'll figure out a reason, make an excuse. Arrangements have been made. Sign. Come." Click.

All and everything and everything else exploded with that phone call. Everything was entirely wrong and it was all my fault. My undoing. My shame. My betrayal. My negligence. My ignorance. My shit.

I should have stayed in that phone booth. Why did I turn the radio on? Why was everything so wrong, so lost, so bitter and blue, so nasty, so heavy with grief and guilt? Where was the JOY, the laughter? Why couldn't this Christmas baby be a blessed event? What was happening? WHERE IS MY BABY? What can I do?

I don't remember how it went down. Everything seemed to speed up and speed by. Everything was moving faster than light.

I think I went to that building to sign those papers. I didn't have a prayer or a choice to do anything other, anything else. I was powerless as a slave.

No one was there to protect the fact of us. No one stood by me to help me stand my ground, or hold out, or buy time. I know I wanted to see you, my baby. I ached to see you just one more time. To kiss, to touch, to bless you. To reluctantly say good-bye for now or . . . good-bye, but I won't forget you.

They didn't think I was strong enough so they firmly advised against a visit. Did someone say, "Make it a clean sweep. Make it easy on yourself. It's better this way . . . "?

"You have other things to think about. Now, here's the pen . . ."

My daughter left Her face in my mind. She left Her total tiny being and Her face in my mind. With a single stroke of my pen, I condemned MY child to . . . life. Another life. A life without her mother.

Everything had fallen apart. I was numb. Empty. Forced to leave. After four days, it would not be for me to feed Her, to clothe Her, to bathe Her, to wipe Her head, to wake for Her when She cried, to sleep beside Her when She was afraid.

It would not be for me to walk out every morning to provide for Her, to come home every night to comfort Her. It would not be for me to tell my little girl, born full of hope, that there was no hope in the world.

But what about guardian angels? Music that heals? GOD? Forgiveness? What about the Love that never dies?

All the days were full of crap from late December to February 15, 1965. Tons of sad-ass emotional, psychologically and spiritually debilitating mysterious crap happened from then on.

Someone took me and my sister to Lord & Taylor's to get clothes for Dad's funeral. (Fashion-conscious Maria's directive was to buy something in a charcoal gray because "they are too young to be dressed in black.")

It was the beginning of the end of damn near everything that contained light. I lost my baby in December. I lost my father in February. I lost my soul.

Then . . . thirty-seven undulating, mischief-making, livelong lifetimes of years later, a relentless, often lonely journey was finally eclipsed in Spring by what Coltrane would call "A Love Supreme."

On March 18, 2002, the day after what would have been my father's eighty-third birthday, the telephone became a lifeline. Her voice was magically musical, mysteriously familiar, soft as rainwater and full of Grace.

William Least Heat Moon says, "A true journey, no matter how long it takes, has no end." The Sioux once chanted: All over the sky, a second voice is calling.

CHAPTER 13

HANG-UPS

*I*t's too much, I fear. All this pain I've stirred up for her is untenable. I beg her forgiveness and tell Cookie I have to see her, to make sure she's okay. She assures me that she is, that there are no apologies to be made, that the process is "difficult but cleansing—and necessary."

So, I'm forced to face the fact that it's me; I'm not okay. The cards, the e-mails, the calls are wonderful, but they are no longer enough—for me—and this eventually leads to our first fight.

I am on a business trip to Nashville, and after calling my parents to tell them I'm safe, I call Cookie, per her request, to let her know the very same thing. Our conversation starts out fine enough, but I am not in a great mood. A storm has been brewing inside me and I'm ready to blow.

For days, Johnny has been urging me to accompany him on a business trip to Los Angeles that's scheduled for early June. This way, I won't have to fly across the country (something I dread) alone. This way, he will be there to catch me if I fall. This way, she and I can meet in person, and isn't that the next obvious step? With this trip on the horizon, why not meet now rather than wait nearly three more months for the Golf and Tennis Challenge? Johnny asks. This time, I welcome his nudging and his eagerness to help orchestrate. My response: Why not, indeed?

But when I raise the idea with Cookie before leaving for Nashville, it doesn't go over well. There is none of the open, eager willingness with which she greeted my first call. Gone are the spontaneity and joy that infuse her postcards. On the contrary, she all but rejects the plan outright—with attitude—so I back off, trying to hide my dismay. I know better than to push her. She's all light and air and openness . . . until she isn't. Once she shuts down—which she does more often than she'd ever admit—she is as closed, done, and immovable as I've ever seen anyone, except maybe myself.

My hurt and anger over her resistance to our meeting simmer just beneath the surface and are building to a slow boil. By the time I reach Nashville, I'm just about there.

"You made it safe and sound," she chirps, after answering my call on the first ring. "Now tell me again what this is all about. You're putting on some sort of entrepreneurs' conference for *Black Enterprise*? This happens every year, right?"

"It does," I say.

"And what does that look like? I have absolutely no reference point for something like this. What happens there?"

I describe the program, consisting of three days of motivational speeches, networking sessions, and seminars designed to educate and inspire small-business owners. I also explain our Kidpreneur component, a parallel program designed to teach children the ABCs of entrepreneurship.

"Do you mean to tell me children will be initiated into some sort of capitalistic mind-set at this event?" she asks, not bothering to disguise her disdain and disbelief. "They'll be taught how to start and run their own businesses and how to think like little moguls?"

"You make it sound like a cult." I laugh, but I feel my edges hardening. "It's more like a day camp, and yes, that's exactly what we teach them. The kids get really into it. Some of them already have their own businesses—and they're profitable. Nica and Carter participate every year. It's never too early to learn how to generate a decent income and manage it."

I know this touches a nerve. Neither Sage nor Harleigh works full-time, and because they are artists, it isn't clear to me if they ever did. John, who seems to work nonstop on household projects, doesn't have a good old-fashioned *j-o-b* either. It is one of those subjects we dance around. Until now, this aspect of my job had been another.

"Well, I'm not sure I agree," she says. "In fact, I'm quite sure I don't. But I suppose it makes sense that that's what a *Black Enterprise* would be about. Is everyone who comes to this gathering African American or of so-called African descent? How many people do you expect?"

"Over eight hundred people registered, and, yes, they are all black," I say, trying to contain the heat I feel rising on the back of my neck. "Anyone can come, but this is our audience. This is who we target, this is who responds. That's why it's called *Black* Enterprise. Is that an issue for you?"

"Of course not! I hear that, although I would hope that who exactly qualifies as 'black' would be open to interpretation. And I'm just not so sure about the idea of indoctrinating children into—"

"We don't 'indoctrinate' children into anything. We teach them about business and explain that this is how the world works. They are learning about entrepreneurship just as they would music or art or any of the things that you view as worthwhile. As for the black thing, yes, they're all black, and that's key, because our children are not exposed to business and other potential vocations the way other children are. Why do you have a problem with that?"

"I didn't mean to imply that I do," she says. "And I do hear what you're saying about the need to expose underserved children more, but I'm not sure that's entirely a racial issue."

"You're right. Underserved children come in all shapes and colors. But at *Black Enterprise,* we are focused on one ethnic group and we don't apologize for it. What is up with your black thing?"

"Ex*cuse* me? My *what?*"

"You know what I'm talking about. You obviously have a hang-up about this. You're always wanting me to fly the biracial flag and go looking for my birth father . . ." I should leave it there. Unfortunately, I don't. "I mean, have you ever even dated a black guy?" The question has been spinning through my mind for weeks but I didn't know how to ask it. Now I have, and it is on.

Cookie springs back, openly angry at me for the first time. She fails to control her indignation as she begins regaling me with stories of her multicultural conquests throughout the years, which, to both my horror and amusement, included "all sizes, shapes, and races of brothas," even Stevie Wonder, she notes in what I view as a brazen attempt to impress me, which it does.

She expresses her outrage that I would dare to ask her such a thing, and that any aspect of what we've shared with each other has led me to believe that she isn't in full possession of her own racial identity and proud of it.

I counter: "Given that my birth father was white, your sons' father is white, John is white, and even your annulled husband is white, it seems like a pretty fair question."

She fires back: "Since we're being so forthcoming about our social histories and sexual preferences this evening, have you ever dated anyone who *wasn't* black or who was, in fact, white?"

"Other than black? Yes," I answer. "White? No. What of it?"

"I don't understand how you came to be so closed minded. So judgmental. So *limited*." I take this as a veiled indictment of my parents' influence, but just in case I don't, she addresses the issue head-on. That's when things get really tense.

"I have been trying to understand why Mommy and Daddy chose not to tell you that you were biracial—and why you have refused to embrace it or even openly acknowledge it," she says in a very carefully controlled tone.

"My parents are not racists," I yell.

"I didn't say that they are," she answers, calmly seizing the upper hand. "I am merely suggesting that your lack of toler- ance for dating outside of your so-called race—or for my doing so—and your unwillingness to view yourself as biracial stem from somewhere. It's logical to assume that your upbringing had something to do with it. That's not a criticism, it's merely an observation, whereas your—for lack of a better word— *assault* on me was clearly a criticism."

"I didn't mean to criticize," I say, beginning to feel my anger give way to truer feelings. "It was a question. I have lots of questions, way more questions than you're ever willing to answer, that much is clear."

She sighs. I sigh. We are both frustrated and hurt and regretful, especially me, since I started it. It was a passive-aggressive, immature move on my part, and I know it. I don't really give a damn whom she dated (although the Stevie Wonder bit is definitely intriguing). I am just frustrated because I want to see her. That's what this is really all about.

The phone calls and all the mail are fine—better than fine—but I haven't seen so much as a photograph of her (despite the albums-full I've sent). I need to *see* her, and as with so many subjects, whenever I broach the idea, she dodges it. *Why? What is she hiding? What is she afraid of? Why doesn't she feel the same way I do?*

"Here's a question that maybe you can answer," I say, as my eyes fill with tears. "Why don't you want to meet me?"

There it is, out in the open. No more dancing around it.

As I struggle not to fall apart in the engulfing silence, I think about calling Dr. Rosen.

In late April, I had taken Cookie's advice from our first conversation, and gone to see a psychotherapist for the first time in my life. Although things were going unbelievably well at that point, it seemed like sheer luck. I didn't know another soul who had ever experienced anything like this, so it wasn't lost on me that I was in uncharted territory with Cookie and had no idea what I was doing. The stakes were high, not just for me, but for my whole family—parents and children included—and I needed a guide, a road map, a guru, someone to help me sort things out so they would continue to go well and not suddenly go terribly wrong, as I feared they were doing now.

Dr. Rosen was recommended by my friend Charise. A social worker and gifted amateur shrink herself, she was a terrific resource, and just as she promised, Dr. Rosen was great. He had a calm, professorial demeanor that I liked; he listened to my story and was duly impressed.

"Every adopted child grows up with a fantasy about her parents and what it will be like when they meet," he told me in our first session. "If it happens at all, it rarely lives up to expectations. Sometimes it's terribly disappointing." I didn't know that, although I suppose it's what I'd always dreaded.

"In every way, you got the fantasy. You do realize that, don't you?"

I did, but to hear him say it made it feel true.

In subsequent sessions—I had been to three so far—Dr. Rosen was as interested in my parents' reactions as he was in Cookie's. He remained quiet as I told him how Mommy had encouraged me to call her and had made me feel confident that Cookie would embrace me from the start. My parents had not hovered as Cookie and I forged a bond, nor did they dwell on news of her. Daddy never brought Carole up; Mommy would ask every so often if I'd heard from her or how things were going, but she didn't pry, and I was grateful for that.

After I described their reactions to my learning about Cookie, Dr. Rosen smiled. In their case too, I got the ideal, he said. Again, this I knew.

"I have another patient who found her birth mother. When she told her adopted mother, the response was as bad as they get. She screamed and cried and said hateful things. My patient was upset, of course, but we talked about it and made a plan for how to work through it. A few days later, she received a large package in the mail. Inside was every photograph, report card, award, and art project she had ever made as a kid. The note from her mom might as well have been a bomb. It said, 'Give these to her. I don't want them anymore.'"

More and more, I was realizing how rare and blessed my reunion story was. Sitting in Dr. Rosen's cozy suburban office, I recalled attending a meeting at Spence-Chapin a few years back where I met a very tall, very pregnant blond woman about my age who told me a recent search for her medical history had unexpectedly led her right to her birth parents. It turned out they married each other and had five other children, all of whom couldn't wait to meet the missing child for whom they'd always saved a space. It sounded like a dream come true, but she seemed totally overwhelmed by it, and not in a good way. She said meeting them was strange, difficult, and deeply uncomfortable because they wanted her to assume what they saw as her rightful place, but she didn't see a fit. She already had a family she loved; she fit somewhere else.

The fact that she was pregnant with her first child throughout this entire ordeal only complicated matters. Her biological family wanted to meet the baby and became a part of her life. She said she had no plans to see them again anytime soon, if ever. I never forgot the flatness of her response when I asked her what she'd tell her child about them: "Not much," she said.

Dr. Rosen called my parents' reactions to my finding Cookie "the linchpin of the reunion experience" for me. If Mommy and Daddy hadn't supported my establishing a relationship with her, I doubt that I'd have been able to go through with it. I wouldn't have had the heart to openly cross or disappoint them.

"It sounds as if things are going extremely well, but you need to understand that it will be a roller-coaster ride." Dr. Rosen's soothing demeanor didn't do much to camouflage the fact that he was issuing a warning. "Experiences like this are multilayered, like an onion. You peel one layer back and there are countless others beneath it, some of which you can't even see. You can never be sure what you're going to find, or how you're going to feel."

His explanation was both reassuring and disquieting at the same time. The roller-coaster imagery took root in my mind. The world is divided into two kinds of people: those who love roller coasters and those who hate them. I hate them, always did, and I knew without asking that Cookie hated them too. So when our smooth, easy little ride flipped upside down in the midst of that awful phone call, with me sitting in a Nashville hotel room and her sitting at her desk in Los Angeles, we both panicked. We had reached an impasse, and I was at a loss for how to get around it while she didn't even seem to be trying.

I never suggested she come to me, even though I secretly wished she would at least offer. She hadn't flown since taking the cross-country trip to her sister Casey's wedding more than twenty years before. Whatever happened on that trip—Cookie only described the flights there and back as "awful"—by the time Timmie got married three years later, Cookie couldn't bring herself to go. Given my own anguished struggles with flying, I understood. But her resistance to my coming to see her was something I just couldn't comprehend, and so far, she had been unable to explain it. Every time I brought up the possibility of our meeting in the flesh, she'd start gabbing about patience and the need to take things slow and how she never responds well to being pushed. She would stutter, stall, backpedal, make excuses, and jam on the brakes or ignore me alto-gether in hopes that I'd back off—and I always did, until now. This time, I would not shrink away.

"Hello?" I demand into the gulf between us. "You still there?"

"Of course I am and of course I want to meet you," she says sweetly, attempting to comfort me. "You really are such a Silly Goose." I love it when she says things like this, but I'm not going to let her distract me.

"That's great!" I say, ready to seize the moment and make her prove it. "How about next weekend? I can hop a flight and come right on out. How about Friday? What time is good for you?"

Silence. I wait for what feels like days before answering for us both.

"Exactly," I say, bitterly. From the start it all felt too good to be true; secretly, we have both been dreading this moment. "I guess the honeymoon's over."

"I hope not," she replies, sounding tired and beaten, "but we should probably say good-bye for now."

I hang up and have just one thought: forget her.

This has become too hard, and too time-consuming, I ra-tionalize to myself. In just two months she's turned my life inside out. She is taking up time and space in my head, in my heart, and in my day. That is time that I used to put toward my work and my kids and my life—*I actually used to have one outside of her*—and now it all revolves around her calls and e-mails and postcards and funny little presents and my constant quest to respond in kind, to get to know her, to impress and please her. But if she doesn't want to meet me in person, what are we doing? *What am I doing?* What's the point of it all?

As I climb into my hotel bed that night, free of the usual distractions of home, I eerily detach from everything, including her. In that moment, it is easy to devise a strategy for pulling way back from Cookie. I decide to gradually force a shift by e-mailing her once or twice a week instead of a few times a day. I'll respond to every third or fourth snail mail instead of every single one. I'll stop calling her entirely, at least for a while.

If she wants a pen pal instead of a daughter, that's what I will be. It's time to face it: our story isn't going to have that fairy-tale ending after all.

As I drift off to sleep I try to steady my mind by thinking about the conference. I'm scheduled to speak to a ballroom full of entrepreneurs at eight the next morning. My life is calling—my pre-Cookie, perfectly fine life. I got carried away—who could blame me?—but now I am ready to go back. Or so I tell myself.

I sleep restlessly, rising at five to find her e-mail, sent less than an hour earlier, awaiting me:

Hi. First things first: OF COURSE I WANT TO SEE YOU! I'm just such a creep sometimes. Guess I'm not as spontaneous about some things as I'd like to (or should?) be. My hesitations are complicated. I feel like I'm trying to process so much stuff all at once. How to explain?

Frustration sets in whenever I realize there are experiences in life that are incomprehensible to other people. Even w/people that have similar experiences, there are always elements that remain unexplainable. Bear w/me 'cause I'm not doing a great job of even formulating these thoughts into sentences.

. . . I just got off the phone with Carla, a good friend

for years. Your ears should have been burning because 99 percent of our conversation was about you/us. Yes, many years ago I shared you w/her. I've now come to realize through people like Carla how very much you have been on my mind over the years . . . more than I guess I allowed myself to realize.

Needless to say, Carla was gushing w/joy for us: laughing & praising the mysteries of the universe; shocked and sorta pissed about Tim & Maria; lecturing me on protecting myself when I talk to Maria; reminding me not to have any expectations of her, etc. In front of & in between all of the above, Carla keeps saying, "So when are you going to see Caroline? We have an apartment in NYC & you can use it! If you want, you can meet there, just the two of you. Just let me know." I'm sputtering and laughing through it all but I'm thinking, ugh.

My point is, I'm trying to deal w/everything and . . . it's been tough.

Our joy & journey of discovery has been profound, uplifting & intense. As much as your phone call changed EVERYTHING, my life & yours continue to be full of everything that was already on our plates. I'm not by any means suggesting that all or any of our life-issues need to be resolved when you and I meet. I think I'm just saying, I'm trying to manage a lot right now and I hope I can feel less weighted down when we meet so that I can totally allow myself the luxury of having you near.

Since I'm in confessional mode, I may as well try to explain something else. This is also not easy for me to talk/ write about, but here goes: We've laughed about the East Coast/West Coast thing . . . California/beautiful people stereotypes, etc., but I guess I figured that you & your family & friends are all NY-chic & dressed to the nines & thin-thin-thin & well-to-do w/perfect lives, blah-yadda-blah . . . and I am . . . none of that. Bottom line: I guess I'm feeling that I don't want to be a disappointment to you and I don't want the physical me to stand in the way of everything we've experienced so far . . . or to alter the me that you're getting to know via phone & e-mails & PCs.

On that note, I had better close. I'm going to try not to stress about any of the things I've conveyed in this e. This wasn't an easy one to write but I think I feel better for making the attempt. Please don't let anything I've said disturb your day. If you have a prejudice against meaty ole me, you'll probably be gentle and politically correct in letting me know. If you still want to see me, maybe I can buy some time & lose some pounds before that day.

Love to you my Caroline, my beauty.

See

I'm stunned. *Is that what this is about?* Heartbroken for Cookie, I sense more of Maria's dubious handiwork. I know from Timmie that her mother is weight-and-looks-obsessed. Maria keeps herself in fighting trim, youthful and impeccably appointed at all times. Her vanity is such that she has Timmie's and Casey's sons call her "Mamaria" as opposed to the less vibrant "Grandma." It's clear from the many gifts Cookie's sent, she inherited her mother's exceptionally good taste. But she has admitted that Maria is often critical of her attire and personal upkeep. Maria also openly disapproved of how casually Cookie dressed the boys when they were little. I barely registered the comments at the time, but they float back to me now.

With minutes to spare before my workday begins, I toss out every promise I made to myself mere hours before and I e-mail Cookie right back:

Where to begin . . .

I love the way you express yourself. I love your deep kindness, softness and sensitivity. I love it that you're so smart and humble at the same time. I love how often you call me "silly goose," because it is so damn cute and sweet and childlike. I guess it makes me feel like a little girl for a second, as I would have been in your presence if life had been entirely different. Understand, it doesn't make me wish for those what-ifs, but it gives me a precious taste, and that's enough, not just because it has to be, but because it truly is.

You think you were muddled, but your e-mail makes everything so clear. I get it. I do.

So, we'll keep taking it day-to-day, riding this roller coaster that we both wish was a kiddy-ride, laughing together when it's fun and comforting each other when our stomachs drop to our toes and we think we can't bear one more terrifying dip or unexpected turn or dark tunnel. We're on it together, just the two of us, and that's all that really matters. So, just tighten your safety strap and know that I'm right here by your side.

I send you electronic hugs and love for real.

Sea

The sign-off is very Cookie-like. Am I just beginning to express myself like this or have I always done it? I can no longer tell.

She calls the next day, and our conversation is brief but it's long enough for me to finally hear her say, "Come."

Before she can change her mind, Johnny and I book a flight to Los Angeles for the first weekend in June. Gamely, Cookie holds on, as our roller coaster picks up speed. Our trip is less than three weeks away.

CHAPTER 14

MAMARIA

$\mathcal{A}$s soon as we are set to meet, Cookie becomes obsessed with confronting Maria. For reasons I don't begin to understand, the two events are connected in her mind and in a distinct sequence: before coming face-to-face with me, she needs to deal with her mother.

Their relationship confounds me, and whenever she broaches the subject, everything bright, strong, and sure in Cookie seems to shrivel and turn cold. Timmie and her family, who live in the same state as their mother but at a purposeful distance, host Maria every Christmas and sometimes on Thanksgiving, and maybe they visit a few other times a year. That, Timmie has always maintained, is plenty. But it quickly becomes clear that, compared with her big sister's, Timmie's relationship with their mother is downright idyllic. Cookie has never been to Maria's Jacksonville, Florida, home; and when Maria visited Cookie in Tarzana a few years earlier, Cookie turned to John and her sons and told them that her mother was never to set foot in their home again. She hasn't.

While Cookie sends flowers every year on her mother's birthday and they communicate about matters relating to the business and Cookie's oversight of Maria's ailing older sister, Aunt Baba, when necessary, that's the extent of it, and—by Cookie's measure—it is still, at times, too much. But if Maria's relationship with her children is strained, at least there still exists some semblance of a bond between them. To her six grandsons, Maria is largely a mystery, and a somewhat troubling one at that. While she has contact with the twins' sons, by the time I reenter Cookie's life, Maria hasn't seen her other grandsons in years. She doesn't even send them Christmas or birthday cards.

Despite not having had a grandmotherly model to mimic, Cookie enthusiastically embraces the prospect of embodying the role herself. I'm touched by her genuine interest in my children, whom she only knows through quickly outdated photos and my stories, which always accentuate the endearing and adorable while skipping past the grating and gross. Her own inner child frequently appears, as when she quizzes me about Nica and Carter in ways that reveal how much she genuinely likes children and reveres the wonders of childhood itself.

"Do you read to them at bedtime? What authors do they like? I adore Dr. Seuss and Roald Dahl. Has Miss Nica been introduced to the wonderful Judy Blume yet?"

From the start, she was eager to send them gifts, which I discouraged, because they didn't yet know about her. (I'm still not sure how to introduce her in a way they'll understand. I also fear confusing them about their other grandparents, especially on my side.) Respectful of my position but wanting to connect somehow, she began sending things for me to share with them—Japanese anime videos, a collector's edition Slinky, and a Nat King Cole CD she produced in 2000 called *Christmas for Kids (From One to Ninety-two)*. It features classics like "Frosty the Snowman" and "Silent Night" as well as the lesser known "Brahms Lullaby." Cookie was thrilled when I told her how much Nica and Carter loved it; I didn't mention that we already owned it and had been enjoying it for years. Nor do I confess how strange I feel listening to it now, knowing what I do. I'm glad she doesn't ask, because I can't aptly describe it, this odd mixture of exhilaration and utter disbelief that rolls over me unexpectedly and often.

In late April, as Nica's birthday drew near, in deference to my still having not told the children about her, Cookie offered to send her granddaughter something from a secret admirer. Again I demured, and although she seemed a bit deflated, she didn't insist. On the contrary, she declared me a "clearheaded and wise-woman-warrior-mom." Such generous heaps of exaggerated praise still catch me off guard, just as her unfettered affection for me, Johnny, and the children often does. For all we've shared over the course of two short months, we still barely know each other, and it isn't lost on me that Cookie doesn't have to care about any of us; she chooses to.

*T*he small circle of friends and family I've told about Cookie and me reacted with sheer awe and delight. Even my parents, who maintain a palpable distance from the subject, rarely inquiring about Cookie, and perhaps assuming—even hoping—that there is precious little to discuss on the matter, responded with mild but duly noted approval to the few details that I volunteered about our evolving relationship.

For the most part, Cookie was enjoying a similar experience on her end, but the weight and ambivalence surrounding her need to talk to Maria and Timmie about why they never divulged what they knew, or at a minimum suspected, hung heavily in the air.

Cookie had finally worked up the nerve to talk to Timmie, in late March. She called me as soon as they hung up. She said Timmie was "beside herself and nearly speechless," as she shared our news. But Timmie found her voice when Cookie confessed that she'd been wounded by her sister's prior reluctance to help bring us together.

"How could I possibly have known that Caroline was really your daughter?" she asked. "Of course, I wondered. Her age, her birthday, where she was born, that she was adopted . . . it was possible, I knew that. But I had *no way to know* for sure or to find out, and *neither did Mother*. If I could have, honey, I would have. You have to believe me." But Cookie didn't.

"You introduced Caroline to Mother," Cookie pressed. "She told me all about her staying at Mother's place in the Ritz, and going with you and Casey to Sweetie's concert in Boston. Do you expect me to believe that you didn't tell Mother you thought she might be my only daughter—the same child Mother forced me to give up?"

"It was such a long time ago." Timmie sighed. "Yes, she met Mother, and I told Mom that I wondered . . . that Caroline could be . . . that it was possible. But Mother had no idea what the truth was. I think I asked her if we should say something to you, but Mother thought it would hurt you to drag all that up, especially since all we had were questions. We didn't have any answers, so what would be the point?"

For Cookie, the point would have been reassurance—knowing for sure that I was okay.

Cookie was seething, but she didn't unleash her anger at that moment. In that sense, the sisters' conversation was like countless others in their family through the years, where hurts got buried, resentments simmered, secrets lurked in the shadows, and important things went unsaid.

I didn't know what to think. I felt empathy for and loyalty to Cookie, but I'd also gotten her phone number from Tim. If Timmie had been conspiring to keep us apart all those years, why would she have so easily—and knowingly—handed me the key to making contact with her sister? Meanwhile, Maria's emotional grip on Cookie was significant. I wanted to be there for her, but I had no desire to get entangled in their complicated knot.

Not wanting to upset Cookie by appearing to defend Maria or Timmie, and afraid of doing anything that might make her more anxious about our scheduled reunion than she already was, I went mum on the subject and prayed that nothing would interrupt our smooth flow. But unexpectedly, in May, Cookie does the thing she most dreads and needs to do: she calls Maria.

Distrustful of her mother as well as of her own memory, Cookie takes diligent notes throughout their conversation, and immediately e-mails them to me.

Called Mother today and told her, "I have really great news that has made me enormously happy."

"What is it?" was said in a tone of preparing to hear bad news.

"I heard from my daughter!" I said. Long pause.

Then: "What? Who?"

"I heard from my daughter . . . the baby I had to give up for adoption."

"Don't tell me . . . you mean, she admitted to it?"

"What? What do you mean? She called me, Mom."

"Oh, well, that's . . . fantastic." Pause.

"Well, I think you know that she and Timmie have been friends for years."

"Oh. Is that the girl that married one of those Graves boys?"

"C'mon, Mom. You've met her and you know the name of her husband because—"

"Now just a minute! What are you trying to say? I only met her once, when Tim brought her to Boston. When she told me she was born on Christmas day, I thought maybe she could be . . . It looked like she had your hair, what we used to call 'good hair,' but I haven't given her one thought since. I forgot about it because I think she lied to Timolin about the year she was born."

"Mother, why would she do that?"

"I haven't any idea, but the year she said wouldn't have been the right year for her to have been your child. I may have asked Tim what else she could find out, but Tim said the girl wasn't interested in talking about it. . . . I'm happy for you. How did she get your number?"

"Tim gave it to her. She fabricated a story about her magazine wanting to do a story on me. . . ."

"Well, I'm glad she found you. That's important. If you had gone looking for her, it might not have turned out well . . . you know how these things can go. She may not have wanted to know you."

"Well, since you've known about her for so many years, did you ever think about saying anything to me?"

"No, never! Anyway, I didn't know for sure."

"But when you and Tim discussed—"

"We never discussed it. Not really. I would never mention it to you. I thought it would hurt you, that you'd say why bring it up, it happened so long ago. Do you remember . . . I think I said something to you once and . . . Well, it's wonderful. Strange too. Hope you'll get to see her. I guess you won't get on a plane but maybe she'll come to you. . . . You know, I won't get into it right now but I don't think that was Kelly's mother that he found."

"Mother, what are you saying? Why would she lie, and what does that have to do with my—"

"You know how people are, how they want to be attached to celebrities. I'm glad you didn't put yourself in that position."

I feel uneasy, like someone trapped in a bathroom stall, unable to avoid overhearing a private conversation. I hang on every word, nonetheless.

When I call Cookie later to flesh out the gaps in her pseudo-transcript, she is still on fire. The conversation with Maria has unnerved and empowered her at the same time. She talks a mile a minute, hurling fury at her mother's responses and overall demeanor. She says Maria had gone on to ramble about the actress Dorothy Dandridge ("Aunt Dottie" to Cookie when she was growing up). "She went on about what a creep her husband was and how they got married at our house and how she was with Aunt Dottie on the way to see her retarded daughter when John Kennedy was killed."

Cookie then abruptly shifts gears, summoning the name of the one relative she has yet to confront, Aunt Baba: "I dealt with Mother today, which got me thinking I might as well deal with her sister today too."

Maria's sister, Charlotte, or Baba, helped raise Cookie. She is the one who answered the phone when Cookie called home after giving birth to me. She is the one who admitted to Cookie that her father was deathly ill and summoned her home. And now Baba, near ninety, is largely in Cookie's care. While she seems to occupy a more comfortable space in Cookie's life than Maria does, it's clear that Cookie still needs Baba to acknowledge her culpability for my loss; she also wants Baba to embrace our reunion and to bless it.

It is clear from the moment Cookie starts recounting the story that, as with Maria, things hadn't gone as she'd hoped.

While waiting outside Baba's doctor's office, Cookie handed her my picture, telling her who I was and how we had come to know each other. Baba became quite agitated. Barely glancing at the photo, she placed it on a nearby table, amid piles of magazines, and began spouting every thought that entered her head: "You've got to be kidding. Lord have mercy, I'm shocked. How did this happen? This sounds like a movie script." If the older woman had stopped there, it would've probably been fine. But she turned an unfortunate corner.

"I hope it's true that she's your daughter. You know, I wouldn't want her coming along because of who you are—or who your daddy was. You know how folks are about the whole celebrity thing. She could be after something else. She could not be your child at all. They have those tests now. Make her take one. Find out her GNA. Then we can figure out what to do."

Even as she replays it, Cookie's outrage is on full blast. "GNA?" She laughs out loud. "I am very sorry, but can we at least get the letters right, Miss Baba? Try *D-N-A*."

Their chat deteriorated from there, but the low point came when Baba attempted to leave my photograph behind, stuck between the pages of a magazine, before heading off to be examined.

Despite feeling "beyond plucked," after her day of dual confrontations, Cookie sounds lighter than she did before, as if she's been relieved of a heavy load, even if only partially.

"Are you all right?" I ask. She takes a moment before answering.

"They're certifiable, but I'm okay," she says calmly. "And you're better than okay, and we just have to laugh to keep from cryin'." At that, we both chuckle and then she utters the words I've most been waiting to hear: "I can't wait to see you."

CHAPTER 15

CAREFUL

*ℋ*aving confronted her family, Cookie may be at last ready to meet me. At least that's my prayer as the days whittle down and stress levels rise on both coasts. In the correspondence that flies back and forth we keep reminding each other to "just breathe."

A week before my departure, my parents are with me in my kitchen when the mail arrives. Inside an envelope thick with postcards, Cookie has included a long-awaited picture of herself. It is black-and-white and decades old. She is seated, wearing a simple dark shift with a circular brooch at her neckline. There's a sweet smile on her face, a sparkling crown on her head, and she wears a ring with a single pearl that catches my eye. Might it have been a small, silent reminder of me?

She looks like a girl, pretending to be a woman, struggling not to laugh. According to her note, the photo was taken in October 1965 as part of Columbia Pictures' earliest promotions of her as one of its new actresses. She'd been signed to a seven-year contract the summer after I was born, along with Harrison Ford, a buddy of hers from acting school. She would become dear friends with his then wife, Mary, and godmother to their first child.

On the eve of her twenty-first birthday, Cookie was crowned Princess October of Hollywood (thus the tiara) by the Los Angeles Chamber of Commerce. In a small yellowed news clipping that she encloses, she wears the same serene smile as well as a white sash, making her look like a Miss America contestant. The clip, from *Time*, says she'd just launched her movie career with a bit part as a waitress named Pussycat who douses Dean Martin with a drink in a film called *The Silencers*.

I finger the photograph, staring into her round face with its smiling eyes. They are large, dark, and set wide apart, just as the Spence-Chapin report described. Her hair is meticulously styled into a chin-length bob. I am entranced, even if slightly disappointed. We don't look alike, moreover, the picture is so old. Before traveling out there, I'd hoped to have a sense of what she looks like now. That she would send this picture, and not one more current, spoke volumes.

One of the only known photos of Cookie with her birth parents, Caro ("Babe") and Kenny.

Flower girl Cookie at Nat and Maria's wedding reception.

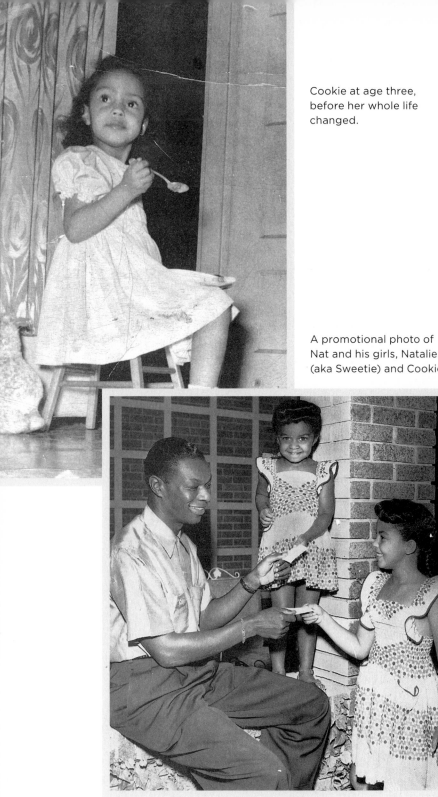

Cookie at age three, before her whole life changed.

A promotional photo of Nat and his girls, Natalie (aka Sweetie) and Cookie.

The Cole family during a rare respite at home in Los Angeles. From left are Cookie, Maria, Sweetie, and Nat, and his beloved boxer, Mr. Cole.

Cookie runs on the beach with Casey, Timolin, and Kelly circa 1965.

Columbia Pictures press shot of Cookie taken in late 1965. *(The Silencers © 1966, renewed 1994 Columbia Pictures Industries, Inc. All Rights Reserved. Courtesy of Columbia Pictures)*

My first formal portrait, one month old.

Daddy, Mommy, and me in front of our house in Liberia, 1966.

Christmas morning, 1972. Months later I would learn I was adopted.

Timolin, our friend Rashid Silvera, and me on the town circa 1987.

Daddy and me on my wedding day, November 10, 1990.

Cookie and her siblings, Kelly, Sweetie, Casey, and Timolin photographed for *People* magazine, 1991. *(© Harry Benson)*

The children, Johnny, and me in the Bahamas with my in-laws, Earl and Barbara Graves, on their fortieth wedding anniversary, July 2000.

Veronica and Carter with their bonus grandma the week they met, August 2002.

Mommy, Cookie, and lucky me.

All in the family. La Costa Resort, August 2006.

Over my shoulder, I hear Mommy say, "Who's that?"

"It's Cookie," I say, offering her the picture.

She takes it with one hand and uses her other hand to cover everything except Cookie's tiara. Slowly she slides her flat palm down the surface, exposing Cookie's face one fragment at a time.

"You've got the same eyebrows," she says.

"Yes, but not eyes," I note.

"No," she agrees, studying the image as she reveals it more and more. "She has real almond eyes, farther apart. But your shape is similar."

"I guess so," I say, fixated as much on Mommy's reaction as I am on the picture. "She has a little nose," I offer.

"Oh, she does! And yours is . . . not little." We crack up.

"No kidding. Guess I got my father's nose. He's Jewish."

"Jewish? He's not Jewish, he's Irish. They told us he was Irish."

"According to Cookie, he's Jewish. She lied to the agency about him."

"Ohhhh," she says, looking as if she has another question to ask. But she doesn't. She returns to the photo. "Different mouth, different chin. She's really cute. When was this taken?"

"1965."

"So that's how she looked when she had you. I guess she looks quite different now. Bob, look at this picture of Cookie."

Daddy, who has not so much as glanced up from his newspaper, takes the photo, squints at it, and smiles.

"Yeah, she's cute," he says. "She looks so familiar, doesn't she, Vera?"

"No," Mommy answers, a bit too quickly. "But she looks nice."

A few days later, my girls come over to check on me before I leave. Cindei and Jeanne and I have been friends since I was twelve years old. I can barely remember life before them. I met Allyson in graduate school, she joined our little trio, and we've been Siamese quads ever since, cheering each other through every victory, life rafts in every storm.

Sitting around my bedroom as I pack, they are full of questions (when am I going to tell my kids about Cookie? How is Johnny handling the whole thing? Have my parents expressed any concerns about the visit? Do I think they'd admit it if they had any?) and observations about my "state" in the midst of it all.

"My state?" I ask, amused and slightly appalled. "I have a state?"

"Yes, honey," says Allyson, with sincere concern. She eyes the others, and I can tell this has been discussed. "You've been so calm, so rational. We know you're the practical one—and that's good—but it's almost as if you're . . . unemotional. And maybe that's not so good. It's never wise to hold these things in."

"These 'things'?" I repeat, trying not to laugh. "What 'things'?"

"The 'practical one'? Who says she's the practical one?" Cindei carps. "For the record, I think *I'm* the practical one."

"Can we please . . ." Allyson sighs.

"Fine," says Cindei, in surrender, a rarity. She turns to me. "Come on, Caroline, you haven't even had a good cry yet. Nobody's *that* practical. You have to admit: you're a crier, and we love that about you. I'm sure you've had your moments, but with us, you've been all la-di-da, cool, calm, and collected about probably the most incredible thing that's ever happened to you, and we know it's really loaded, emotional territory. It makes *us* cry, so for it to not have *you* crying, *right now* in fact, as you pack to go out there and finally *meet* her, let's face it: for you, *that's just weird*."

Cookie thinks I'm the queen of directness but that's only because she's never met Cindei. In the dictionary under *blunt objects*, there's her picture. The entire time Cin speaks, Allyson nods in silent chorus. Jeanne is uncharacteristically quiet as she sifts through Cookie's latest batch of postcards. Then she spots the picture.

"Oh my God! Rice, is this her?" In all the world, only Cindei and Jeanne and Jeanne's husband, Tommy, call me Rice, as in the Carolina brand of the long-grain white stuff. Allyson never uses the nickname; it started before her time.

"That's her," I say. Cin and Allyson race to Jeanne's side. They have the same response as my parents and I had: the picture is so "old" and Cookie is so "cute." Of course, Cin nails her on the headgear.

"What's up with the crown? Because she's Nat King Cole's daughter, she wears a crown? Natalie Cole doesn't wear a crown." I throw a pillow at her and we all laugh.

They dig into her postcards, commenting about how "cool," "eloquent," "descriptive," and "incredible" they are.

"Well, she's smart as hell," Allyson says. "You got that from her."

"I know," I say, only half-joking.

"Oh, give me a break," Cindei says, tossing the same pillow back at me. She returns her focus to the postcards. "She missed you, Rice," Cin says. "It shows."

Jeanne begins to weep, and we all turn to stare at her, dumbfounded. I put my arm around her and ask, "What's wrong?" although I think I know.

"I'm sorry." She chokes. "I can't help it. It's just so incredible."

A year earlier, Jeanne and Tommy adopted their daughter, Karinne, my goddaughter. It was an emotional journey that involved meeting her birth mother, who chose them from among several candidates. That's how most adoptions work nowadays. Karinne's adoption bore almost no resemblance to mine except that Jeanne and Tommy and their biological sons, Andrew and Russell, were completely besotted with this child. She was the perfect addition to their family; she completed them.

"Aww, honey." Allyson rubs Jeanne's back. "It's okay. We understand."

Cin turns to me. "See! This is what you should be doing: blubbering!"

I'm reminded of Johnny's similar comments a few months earlier. Apparently everyone thinks I should be an emotional wreck over all this, including Cookie, with all her urging me into therapy. But I don't feel that way; I'm just . . . grateful. Am I missing something?

Jeanne composes herself and they begin asking about the details of my visit. They think it's wonderful, but Allyson is also worried and she insists it's important that plans and expectations be carefully set.

"You should have an exit strategy," she says.

"I like that," says Jeanne. "That makes sense." Not to Cindei.

"An exit strategy! She's flying clear across the friggin' country after thirty-seven years and she needs an exit strategy? Where the heck is she exiting to?"

"Well, you know what I mean," Allyson tries to explain. "This first meeting could be so emotional. She may need to take it slow-ly," she says, dragging through the word for emphasis. "She might need to cut things short if she gets overwhelmed or take a break until the next day. That should be allowed, so she can get herself together, keep things cool."

"What the hell are you talking about?" Cindei cries. "She's meeting her mother for the first time. It's a big deal. It's going to be emotional. Why does she have to keep things cool?"

"Oh, I don't know," says Allyson, exasperated with Cindei and her own inability to be as direct. "I just think you always need an exit strategy!"

They go on like this for a while, lobbing that dumb ball back and forth, forth and back, as I sit there, a spectator in a debate about my own life. Jeanne just watches them too, laughing now, but still clearly full with emotion as she thinks about me, her near-sister, and her own daughter, who has another mother somewhere.

Ultimately worn down by Cin's refusal to budge on the matter, Allyson throws up her hands, then she wraps them around me and holds on tight. "Don't listen to me, with my crazy ideas about all this," she says. "You know how I am, I'm just a worrier. We want to protect you. We want to make sure it's all perfect for you, and it will be. It's going to be fantastic. Just please, *be careful*, and pay close attention because you know we're going to want to hear every single detail!"

CHAPTER 16

LIFT-OFF

$\mathscr{I}$t's early Friday morning, May 31, when a Town Car arrives to take Johnny and me to the airport. My parents stayed over at our house the night before and are up with the children when we leave. I hug and kiss Nica and Carter and quickly turn away so they won't see my tears. We rarely leave the children behind when we travel. When we do it is always hard.

Only when Johnny and I are strapped into our seats and zooming down the runway at JFK does it occur to me that I have been too consumed with thoughts of Cookie and this day to stress over the plane ride as I normally would have. My typical preflight list of obsessions—the weather, wind speeds, airline safety record, national security alert color of the day, pilot's voice (Too young? Too old? Calm and unflappable?

Hyper and nervous?)—never entered my mind because, for once, none of it matters. I would have flown myself through enemy territory in a crippled helicopter during a category-six hurricane to make this trip. The fact that I am able to do it on a beautiful day sitting in business class (a surprise from Johnny) makes it an absolute breeze.

After he falls asleep, I busy myself by watching the in-flight movie, writing in my journal, and trying my hand at haiku. In a nod to Cookie's love of poetry, I purchased a book of haiku to give her, but I need to inscribe it appropriately. My attempts are plodding and hopeless:

> If by chance we meet
> before we each intended
> let us laugh, not cry.

Although we land at LAX before noon, the reunion is not due to commence until the next day. Not that there is much of a plan. After her fretting for weeks over where we should meet, who should be around, what we should do, and where we should go, Cookie and I agreed to just play it loose. We'd meet at her house or my hotel, initially alone, and take it from there, based on however we feel.

Johnny and I have an event to attend the evening of our arrival, and Cookie seizes upon that as an excuse to delay our meeting, insisting that I'll need "at least a day to rest after such a long trip" and that it will be better if there is nothing to interfere with our time once it officially begins.

I don't say "BUT I WON'T REST" until I see you." I don't say "I can't wait another second." I don't object or make a fuss. Even with the distance between us reduced from three thousand miles to twenty, she needs to take it slow, and so I try my damnedest to understand and be patient.

Johnny has us picked up at the airport by a limousine and driven to the Peninsula Hotel, where he has booked a beautiful suite. Without saying a word, he is trying to make this trip as easy, as lovely, and as memorable for me as he can. He is showing his love for me in the best way possible: he is taking care of me.

The day drags a bit, but we have a fun night out at the Essence Awards. He keeps me laughing, if not entirely distracted. We get back to the hotel after midnight and make love (another great time-killer), but then he falls asleep as I lie wide awake, pulsing with anticipation. If we had rented a car, I would have gotten up, gotten in it, and driven to her house right then.

Always a morning person, Johnny is awake and dressed by five, heading to an early tee time at a golf course about an hour away. He has a meeting scheduled after that and then he is to meet me at Cookie's house, late that afternoon. I'm sorry that he has to leave because I want someone to hang with and focus on while I wait for the hours to tick down. At the same time, I can't wait for him to go because it will mean this day is finally in motion.

He kneels beside the bed before he leaves and kisses me several times. "I'm really happy for you," he says. "If you need anything, or if anything changes, call me."

"Okay," I say, feeling lucky to have him with me in that moment and in life. "I will."

Time has never moved as slowly as it does that morning. Unlike Johnny, Cookie is a night owl, late to bed and late to rise. We haven't set an exact time for our meeting for that reason. We plan to touch base on the phone sometime after ten (which, in my mind, means two minutes past, at the latest).

I can't get back to sleep after Johnny heads out so I read. I write in my journal. I order a big, extravagant breakfast in bed, and while waiting for it to arrive, I call the kids at my parents' house. Carter and Veronica sound fine. My parents sound anxious.

"Did you meet her yet?" Mommy wants to know, forgetting about the time difference. She'd barely said hello.

"Not yet. We won't meet until later today."

"Okay, well don't forget to call us," she says.

"You have a good time, Boop-Boop," Daddy says. I'm glad the children are with them. Having that distraction this weekend is probably my parents' saving grace.

Ten o'clock comes and goes. Fifteen minutes pass, then a half hour. At exactly forty minutes past ten I grab the phone and call her. I can't wait a second longer. She picks up and is all over the place, unable to make a simple decision or take a single step forward. It is frustrating as hell. After some wrangling over where to meet and how to get there, we agree on half-past noon at her house.

I hang up and stare at the phone panicked for a moment, afraid she might call back and cancel outright. With nothing else to do, I allow the feelings I'd been keeping at bay to come crashing in. This isn't going at all as I'd hoped.

I wanted her to be so eager she couldn't sleep. I wanted her to be camped out at the airport, hiding in a corner, just to see me from afar. I wanted to catch a glimpse of her peering out from behind a big newspaper in the hotel lobby. I wanted her to call just past dawn today and whisper, "I can't sleep. I need to see you. Let's go grab breakfast." I wanted her to be unconflicted, irrepressible, and overjoyed. Instead she sounds tentative, tense, terrified, and totally unready for our date.

A.C.
(AFTER COOKIE)

CHAPTER 17

BELIEVE

$\mathscr{I}$ ask the cabdriver to let me out at the foot of Cookie's long, steep driveway, in front of the neon-yellow mailbox that marks the spot. I don't want my arrival announced by a screech of brakes outside her door. I want to walk up to her house alone, to take my time, feel my way, and leave room to pace or turn back if I need to. I've been a mess of jumbled emotions all morning and I want to arrive calm. Besides, even with traffic that made the drive a bit longer, I'm still about twenty minutes early.

It's a bright, flawless day in Tarzana. The valley is far clearer and a good bit warmer than smoggy Los Angeles.

Her shared driveway feels even steeper than it looks, but as I near its top and her house comes into view, everything else ceases to exist. It's charming, enchanting, magical. No one label will do.

It's an adobe—stucco with a flat roof trimmed in red clay tiles. A trellis-covered porch runs the length of its front; there are cacti in large terra-cotta pots; climbing rosebushes and flaming pink bougainvillea shimmy in the breeze, framing the earth-tone house in a blaze of brilliant color. Although we are supposed to meet alone, there are two cars parked in the carport. I no longer care. I am finally here, and I'm ecstatic.

As I climb her few porch steps, a half-dozen little birds flutter away from a large collection of feeders. No doubt they are urging me to hurry, so they can return to their lunch. My senses are heightened, as if I am seeing, hearing, smelling, touching, feeling everything for the first time. I suppose, in a way, I am.

Everything—the beating of bird-wings and complex harmony of their songs, the smooth tiles under my feet, the colorful metal sculpture in the front yard, and the large stones scattered about with words etched into them like IMAGINE, BELIEVE, TRUST—all of it comforts me and reassures me that I am in the right place at the right time and that everything will be better than fine.

I move slowly, peering into each window as I pass it. I can hear the moan and tinkle of wind chimes in the distance, the buzzing of cicadas; a cluster of butterflies dance nearby. I want to take in each and every sight, smell, and sound. After all my weeks of impatience and rushing, I want to linger here, alone and alert in a way I have never been before. I want to savor these last precious minutes B.C.—Before Cookie.

Suddenly, a shadow moves on the other side of a window screen. I hear her voice, now so familiar, a slight gasp, and her "Oh . . ." as she moves quickly to the front door. Just as I reach it, before I can knock, the door opens wide and she takes a few steps back to let me in. Suddenly self-conscious, I step inside.

"Well, look at you," she says and I barely catch a glimpse of her before diving into her embrace. We hold on there for a while, each of us weeping softly. It's an odd feeling after waiting so long. It's relief . . . release . . . it's gratitude and disbelief and a massive mix of other emotions, none of them conflicting, all of them good.

We let go; laugh a little at ourselves, nervous and elated; then reach for each other again. This is real. She is real. Overcome and deliriously happy, I could have held on to her for all time. The warmth and fullness of her embrace calm me. Her home smells of incense and is flooded with diffuse light; the combination reminds me of church. More than blessed, this moment feels holy.

We step away from each other finally and laugh, harder now. But my nervousness is returning as I'm not sure where we go from here. I've thought only of this moment, never much beyond it.

We're grinning through our tears.

"Just look at us," she exclaims, reaching to grab tissues for us both.

Just look at you, I think, taking in her warm, lovely face, searching it, as if to trigger some memory that's just not there. She is physically small, but her presence is large, magnetic, and very maternal and I know right away that this is how everyone sees her, not just me. I go quiet; I feel suddenly shy.

"Well, hi!" she says, still smiling. "I can't believe you made it. You're finally here."

"Hi," I say, noting that she really is several inches shorter than me and many years older than the only image of her I've seen. She bears little resemblance to that picture but I am utterly captivated by her. "You are so beautiful."

"Oh puh-leeze," she says, laughing and turning away to dab at her eyes. I smile to hear her mouth that word precisely as she has written it to me so many times. She turns back to me, takes both of my hands in hers, and looks me over deliberately from head to toe. "You! You, my beauty, are divine."

She wears all pale, airy linen: a pink tunic over cropped white pants, with little flat shoes (almost like Mary Janes) on her little feet. A bunch of gold charms hang from a chain around her neck; I make out a G clef and a magic wand with a tiny diamond star at its tip. I can't believe how worried she was about how I would view her or that she almost allowed insecurities about her weight to keep us apart.

Her face is round and full and she has apple cheeks that make me think of Shirley Temple, whose movies I loved as a child. Her mouth reminds me of Carter's, and that cute nose, so unlike mine, is, I realize, much like Veronica's. Her eyebrows are thick but her hair is quite thin; its dozens of sliver-skinny shoulder-length braids perfectly suit her, although her scalp is visible in spots. I can't help thinking of Mommy, who lost much of her hair to radiation in her twenties, and who has worn wigs my whole life.

Everything that has started to become familiar to me from a distance—Cookie's deep, throaty laugh, her frequent sighs and oft-used expressions—becomes fuller, richer, and even more disarming in person. Cookie gives off this beguiling earth-mother vibe, kind of like the rocker Stevie Nicks with a tan. She has mammoth undeniable charisma and she is mine. I am here and she is real and she is mine.

Here, in the flesh, I'm struck by our lack of a resemblance but not enough to dampen my high. I'm not much of a drinker, never even tried pot, but if there were a drug that could give me this feeling, I'd happily surrender to it, addicted for life.

I used to dream vivid dreams as a child, intensely felt dreams that would repeat often, becoming more familiar but no less dreamlike each time. I never wanted those dreams to end but felt comforted by the knowledge that I would dream them again. Standing in Cookie's home, surrounded by her things, inhaling her incense, finally knowing the warmth and texture of her touch, that's how I feel, as if I'm in a familiar place that only exists in an imaginary realm, as if I am dreaming a dream that I don't want to end and don't quite understand but know well, having dreamed it before. I try hard to stay focused and alert, not wanting to miss a single detail by second-guessing it all.

Her light-filled home is not to be believed. The wonders out front offered barely a taste of the feast for the senses that lies beyond her door. There is music playing, the specifics of which I don't register, but I like it. The burning incense—sandalwood maybe—is intoxicating, and everywhere I look there is some small special touch of whimsy, creativity, great care.

"This is incredible," I say, taking in the bright open space with its eclectic mix of treasures and spectacular garden view.

She claps her hands together, clearly delighted by my reaction. "Aww, thanks," she says, giggling. "I'm glad you think so." She offers to give me "the five-cent tour," and I eagerly accept.

We walk together from room to room—her bedroom, with its cozy fireplace and private little garden on the side; a guest room with hand-carved antique mahogany furniture that I instantly love; the open kitchen where two skillets painted with portraits hang like cast-iron cameos over the deep, wide sink. Her walk-in pantry is home to the usual household staples, but alongside the bottled water and olive oil is a large vintage toy collection artfully arranged, including a red kaleidoscope, a plastic Godzilla, and an Etch A Sketch whose image of a pair of musicians has been frozen in place, unshakable.

She is everywhere in this house: in the assortment of miniature chairs scattered on ledges and mantels and tabletops; in the expansive album and CD collection housed in a rustic armoire beside the front door; in the solid, beautifully crafted coffee table John designed and built himself and the delicate homemade mobile of shiny little hearts suspended from the light fixture above it. The table is home to an assortment of treasures from books and small statues to a collection of mini-crowns fit for a tiny king (as well as the votive candles Cookie has placed in a few of them).

Although John doesn't work outside the home, he clearly does a whole lot of work inside this one. In addition to building furniture and doing spectacular ironwork, masonry, and tile, he's an amateur landscape architect. Their garden is his creative playground, and Cookie is his muse. She's confided that their decades-old union is rocky at times and the blended family dynamic between them and their sons is fraught with tension, but their collaboration on this house has resulted in a haven unlike any I've ever seen. I'm not well steeped in the ways of Eastern religions, but this home has good karma; the Buddha himself would love it.

To get to her office, we step through a beaded curtain reproduction of the *Mona Lisa* and climb a Mexican tiled staircase to an airy room with a wrought iron balcony that overlooks the pool. Any wall that lacks a window is lined with floor-to-ceiling shelves that house more albums, CDs, and, of course, books—tons of them. Beside a vintage leather love seat is a white wire rotating rack, like you'd find in a card store. I'm delighted to note that its dozens of pockets are stuffed with postcards, waiting to be sent.

She sees me eyeing it and laughs. "Isn't that brilliant?" she says. "I bought it from a store that was closing down. I wish I'd bought three more. Especially now that we have each other, I'm constantly picking up new PCs. I can't send them to you fast enough."

Together we sit and look through her photo albums. I'm mesmerized by the gorgeous images of her through the years. She seems uncomfortable, embarrassed perhaps, as she turns from one to the next too quickly, dismissing my admiring comments and offering few details to flesh out the scenes in response to my inquiries. I love old photographs and want to linger. I long to get a real glimpse of her life and the years we might have shared. But she's eager to close her albums and move on.

We chat. We sigh in the silences, and there are many. For nearly three months we've been having an almost constant conversation in writing and on the phone. There's not a lot to say now; it's simple nearness that we crave.

We hold hands, even when we're seated, and I keep finding reasons to put my arm around her, lean into her, brush past her, scoot in beside her, extra close. She does the same, stroking my back, my hair, my hand, my cheek. It's both involuntary and deliberate, each gesture born of our own needs as well as our responsiveness to each other's.

Slowly I'm regaining my equilibrium as I become accustomed to her and this magical place. But when we step out into her garden, I'm moved to tears again. Whatever you've imagined heaven to be, it's that, only more funky and more fun.

As with the inside of the house, there is nothing forced or fabricated about it and yet there are countless special touches, all rendered with palpable precision and care. A little fountain peeks from between two potted bamboo plants. It consists of a spout that pours into a cup that, when full, empties into a bucket with a little bronze bird sitting on its rim. It charmfully embodies the notion carved at its base: MY CUP RUNNETH OVER. Imperceptibly I mouth, Amen.

Everywhere I look there are flowers and plants that take my breath away; birds-of-paradise, white calla lilies, bright yellow daisies, roses of various shapes in vibrant hues; there's a clutch of gorgeous succulents in tiny mosaic pots and a spread of feathery pink and purple blooms that she tells me is actually called heaven. A symphony of wind chimes—they are hanging from trees like Christmas ornaments—plays to the seeming delight of colorful birds that dive and soar and sing.

Just beyond the turquoise pool, with its cheery surround of bright red cement and Adirondack lounge chairs painted in mismatched shades, is the centerpiece of this landscape, a functional piece of art called the M-velope. The same deep summer green of the grass it sits on, and made entirely of wood, it's a massive piece of origami you can rest inside. The M-velope's panels open and close, morphing it into countless shapes that allow prisms of light to play inside. We sit together on its cushioned bench, entranced. Beyond the M-velope, through a succession of garden gates along a rock-strewn path, is John's latest work in progress: a labyrinth. No wonder Cookie never wants to leave her home. Neither do I.

Although we get to spend a couple of hours alone together, it feels like far too short a time before John returns. With his long, thick, salt-and-pepper hair, full beard, faded jeans, and work boots, he looks like an aging hippie, an unprimped, unfashionable Kris Kristofferson. Unlike Cookie, he's sparing with his words. When he does speak, he is a bit awkward but kind. He says he's deeply happy for us both.

His life seems built around Cookie and this house. He circles her constantly, asking if she needs anything, making suggestions about what to do next. His quiet surface can be misleading, though; it camouflages a churning mix of anxiety and impatience that, given time, reveal themselves. She seems to need that prodding from him although at times she bristles.

Not long after John arrives, Harleigh appears. I'm standing with Cookie by the pool when he steps out of the house alone. I watch him walk toward us and can't help but smile. He's about my height and fit. Wearing gym shorts and a T-shirt, he appears a lot younger than his thirty-two years. His dark hair, the same fine, curly texture as mine, is long enough to bounce as he moves. He's handsome.

"So, you must be Caroline," he says, in a deep smoky voice reminiscent of Carter's. Like a few other musicians I know, he gives off a low-simmering cool vibe. He offers me a broad smile and a light hug. "It's great to meet you," he says.

"You too," I say, feeling a natural pull I can only liken to the instant chemistry you have with a new best friend or great love. It catches me completely off guard but I yield to it, relieved by the surprising ease of this first encounter.

Meeting Cookie is one thing; we have a shared history, splintered though it may be. We've spent months developing a relationship that is already solid, a bond that was mutually desired and nurtured from the moment we first connected on the phone.

This is different. I never had siblings, so I have no instincts to rely on. The only times I even wished for or imagined having any, they were sisters. Although Cookie has shared mostly positive feedback about us from her sons, I don't assume that they're thrilled by my visit, or by my existence at all. I've worried that they'll see me as an interloper, infringing on their territory. I don't envy them having grown up with an awareness of me, their mother's lost daughter, a sadness from her past—the memory of which she already told me marred their Christmases.

Cookie watches us with one hand over her heart. The other covers her mouth but is unable to hide her smile, which soon bubbles over into laughter; Harleigh and I exchange a glance, a silent satisfied acknowledgment that we've made her happy. As the three of us walk toward the house, we diffuse this big moment with small talk. I feel relieved but not for long.

When John announces that Sage and his girlfriend, Jen, have pulled into the driveway with their friend Tim, Cookie jumps up anxiously, and I excuse myself, escaping to a bathroom. I close the door and wash my hands, splash my face, and try to gather myself. I'm not just nervous about meeting Sage; I'm worried.

Jen and I have spoken enough that I can't wait to see her. Because she's Cookie's assistant, and they share an office, she often answers the phone when I call. She has been every bit as warm and welcoming as Cookie was from the start. She is one of those people who is so incredibly kind and seemingly pure-of-heart that you wonder at first if she's for real. I already consider her a friend, and I appreciate her openness to me all the more because I understand her vulnerability.

Jen's parents are unwell, their relationship is ceaselessly stressful, and Cookie has offered her a center of stability she craves. Jen's not just Sage's "lady," she's also Cookie's ever-ready right hand. With their desks three steps apart, and their unconditional love and concern for Sage, they are joined at the hip and the heart. No one ever says as much, but I instinctively know that Jen has been a surrogate daughter to Cookie and I want to assure her that I'm not here to take her place; I just hope to establish my own.

Sage and I have spoken on the phone a few times, and he's been nothing but kind, amazed at all that's happened, and seemingly pleased for Cookie and me. But our few conversations have been brief and a bit stilted.

Based on things Cookie has shared, Sage seemed to take on all the attributes—best and worst—of both first and middle children. He is a natural leader, generous, caring, and dutiful. But he is also burdened by heavy baggage—resentments, hurts, disappointments, and God knows what else, carried over from an entire lifetime I wasn't a part of, causing him to be confrontational and deeply cynical. Like Cookie, he's a smart and sensitive seeker, but he seems to reside behind an emotional wall that is tough to scale. Aware that he's also in the throes of the early total-immersion stages of recovery, I worry that my appearance out of nowhere has complicated his journey.

On the day I first called, Sage walked into Cookie's office in the midst of our conversation. He was thrilled to hear it was me on the phone and eager to soak up every detail once she hung up. But that same afternoon, when Cookie found my book and bio on Amazon.com, Sage's reaction was blunt: "Well, at least one of your kids is successful."

It was a knife in Cookie's heart—and in mine when she

told me. I wasn't ready to deal with jealousy or resentment, especially when we had nothing yet to counterbalance it. The thought of walking into a relationship, already complicated, scared me. But the time had come to just handle it, and I couldn't stall much longer without being obvious.

I hear their voices in the kitchen and strain for a few minutes to try to make out what is being said. Sage is asking Cookie how things are going so far, what she is feeling, if she is okay. Cookie is purring like a cat, going on about "how great" it's all been. Sage sounds relieved for her and genuinely pleased.

As I head toward the kitchen, I spot freckled, bright, auburn-haired Jen, who offers me a big hug and an even bigger "Hello!" Awkwardly, Sage and I hug too. I think instantly of my Nica, who is so deeply compassionate and intuitive but at times uncomfortable expressing her softer side.

"Wow," he says. "You're actually here, finally. I can't believe it. We've been after her to do this for so long. Glad you made it. How was the trip? More to the point, how's it going with you two?"

He is anxious for us and wears his tender heart on his sleeve. I want to hug him again, but I wouldn't dare. Harleigh, I can tell, will be easy; Sage will take a little time. Both of them are struggling in their own ways, but they are more open to my presence—and even my inclusion—than I could have dreamed, or than I would likely be if I were in their position.

The day slips by without my having any sense of time or space other than what exists inside the bubble of Cookie's self-created world. The entire weekend goes that way. I eat, sleep, walk, and talk, but none of it registers in the usual sense. During the hours when I'm not with her, I sleep like the dead—spent and dreamless; my dreams have already come true.

From the moment I awaken, I just want to be there in her home, in her garden, by her side, *with her*. Not at the luxurious Peninsula Hotel with its spa and our grand suite, not at the peaceful Japanese gardens she and John take me to see or the restaurant in Malibu overlooking the Pacific Ocean where she and her John have dinner with me and mine. I just can't get enough of her amazing home or of this woman, who, with incense swirling around her braided head and a skinny brown French cigarette dangling between her fingers, presides over it all.

But after a few short days—just seventy-two hours—it's over. Johnny is set to head to a meeting in Palm Springs at five-thirty on the same morning that I'm due to fly home alone. He'll be in California for another three days. Waking me before he leaves, he sits on the bed beside me and gently strokes my hair.

"Hey," he says as I pry my eyes open. "You okay?"

I'm not sure if he's asking how I am in the wake of meeting Cookie or how I am on the verge of having to endure five nerve-racking hours on a cross-country flight without him.

"I'm good," I say sleepily, which I am in either case.

Meeting Cookie and her family has exceeded my every expectation. As for the flight, God has been so good to me from the very moment I was born, how dare I question His plans now?

Cookie and John arrive at ten (early for her) to take me to the airport. John drops Cookie off and disappears so she and I can have breakfast alone. I'm grateful for this; if I could change anything about the weekend, it would be that she and I had more time alone.

At a café table set beneath the palm trees in the Peninsula's sun-dappled courtyard, we talk about lots of nothing, keeping the conversation light. I'm intrigued by her jewelry, which includes a funky necklace made of big primary-colored plastic beads. With her denim tunic and black leggings, she looks like an art teacher who proudly decks herself out in her students' designs. Her assortment of rings also catches my eye. We compare the gold bands we wear on our thumbs. I take her hand to look more closely at the engraving on the outer edge of another ring.

"Don't . . . forget . . . to remember." I read it aloud, turning the ring in place on her finger. It's open-ended. I'm thinking the obvious: don't forget to remember I love you, probably a gift from John, who no doubt mined the gold, designed the ring, and engraved it himself. But I ask anyway, allowing her the thrill of sharing the story. "Don't forget to remember what?"

". . . Who you are," she says, looking straight into my eyes. I blink back tears. "My friend Lois Sasson made this ring for me a thousand years ago. I had one made for Harleigh and for Sage as well. And, in a perfect segue . . ." She reaches over to what I thought was an empty chair and passes me a little gift bag she'd hidden there. "This is something else that Lois made for me eons ago. I hope you like it."

I reach into the bag and pull out two postcards, handmade from photos we took the day before of the Japanese garden we visited in Van Nuys, and a small felt jewelry bag from which I extract a gold necklace with seventeen tiny bezel-set diamonds. As I place it over my head and finger it, she's fretting, which I've come to understand, is her way: "It's a precursor to Elsa Peretti's Diamonds by the Yard at Tiffany. I love Lois's work, but if you don't like it, tell me—I have so many other things. Maybe you'd like to choose something else. And if it's too long, you can shorten it. I wish there was some significance to the seventeen. I can't remember but it probably had something to do with my thing for the number seven. If only there were eighteen little diamonds, then it would be for March eighteenth, the day you . . . well, Our Day. . . ."

I rise from my chair and wrap my arms around her from behind as she stops talking and starts giggling.

"I love it," I say. "I will not be shortening it or trading it or doing anything to it. It's perfect."

I check my watch and realize our time is running out. I hand her my own little felt pouch.

"What have you done?" she asks, looking stunned and delighted as she pulls out the small square of tissue paper within and gingerly unfolds it. Inside is a gold filigree ring from West Africa that my Aunt Joy gave me when I was about eleven years old. It was part of a twin set, one small, one large, or as she put it when she presented them: "One to wear now, one for later, when you've outgrown this one." I never outgrew the smaller of the two; it just moved from my index to my middle to my ring finger to my right pinky, where it remains. I tell Cookie the story as she examines its larger twin, grinning broadly. "I don't believe you did this," she says. "It is perfection! But I have such big fingers, it probably won't fit." As she says the words, she slips the ring onto her pinky, where it fits with ease. She gasps and bursts out laughing. "Well, will you look at that?" she declares, holding out her hand to admire it. I place my ringed pinky beside hers, and she beams.

Once again, we'd had identical impulses—each to give the other a piece of jewelry not purchased for the occasion but time tested and our own.

On the drive to the airport, John plays chauffeur as Cookie sits with me in the back seat. He parks the car, they both walk me in, and the three of us linger near the security check, gabbing, avoiding the inevitable for about ten minutes before we hug and I have to go.

"I won't say good-bye, little C, I'll say, see you soon and trust the universe to make it happen." Of course, she knows already that I'll be back for the BE Golf & Tennis Challenge in August, and that I'll be bringing the children to meet her. Johnny and I floated the idea when we had dinner together on our first night, and this time she didn't hesitate; she just clapped her hands and exclaimed: "I can't wait!"

When Cookie returned home, she discovered the haiku anthology I'd left behind on her desk chair. I inscribed it with my original poem, written on the plane en route to our meeting:

> miracles abound
> in ordinary spaces
> what once was lost? Found.

CHAPTER 18

FRET NOT

*G*uess what," Johnny says to the kids in his most animated voice.

"What?" they chime.

We are spread out on the floor of our master bedroom. It's mid-July, school has ended, summer's begun, and Johnny and I have booked our tickets to go back out west in mid-August. The plan is actually for the kids and me to go first, spending a week in Los Angeles with Cookie and her crew. Johnny will join us for a weekend, then our family will drive to Palm Springs for the BE Challenge. I'm intensely nervous, unsure of what Nica and Carter will think, not just about the trip but also about the whole idea of Cookie and this new branch of our family tree.

There's no moment of reckoning I can recall when my children learned I was adopted. They've just always known and accepted it. Then, out of the blue, Nica confronted me about it in my car one day as we drove home from her school.

"Have you ever wanted to find your real mother?" she asked me.

"No," I answered, reflexively. "Not really. Why do you want to know?" I was slightly taken aback, but I'd already been a parent long enough to realize that children do this; they catch you off guard on the most random topics at the most unexpected times. In this case, though, the timing was truly confounding, as I'd met with Amy Burke and figured out who Cookie was only days before.

"I just do," she said. "Do you have any pictures of her?"

"No," I replied, growing uneasy. Where was this heading?

"Why don't you want to find her? You should want to find her. I think she wants you to find her." She was starting to assume an eight-year-old's attitude, and I was trying to keep the hair on the back of my neck from rising so dramatically she could see it. Where was this coming from?

"She's never tried to find me, Nica," I said, aiming for evenness. I knew my child was intuitive, but this was just bizarre. "You don't know if she wants that."

"Yes, I do," she answered, indignant now. "And I want that!"

"Well," I said, stunned, "you never know. Maybe one day." Thankfully, she dropped it. Now that day had arrived.

*A*fter discussing at length how best to introduce the whole idea of Cookie to the children, Johnny and I decided to give them enough time between finding out about her and meeting her to grow accustomed to the idea, but not so much time that they'd start to ask too many questions and grow impatient. I'm especially concerned about what they might say about her to my parents. I know they'll be excited to meet Cookie, but I need them to know why that might be hard for their Amma and Poppie to take. Precocious Nica may get it; newly five, Carter probably won't. Luckily, he's not the chatterbox she is.

"You know how some people have one grandma and, if they're really lucky like you guys, they have two?" I ask, attempting to ease them into the big news.

Carter is bouncing with anticipation. "Yes, Mommy! I have two grandmas!" He holds up two fingers on each hand, making double peace signs, like Nixon. Nica is eyeing Johnny and me suspiciously; she knows something's up. Ignoring our loosely planned preamble, Johnny cuts to the chase.

"Actually, you have three grandmas, because Mommy has found her birth mother," he says.

Carter stops bouncing. Nica's eyes become as big as headlights; her mouth drops open and quickly spreads into a smile.

"You know who your birth mother is?" she asks, launching her interrogation. "You mean, the lady who had you? The one who gave you up for adoption? You *know* her? That means you met her. *You met her?* When? Who is she? Where is she? What is she like? Does she look like me? Is she coming over? Can she come for dinner? Is she coming today?"

The children have switched places. Now Nica is a bouncing ball and Carter is the one who appears unsure of what's happening or how to respond. But taking his cues from the rest of us, Carter is soon bubbly again and echoing Nica's questions but with his own twist: "Did you meet your *dad*? Is he coming too?"

"Shhh!" Nica admonishes him, sounding closer to eighty

than eight. "No, Carter! She did not meet her father," she says, as if it is the most obvious thing in the world.

"Oh," he says, chastened at first. But he quickly recovers. "Why not? Where is he? I want to meet your daddy *and* your mommy!"

"I don't know who my father is," I offer, knowing that this is too much for a preschooler to fully understand. "My mother and father didn't get married like Amma and Poppie. They knew each other, a long time ago, but they don't know each other anymore. I only found my mother."

"Yeah," Nica says, rubber-stamping my explanation, as if she'd known these details all along. Carter's face falls. I look at Johnny, silently pleading for help. He jumps in.

"We're going to call Mommy's birth mother so you can talk to her," he says, pulling Carter onto his lap and giving his belly a tickle. "Maybe you can ask her some of your questions, Bops. She lives in California, and it's pretty far away, even farther than Colorado." They know Colorado from our annual ski trips. "She's waiting for our call. Are you ready?"

"Yes!" Carter is back and all in. Suddenly, Nica seems nervous. She scoots over to me and snuggles in close.

Johnny puts the phone on speaker and starts to dial when Nica's hand shoots out in his direction: "Stop!" she shouts.

"What's wrong?" he asks.

"What do we call her?"

Johnny looks at me, stumped.

"Cookie," I say, thrilled to have at least one ready answer. "You can call her Cookie."

"What do you call her?" Nica's big brown eyes pour into mine.

"I call her Cookie too."

"I like it!" Carter claps his hands. "Coo-kie! Coo-kie!" he chants in a gravelly voice, like the Cookie Monster on *Sesame Street*. Nica, with a little smile, nods her approval.

"Okay," she says to her dad. "You can call her now."

Cookie is no doubt nervously waiting for her office phone to ring. We prearranged the time of our call. As with the first call she and I shared, she handles it beautifully.

"I can't wait to meet you," she says. "I am so excited to have you visit us. We're making lots of plans for fun things to see and do when you're here!"

The children are quiet, mostly staring at the phone as her voice bubbles out of its speaker. They have a bit more to say when Johnny picks up the receiver and has each of them talk to her privately. Then it is my turn to stare, registering the shy, sweet expressions on their faces as they try to figure out exactly who this brand-new figure on the phone is—their extra grandma, their mother's mysterious *other* mother.

*I*f I thought that my meeting with Cookie couldn't be outdone, I was wrong. Witnessing the first meeting between her and my children a month later takes me to another plane of gratitude and wonder. Cookie once sent me a sign that said, LIFE IS NOT MEASURED BY THE BREATHS YOU TAKE, BUT BY THE MOMENTS THAT TAKE YOUR BREATH AWAY. Their meeting offers several of those.

We spend eight days together. I insist on staying with the children in a nearby hotel, knowing how demanding young kids can be and how unaccustomed to that level of activity Cookie is. Also, her house is full of alluring enticements for little hands, and I want to avoid dealing with that as much as possible. Although the aesthetic is totally different, my in-laws' home is also jam-packed with trinkets and collectibles, and as much as they love having their grandchildren around, their don't-touch rules are strictly enforced and a frequent source of tension.

In Cookie's case, I needn't have worried because she doesn't care. On the contrary, she encourages the kids to explore her home and to touch whatever they fancy—which turns out to be nearly everything. She ushers them into her pantry full of vintage toys, pulls out her board games and vast marble collections, and gives them little Buddha boards that they paint on with water, watching their artwork come to life and then disappear. She rolls out crayons and checkers and Slinkys, books and videos featuring the Simpsons and Japanese anime, and the entire British video series of *Wallace & Gromit*, which she delights watching on the couch with them, although they aren't nearly as enthralled as she is.

The hotel ends up as nothing more than a crash pad, as we spend every waking moment together with Cookie and her crew. We go to the movies, to Balboa Park, Venice Beach, the Getty Museum, and a small amusement park near her Tarzana home. Perfect for the pint-size set, it features a castle that houses an arcade, and miniature golf, which they love. We eat at IHOP (a perennial fave) and P.F. Chang's, where Carter and Cookie laugh themselves into a fit by simply repeating one menu item over and over: "Mongolian Beef! Mongolian Beef!" Mostly we get takeout, though (cooking is apparently not Cookie's thing), because no place else has the comfort and allure of her home.

The kids swim in her pool and romp in her garden among the wind chimes and wild rosebushes. They do art projects with Cookie and Jen, play Frisbee with their uncles Sage and

Harleigh, pick out marbles that she says they can keep, and learn to play table tennis and air hockey, which they do for hours in her garage with anyone they can collar into competing. Like my parents, who never tire of engaging in endless rounds of Candy Land or Operation or Battleship with my children, the adults in this house seem genuinely thrilled to draw on their inner child and play. They also seem to never say no; Nica and Carter are in heaven.

The kids capture the entire week in postage-stamp-size pictures taken with Polaroid cameras Cookie gives them. She almost instantly manages an easy and genuine rapport with them and is soon snuggling and whispering secrets with Nica and huddling up with Carter, fascinated as he teaches her how to use his Game Boy. She moves as brilliantly into the role of full-immersion grandmother as she has moved into a freshly carved-out place in my life. If there is effort or angst in it, it doesn't show; she is a marvel.

The two of us steal glances, hugs, and snatches of time alone, but it is hard to snag more than that. The house is always full; the kids are always nearby and clamoring for her attention or my attention or both. We bathe them together in her big teal-tiled tub one night, then tuck them into bed in the guest room, not because it's late, but because they are worn completely out after a day of exploring and exhausting every chance to be loved on by someone new.

Sage, Jen, and Harleigh are fantastic with them, offering up boundless energy and ideas for things to engage and delight them. Sweetie and her son, Robbie, come by, and they are equally full of fun. Nica is especially captivated by her new great-aunt. Only vaguely aware of Natalie's fame (the kids know her hit song "This Will Be" from the movie *The Parent*

Trap), Nica gives her heart when she allows Natalie to blindfold her and lead her throughout the house with the constant
encouragement to "Trust. . . ."

After Nica has roamed from room to room with her skinny
little arms outstretched, guided only by the sound of Sweetie's instructions, Sweetie finally lures my little girl outside and,
after several steps, has her come to a dead stop. "Okay, Nica,"
she says. "Now you really have to trust. Do you?"

"I think so," Nica replies, unsteadily.

"Okay, then fall back. Quickly! Just let yourself go."

Nica allows herself to tilt and before she's off her feet,
Sage and Harleigh catch her. Sweetie pulls off her blindfold
and Nica sees that she would have tipped right into the pool.
"Whoa!" she says, grinning broadly and then doubling over,
in a fit of laughter.

"See, you trusted," Sweetie congratulates her, pulling her
close. "How cool is that?"

As Nica wraps her arms around Sweetie's neck, I feel an arm
curl around my waist. Beside me, Cookie is beaming. I put my
arms around her and squeeze. Together, like Nica, she and I are
learning to trust the process.

Before we depart, Cookie throws a party in our honor.
It's an all-day affair held during our last weekend there, once
Johnny has come to town. Cookie is nervous about it, and so
am I. She'd invited her closest friends and extended family—
maybe forty people in all. Almost everyone is coming, from
Sweetie and her son, Robbie, to John's son Seth and his wife,
Stacie, to Uncle Dinky, Nat's baby brother (Freddy Cole), who
is in town from Atlanta, and his son, Lionel, and grandson,
Tracey, to Maria's sister, the infamous Aunt Baba, who acts as if
every time Cookie mentions me is the first.

I want to make a good impression. I also want to run and hide.

As if sensing my uneasiness, not long after the first guests arrive, Cookie pulls me into her bedroom and closes the door behind us.

"I hope all this won't be too much," she says, clearly wrestling with her own mix of emotions. "I wanted you to meet everyone, and they couldn't wait, so I thought it would be best to just jump in and do it one time. They've all been so thrilled by this miraculous story of ours, but now everybody's starting to show up and I wonder if you're ready. I should have asked you first, I guess. What was I thinking? I wasn't thinking. I just want to make sure you're okay."

"I'm okay," I say, and give her a hug. "I'm nervous, but I'm okay."

"You're nervous? I'm a fucking wreck! Look at me, I haven't even changed my clothes yet and they're here."

"You look fine," I assure her. "Fret not." We lean into each other and laugh.

The week before we arrived, when Cookie was especially stressed over business matters pertaining to the Cole estate and tensions with Maria, I sent her a basketful of Origins body care products called Fret Not: bath oils, lotions, and potions that claim to soak and slather your cares away. Now, "fret not" has become part of our secret code.

"I want to show you something," she says as she stands and lifts the lid off of a large white box on the floor beside her bed. Inside is a huge sheet cake that smells of butter and sugar and love. It's decorated with delicate pink buttercream flowers and homespun letters that read, *Welcome Home Caroline, Nica, and Carter.* I break down.

She takes my face in her hands, gently wipes away my tears, looks into my eyes, and says, "This is why I wanted to show it to you first. When I saw it, I reacted the very same way."

Hours later, when the cake is placed on her dining room table and everyone gathers 'round, Uncle Dinky starts to sing. *"Welcome home, welcome home, we've been waiting for you . . ."* The room is still, no one speaks, no one moves. I've never heard the song before, and his rich, smoky voice bears an unmistakable similarity to his brother Nat's. Everyone, myself included, is overcome. Carter climbs into Johnny's arms and Nica draws close to me, pressing herself into my side, both of them unsure of what is happening.

When Uncle Dinky is done, he walks over to me, puts his hands on my shoulders, and says, in front of Cookie and his son Lionel, "You know, you were supposed to be my girl, Margaret's and mine. We wanted to adopt you, but Maria would have none of it. We went on and adopted two of our own, including this one, here," he says, pointing at Lionel, "but I want you to know, we always wanted you in this family, and I'm so glad you found your way back to us. This time, we're not letting you go."

*T*he day before we are due to leave for Palm Springs, I'm in a bathroom with Carter, helping him change out of his bathing suit, when I hear the sound of familiar music coming from the living room. *My wedding video*, I realize as sheer dread rises in my chest. I throw Carter's wet suit on the floor and rush out to find everyone—Harleigh, Sage and Jen, John's son Seth and his wife, Stacie, our new cousin Pam (with whom the kids and I have become fast friends on this trip), John, Johnny, and

Cookie—staring at the television and my dad walking me down the aisle.

Everything seems to move in slow motion, the way it does when you're in the midst of a disaster. Johnny had tucked the video into my suitcase and I'd found it when we arrived but left it in a drawer at the hotel, not wanting to show it. I loved my wedding day. With the exception of a torrential rainstorm, it had been everything I dreamed of. But I didn't want to share it with Cookie. It was so lavish, so formal, so unlike anything Cookie would have done and so very like . . . Maria. I had hoped to hide this glaring evidence of the fact that my life was in many ways more like the life Cookie had turned her back on than the one she'd chosen to lead. But now it's out.

Fast-forwarding through the minister's homily, Johnny is oblivious to my distress. He waves me over and pats a space on the couch by his side. He is in his element, holding court, commentating with gusto as the video plays on.

"They don't want to see this," I say, hoping to shift everyone's attention and get Johnny to shut it off. "It's so long."

Johnny throws me a vexed look. "What are you talking about? Of course they want to see it."

"We do," Stacie volunteers, her eyes never leaving the screen. "I love it."

I glance at Cookie. She sits staring at the television, straight-backed and smiling slightly, but I can't read her expression.

The sound of the band playing "Isn't She Lovely" draws me back to the screen. There we are, my proud grinning daddy and me, the full skirt of my ivory gown swaying in time to the music as he spins me with expert grace. We fall into our Lindy, and the crowd goes wild.

I bolt through Cookie's den into a bathroom, close the

door, and sink to the floor crying. It's too much. Too much to watch me and Daddy dancing and to think of that day and our whole life together on what might as well have been the other side of the world; too much to watch this family—my whole other family—experience one of the most pivotal days of my life through a video that is already more than a decade old; too much to watch Cookie and realize how different my wedding—and I—would have likely been if I had grown up as her daughter.

There's a knock at the door and it opens tentatively as I scramble to quickly wipe my eyes and rise to my feet. I have only gotten to my knees when I see it's Cookie. She takes one look at me and wraps me in her arms.

"Awww, Little C," she coos. "I know how you feel. It's okay."

I bawl into her waist, soaking her linen top. When I'm done, she hands me a wad of tissue and takes a seat on the toilet while I remain on my knees.

"Did I ever tell you that I was a hand clapper on 'Isn't She Lovely'?"

I look at her, uncertainly, my eyes wide and still wet.

"I was!" she repeats, as if I doubt her. "In the intro to the song, I'm one of the clappers you hear in the background. I was in the studio with Stevie when he recorded it. I told you I used to date him." I am incredulous.

"That's always been Daddy's song for me," I say, sniffling.

"I see that," she replies, smiling through a few tears of her own.

I envision the countless times Daddy and I have danced to that song, the Saturday mornings when he belted it out, serenading me as Stevie Wonder's album *Songs in the Key of Life* album played in the background and we spun and dipped and laughed and clapped along with . . . Cookie.

CHAPTER 19

BLESSED

$\mathscr{I}$n a rare moment alone together on our last night in Los Angeles, Cookie places a white, legal-size envelope on her rustic dining room table and slides it across to me. The last thing I want to do is read anything, but then I see Mommy's unmistakable script. Postmarked August 14, 2004, the letter must have arrived the same day we did.

"Mommy wrote to you?" I can't believe it. Mommy is a big caller, but she rarely writes. "What did she say?" I ask, realizing that I'm unnerved to see evidence of my mom in this house. I'm suddenly self-conscious, uneasy, feeling almost as if I've been spied on and got caught in the act of doing something wrong. I fit here. The kids fit here. Mommy belongs at home.

I was aware that this visit was fraught with worry for my

parents, Mommy in particular. Just before we made the trip, the children and I spent an afternoon with my mother-in-law. As she and I watched them playing in her pool, she asked how the children were feeling about our impending visit and how they were processing Cookie's and my reunion.

"We're very mindful of trying to keep it simple, Mom," I assured her. "They're looking forward to it, but more the trip itself than the meeting. I do think Carter is struggling to understand the whole birth mother thing, and I've tried not to make it a big deal, because I don't want them bursting with excitement about it around my parents. My folks have been so great about all this, but I know it can't be easy."

I registered the change in her expression and instantly knew there was a Barbara Graves reprimand coming.

"I'm glad to hear you say that, Caroline, because it hasn't been easy—especially for Vera."

"What?" I asked, shocked. Mommy wasn't in the habit of confiding in my mother-in-law. They respected and liked each other, but they weren't exactly girlfriends.

"She doesn't want to upset you," Johnny's mom went on, "but she called me yesterday to ask how I was feeling about all this. I told her I think it's all absolutely wonderful—and you know I do—but what she said to me broke my heart." I held my breath. "She admitted that she's afraid of losing you and the kids. She's worried that you'll fall in love with Cookie and her family and things won't be the same here at home. I think she's especially fearful about the children, that they'll be excited because it's California and Cookie has other children, and everybody's so young and"—she snapped her fingers and did a little groove in her chair to emphasize the point—"hip, and there's the celebrity part of it too. You know, Caroline, children are very impressionable."

My jaw went slack as Johnny's mom transmitted Mommy's list of secret insecurities.

"This is harder for your mother than she'll ever admit," my mother-in-law said as Nica ran past us with Carter in hot pursuit, both of them oblivious and laughing. "I know you're never going to forget about your parents, and no one would begrudge your developing feelings for Cookie too. She sounds like a lovely person. But I'm glad she lives so far away, and I'm telling you all this because I think it's important for you to know how your mother feels. You have to reassure her, and you'll probably have to keep reassuring her and your dad as time goes by."

Hearing the truth about Mommy's feelings shattered me. But she never showed her cards to me directly, and I pretended not to know. Now, three thousand miles away in Cookie's home, potentially having to confront those feelings again, I want to flee. If she confessed such painful misgivings to my mother-in-law, what in the world has she written to Cookie?

"It's very sweet," Cookie says, perhaps trying to offset my obvious reluctance. She pushes the envelope a bit closer to me.

I drag it over and open it. Slowly and with mounting trepidation, I unfold several white pages that were crudely torn from a legal pad—one of the thousands Daddy lifted from work over the years. No special card, I note bleakly. No nice stationery or decorative little touches of any kind as I—or Cookie—would have incorporated. But I'm not surprised. This is vintage Mommy: direct, no airs, imperfect perforated edges on full display.

Her words, written in that lovely slanted cursive so distinctive of teachers of a certain era, seem random at first, a careless stream-of-consciousness list of recollections, told straight with no chaser, Mommy-style. But I sense that the lack of cohesiveness or warmth is also a sign of stress.

Cookie sent my folks a long note back in early June, just after my first visit to her. On a card of handmade paper with dried flower petals pressed into the shape of a heart, she thanked them for everything: loving and nurturing me, teaching and guiding me, supporting and believing in me, and, ultimately, sharing me with her. The note was written with great care, and they were touched. But I wonder if Mommy, given her fears, was also a bit intimidated.

Mommy put off responding for months, and with me and the children due to leave for Los Angeles, she obviously rushed to get this to Cookie before we arrived.

She went on for three pages, describing how, when I was an infant, Daddy would creep into my nursery with friends, aching to show them how I smiled in my sleep whenever I heard his voice. She told Cookie about the one beating I got (for throwing a book down the stairs when I was six), that I skipped the third grade, and sang (*incessantly*, she noted) before I could talk.

The chronology is off and her delivery is static. Mommy had suffered a series of ministrokes on Mother's Day eve, three weeks before Carter was born, and since then her memory was not as reliable or free-flowing as it once had been, and neither was her ease in expressing herself. These then were the memories she most held on to of me; for all that she's lost, these are what remain. She closed by recounting how she bawled at my wedding as she realized that I was leaving home for good.

As I read her final line—"Caroline has been a total joy"—I am stabbed by the realization that for her, my going to California again raised the specter of my potentially leaving her and Daddy behind. As I drive back to the hotel where Johnny, Leeba, and the kids are already packed and snoozing, Mommy stays in my mind. This trip has been another answered prayer, but I need to hug and reassure her, to let her know that no one will ever mean to me what she does, that Cookie can never take her place.

*T*he next four months fly by as Cookie and I balance the joys and demands of our nonstop correspondence against those posed by the many other facets of our lives.

By the time Christmas rolls around, we've already marked so many firsts that we've stopped keeping track. But our first Christmas is a big deal, if only to us.

This Christmas there will be no self-pity or silent mourning on either coast. This year, Cookie and I are an integral part of each other's lives, and even though the day is filled with all the same traditional fuss, food, and festivity as those that went before it, our quiet, indelible bond makes it all feel brand-new.

Late in the evening, just as my family and I return home from dinner up the street at Charise and Michael's house, the phone rings and I race to answer it.

"Happy Christmas, my darling," Cookie greets me in a singsong voice. "Merry Birthday!" Like so many brief moments we've shared already, this is another that I'll never forget.

As she describes their day, which is just getting started as ours is winding down, I picture her as she appears in photos she sent from her own birthday celebration in October. There'd been a striking physical change in her since our visit in August. Her braids were longer, thicker, and a richer mahogany color (thanks to her beloved hairdresser Demann, who was known to take her tresses from pink to purple to blue on a whim) and she had on makeup, which I'd never seen her wear. In a word, she looked stunning.

More than that, though, she appeared confident, content—powerful, even—and she looked ten years younger. Apparently I'm not the only one who noticed. In the note she enclosed with the pictures, she wrote that random people were constantly commenting about how changed she seemed, and how happy.

In the swirl of creating Christmas magic for my kids—all the shopping and hiding, assembling and wrapping, baking and faking and staying up late that go with keeping Santa alive and well—I can't say that I look or feel more youthful, as she does. But I am happier. There is a deep calm, a quiet pleasure that comes with knowing Cookie, and how fully she accepts me and mine.

I wish we could be together more often, but at the same time, the physical distance between us keeps life on the home front—especially in regard to my parents—fairly simple. In Los Angeles, I'm Cookie's daughter; in New York, I'm still Vera and Bob's only child. Internally, so much has changed for me; externally, if you didn't know what has occurred (and precious few did), you would have no idea.

Cookie is dying to hear how her gifts went over, especially with the kids. She'd sent them *The Chronicles of Narnia*, about which Carter was ecstatic. I received faux fur bedroom accessories (a joint gift with Johnny), and a beautiful coffee table book on the history of the pearl, a touching nod to the meaning behind my original name. She also sent me a second book, a small, weathered volume with a faded cardboard cover the teal of oxidized copper. It bears an illustration of a frail little girl surrounded by sprigs of holly. Obviously quite old, the book is fraying at the edges, its glued spine is cracked, and there's a stain above the author's name: Kate Douglas Wiggin, best known for writing *Rebecca of Sunnybrook Farm*. Printed within the lines of a musical staff is this book's title, *The Birds' Christmas Carol*.

It's the story of young Carol, born on Christmas day in the bustling all-boys household of the Bird family. Sickly from the start, the child is nevertheless a source of joy and inspiration: "Her eyes were bright as stars; her laugh like a chime of Christmas bells, and her tiny hands forever outstretched in giving. Such a generous little creature you never saw!"

In the midst of Christmas, on her tenth birthday, Carol hosts her final party and then drifts to sleep and dies. I can only imagine how Cookie, as a little girl herself, must have wept to read this ending and been affected enough by the bittersweet story to never forget it.

On a card tucked inside she wrote:

Dearest Little C—

Can't remember how old I was when someone put this little book into my little hands. As you'll see, this is a first edition, published in 1893! This story touched my heart and somehow planted a seed of desire in me: I wanted to have a little girl born on Christmas day. In some ways, I suspect the story must have resonated for me in terms of the loss, the absence of my mother, Caro . . . our Babe . . . This children's story is somehow connected to us. I marvel that I held on to it all these years. It can only have been so that I could give it to you now.

Happy, Happy Birthday, my Christmas Caromine. Merry, Merry Birthmas!

Love forever,
Cookiema

She instructs me in a postscript to "see page six," and I quickly identify why, as the narrative describes a choir of children singing Christmas carols outside the window of the room where Mrs. Bird had just given birth:

> . . . and so Carol came by her name. Of course, it was thought foolish by many people; and Grandma, who adored the child . . . was glad that people would probably think it was short for Caroline.

Opposite the passage, on page seven, is the portrait of a mother, cradling her newborn daughter, as they gaze into each other's eyes.

CHAPTER 20

WHAT NOW?

A week into the new year, Natalie comes to New York to perform at Rockefeller Center's storied Rainbow Room and invites me and Johnny to attend. It is an intimate performance, and she reserves us ringside seats. During the set where she introduces the members of her band, including her son, Robbie, on percussion, she swings the spotlight our way.

"I'm happy to have some more family here tonight," she announces. "That's my niece and her husband, right there in the front!" I am taken aback.

By then I'm all but begging Cookie to join us in Vail, Colorado, on our ski trip in February. I swallowed my own fear of flying, my ambivalence about meeting her, and a bit of my pride, and went to her, *twice*. Now it's her turn. Yet she keeps saying no and has a million reasons why: work, the weather, the altitude, cost, timing, lack of the proper clothes . . . she can grow that list all day. Of course, there is also the ever-present big unspoken reason: she'd have to take a plane to get there.

I offer to pay her fare and put her up, to bring her some sweaters and a warm, comfy coat, but nothing I say sways her and it finally dawns on me that nothing will.

Part of me feels angry; part of me feels taken for granted (already); part of me just feels bereft. With no other recourse, I give up and decide to wait her out.

In the meantime, I have lots of other Cole family company. In early spring 2003, Sage's girlfriend, Jen, flies east to visit a friend who lives about forty-five minutes away from me, and they spend a rainy evening in our home, eating Chinese food and playing with the kids.

A month or so later, Sweetie is back in Manhattan for the engagement party of a mutual friend. Timmie and Casey fly in from Florida to attend. It's my first time seeing or talking to the two of them since they learned the news.

There has been no dramatic downshift in Tim's and my relationship since Cookie entered my life, but there is no denying things between us are different. So I'm nervous to see the twins, unsure of how they'll behave now that our blood ties have been confirmed.

I needn't have worried. Their embrace is warm and genuine. They hug me tight and fuss over me excessively, tag teaming me in their inimitable way, talking about me almost as if I'm a pet.

"Isn't she adorable?" Timmie exclaims to Casey. "Just look at her!" Timmie takes my hands in hers and stands inches in front of me. With Casey right beside us, we form a tight little triangle.

"She's darling," says Casey.

"Can you believe it?" Timmie asks me.

"I can't," I answer, truthfully. Casey is shaking her head, united with us in disbelief.

"It's like a miracle," Timmie says, sweetly, as I nod in agreement.

"*It is* a miracle," Casey chimes in. "That's exactly what it is."

"Have you talked to Cookie lately?" Timmie wants to know.

"I have," I say. "We talk all the time." It feels weird to say this. In fact, I speak to Cookie far more often than either of them do, or ever did.

"That's wonderful, honey," she says; then, turning back to Casey, she adds, "She's just precious, isn't she?"

"Precious." Casey looks as if she might tear up. "Can you even stand it?"

I'm relieved by their kindness and by having finally faced them. But out of everyone in the extended family, I feel most awkward around the twins, whom I've known longest, and especially around Timmie, whom I once knew best. Their ardor and affection are comforting, but they also offer a rather hollow cover for the fact that we have yet to have a candid conversation. For that, I am as guilty as Timmie. I could have as easily initiated a call or note, raising all the obvious questions: When did you first suspect . . . ? What did you tell your mother . . . ? Why didn't you ever say anything to me, in all those years? But I didn't, and she didn't—as days became weeks, then months— and now here we are in the midst of a party, pretending that everything is fine.

By the time the party ends, we have broken the ice, but it's still frozen as we go our separate ways, and I won't see Timmie or Casey again for some time.

Out of everyone, Uncle Dinky—the fabulous jazz man Freddy Cole—comes to town most frequently, old road dog that he still is in his seventies, and he never fails to call when he arrives. In June 2003, he even brings his wife, Aunt Margaret, to meet me. Johnny and I join them at a black-tie party for a friend of theirs, where Uncle Dinky is also performing.

He eagerly introduces us to everyone, starting with our host, the guest of honor: "Hey, Bill, this is my great-niece who I was telling you about—Nat's daughter Cookie's girl— and this is her husband"—Uncle Dinky pats Johnny warmly on the back—"he's Earl Graves's son. You probably know him, the publisher of *Black Enterprise* magazine. You know, this little lady was supposed to be mine and Margaret's girl. She got away from us for a little while, but that's all right 'cause now we got her back." He winks at me, Aunt Margaret beams, and my heart swells with affection as it occurs to me that I've done nothing to earn theirs.

Uncle Dinky's nickname for Cookie is "Number One," Sweetie is "Number Two," and he takes to calling me "One-and-a-half." His unbridled embrace is welcome, but I can't help but question at times why he is so ebullient. I come to understand that he has a special affection for Cookie that he readily extends to me. Also, as Nat's only living sibling, he has stood in for his late brother several times through the years, giving both of the girls away at their weddings (he's quick to note he's given Sweetie away three times and "she keeps coming back"). Maybe he is subconsciously standing in for Nat again, stepping into a sort of grandfatherly role with me, even though he's actually a few years younger than my dad.

Uncle Dinky and Johnny hit it off right away, discovering they have several acquaintances in common and a shared obsession with golf. Although not close, he has known Johnny's parents for years and is tickled by this new connection to old friends. He's eager to know my parents and says so often, offering to give them front-and-center tickets to any show when he's in town. I don't know when they will meet, but Uncle Dinky will fit right in. In fact, he reminds me a little of Daddy. Funny and down-to-earth, they also have the same October fifteenth birthday, and both are the babies in their families of five.

Aunt Margaret is a sweetheart as well. When we meet, she holds me for a few moments and, with dewy eyes, whispers that she can't get over the miracle of my reappearance and all the memories it has sparked of Cookie, who had no idea at the time that Uncle Dinky and Aunt Margaret were among the few who knew she'd been pregnant and given up her child. Aunt Margaret longed to console her, but owing to Maria's demand for silence on the matter, there was no way she could.

"I felt so sad for that child," she says. "She had lost you, then her father. She was just so broken."

$\mathscr{T}$he summer of 2003, as much as I want to see Cookie, I refuse to initiate another trip to Los Angeles, even though the kids are asking to go. I'm being stubborn, maybe even childish, but I am resolute, convinced of a need to be cautious where Nica and Carter are concerned. Cookie was introduced into their lives as their bonus grandma, another loving woman in the world on whom they could depend. But could they really, given the distance between us and her difficulties spanning it?

Cookie is endlessly interested in hearing about the kids' milestones and mishaps, she exclaims over every photo, finger painting, and handmade card they send her way. But a year has passed without her seeing them in the flesh, and she has made virtually no effort to do so. Children are taught that it's good to take turns. As she rejects one invitation after another, I wonder if Cookie will ever take hers.

I ask her and John to come stay with us during the warmer months. For added enticement, I send an entire book of postcards of the Hamptons, packed with detailed notes about how blissful it will be to relax in the Sag Harbor sun. She declines. I offer up the possibility of a fall visit, perhaps just before or during her October birthday. "I used to love autumn in New York," she says wistfully. "But this year's no good, maybe next." Just before Thanksgiving, I float the idea of their coming for Christmas, hoping that might do the trick.

"Uncle Dinky plays Birdland every year during Christmas week, so he's going to come spend Christmas day at our house before his show," I tell her, hoping she'll make her move. I mean, how could she let Uncle Dinky spend Christmas with us and not be there? It turns out she can.

I'm devastated but I am also beginning to understand that the problem is not that she doesn't want to see me or my family—I know she does, and it pains her to disappoint me. The issue—which she never openly admits—is that she doesn't leave her city; she hasn't in twenty years. In fact, she doesn't leave her house unless driven by someone else. She owns her own car, a Lexus. She even squealed with delight when she discovered that I drive a Lexus too. But here's the rub: *she never drives.* She stopped at some point, and when I ask why, she gets quiet and struggles to piece together a convoluted story about a trip to the post office during which she lost her way or had a fender bender or . . . something . . . she can't quite explain.

Like the reasons she stopped flying and swimming in her own pool and venturing with ease more than a few miles from her own home, it's all murky, uncharted territory that she simply doesn't want to explore—and not just with me.

When I ask those who know her far better than I—Sage and Harleigh, Natalie, Jen, even John—no one can explain any of it. Sweetie blames an overdependence on John and laments that Cookie was nothing like that before he entered her life. The guys are mystified, as is Jen. But unlike me, none of them confronts her, perhaps because they just don't seem to care all that much. Why should they? Her quirks and phobias inconvenience them at times, maybe even frustrate or worry them occasionally, but these things don't prevent them from *seeing* her.

Beyond my distress about how her challenges impact her life, I'm increasingly concerned about what they may mean for mine. I already struggle to fly and am prone to excessive worry. If that's genetic, what else might be in store? As much as I love and admire her, I begin to fear becoming just like her.

Despite seeming to be a calm and centered soul, beneath her easy charisma and constant encouragement to "trust the Universe," she is a cool wreck. For all of its beauty and incandescent light, her life is also strange and stormy. She is alluring: her charm and intelligence are irresistible. However, as Aunt Margaret noted, she seems to be broken, still.

Our second year without a visit wears on, and Cookie and I begin talking on the phone less frequently, as our conversations (we seem incapable of ever talking for less than an hour) cause stress on both ends of the line. After all, our immediate families need us. To avoid discord, when we do talk, Cookie and I start coordinating times when no one else will be around. Or, like secret lovers, we steal away and hide the reason why. I call her from the car on my way home from work, and if the call goes on too long, I pull into a lot or drive right past my house and park around the corner until we are done.

Mostly, though, we just keep writing and thrilling over each newly discovered nature-over-nurture victory (like the fact that we both *love* ripe bing cherries and the color red, Audrey Hepburn and Willa Cather, Mary Janes—the shoes, not the candy—and sweet potatoes in any form, from baked to candied to fried to pie). Unable to explain or adequately articulate our feelings about all that we have in common in spite of our decades apart, one of us would say simply, "There you go," which we soon shorten further to "TYG."

We both venerate books and we collect quotations—famous and not. We each save our journals along with most of our personal correspondence, no matter how ancient or trivial. But for all of our so-called synchronicities, as time wears on, I also come to understand how much I am a product of my geography, my home, my world away from hers, and the people there who raised me—my people.

CHAPTER 21

STANLEY

*B*y the spring of 2004, Cookie and I aren't down to sending postcards that simply say, "Wish you were here," but we're getting close. Eventually, like milk, well-loved shoes, and jokes too often told, absence just gets old.

No longer able to quell my desire to be near her, in July I finally relent, and the children and I head to Tarzana. We go full immersion this time, staying at Cookie's magical home in the bedroom next to hers. She's purchased a new set of bright orange sheets for the carved mahogany bed the children and I sleep in together. It is the most saturated, delicious shade; even Nica and Carter comment on how much they love it. Something about waking up wrapped in each other and that burst of tangerine color every day sets the tone for the entire week.

There is no big welcome party this time, and Sweetie is out of town. But her son, Robbie, hangs out with us a lot, as does our other cousin, tender-hearted Pam, whose dry wit, and dead-on Aunt Baba imitations keep us all in stitches. Sage and Jen come and go each day, game for everything any of us wants to do, and Harleigh is ever present—something everyone insists only happens when I'm around.

Although I try to maintain the kids' normal early-to-bed-early-to-rise routine, I make a daily effort to stay up into the wee hours with Cookie and her flock of night owls. It's the best way to snatch some private time with her, and I crave those moments all the more because they are so rare.

Late one night, we find ourselves huddled together on the couch. John and the children are asleep; Sage, Jen, Harleigh, and Pam have left for the night. Except for the television, all is quiet. I can barely keep my eyes open, but not wanting to waste the chance, instead of going to bed, I lay my head in Cookie's lap and curl into a ball. She chuckles and begins to slowly stroke my hair. It is blissful and I want to savor it, but I feel myself drifting away.

"Are you asleep, Little C?" I hear her ask through my semi-conscious haze.

"Hmmm?" I struggle to draw myself back toward the sound of her voice.

"I want to ask you something important," she says.

"Okay," I mumble. With my eyes still closed and my senses still languid, I snuggle in closer to her warmth.

"Why don't you want to know more about your father?" My eyes fly open, but I remain stock-still. "I really do find it odd. Is it because he's white, or Jewish? Is it because you think he hurt me in some awful way? He didn't, you know. He was really quite wonderful, and you remind me of him in the most amazing ways."

I lift my head off her lap, let my feet drop to the floor, and swing my body into a seated position, then pause for a moment, readying myself for a conversation that is going to require me to be more alert than I am at nearly half past two in the morning. I purposely don't face her but I can feel her gaze on me as she waits for a response.

"I told you before, I have just never been that interested in him," I say, honestly. "It's not personal. It's not racial. I don't even think it's odd. It just is."

"You can't be serious," she replies, dismissively. "I'm not saying we have to find him. I leave that entirely to you. I just want you to know about him, and I'd expect you would want to know—just as you insist I must be more curious about my original parents than I tend to admit."

"That's different," I say.

"No, it's not," she replies. She then proceeds to tell me all about my father.

His name was Stan—Stanley Goldberg—and they met through a classmate of Cookie's at Cazenovia named Lydia. If her memory serves, Stan and Lydia were from the same Long Island, New York, hometown.

He attended nearby Syracuse University, where Cookie thinks he was a journalism major; he was a few years her senior. By her own admission, she was quite smitten from the moment they met. Even describing him these many years later, she appears to be still caught in his spell.

He was particularly charismatic, she brags, and also witty, and well read; he wowed her by frequently quoting the likes of Genet, Camus, and Proust. And yet, she insists, he was also unpretentious and street-smart, not that I imagine it took much to impress her on the latter front. Cookie's expression turns downright moony as she describes Stan's appearance: tall and lean with "a killer smile," straight black hair, and long lashes to match. His fashion sense? "Snappy but effortless."

Every time she says something that could even broadly be construed as a negative, Cookie is quick to give it a positive spin: "He was ultraconfident but never full of himself," she says. "He was sensitive way before the call for men to nurture their female sides and—" with a sassy toss of her braids, she laughs and lowers her voice a few octaves for emphasis, "this dude was deep." He befriended underdogs and outsiders even though, in her estimation, he was neither.

Cookie may have considered herself one of those outsiders. As the only African American student at Cazenovia (and probably the only one who arrived in a limousine), Cookie had to have been conspicuous. She said she enjoyed the junior college, but she was sure that her famous name gave her a popularity she might easily have lacked without it. While she had no shortage of friends, something about her relationship with Stan stood out—and not just for the obvious reasons.

She was thrilled to have been part of an exclusive triangle with Stan and his running buddy, Mark. With lingering reverence, she recalls them as "partners-in-cool" and was proud to be the girl they let into their tight sphere.

Unlike most of the guys from Syracuse and nearby Colgate, who were fairly preppy and conservative, Stan and Mark were notorious pool hall junkies who owned their own personalized pool cues encased in leather pouches. This impressed their peers, both male and female, according to Cookie, but she was utterly fascinated by them, especially Mr. Tall-Lean-

and-Deep. She had dined with movie stars, debuted before the president, and sailed the French Riviera, but Cookie had never met anyone quite like Stan.

Eyeing me intently, she says: "He was a caring and an amazing, accomplished lover."

"Okay, I'm done," I say, starting to rise from the couch. Grabbing my hand, she pulls me back down. I really don't need to hear more. "Cookie, I'm tired," I plead. "Can't we take this little trip down memory lane over breakfast at a decent hour?"

"No," she says.

I sink back into the couch's deep cushions and throw up my hands in surrender.

"To my knowledge, he never misled any woman into thinking he was interested in fidelity," she continues. "He may as well have announced that he was not inclined to be a one-woman man. He was about fun and being entirely with the one he was with when he was with her. He made you feel you were only the most intelligent and fabulously beautiful and wittiest female on earth. Beyond that, there were no promises, no bets, no future plans, no BS."

It's clear that she wants to do more than erase any misgivings I might have about Stanley Goldberg; she wants me to like him.

"When's the last time you saw him?" I ask. She has to think for a moment.

"The last time I saw those guys was when I played Doris in the comedy *The Owl and the Pussycat*. Mark and Stan came up to New Hope, Pennsylvania, one of my favorite cobblestone towns, to see me in it. They stayed the weekend at this inn where we were told George Washington slept. I just now realize that was a few years after you were born and I didn't say a word to Stan about you or me. He never knew."

CHAPTER 22

PARTY ON

*J*ohnny has one hand in mine and he dials his cell phone with the other as we hustle at full speed toward a boutique hotel I've never heard of called The Library.

"I want to warn Jimmie Lee's assistant that we're on our way up," he tells me. "I don't want us to run into him on the elevator."

We are racing through the bitter cold to a surprise party for a friend, in celebration of his promotion. Charise and Michael have taken our kids with theirs to see the Christmas show at Radio City Music Hall, and I would have preferred to stay home alone with Johnny enjoying a rare evening in peace.

We walk through a swank little lobby and step into a tiny mahogany-paneled elevator, and Johnny presses the button la-

beled READING ROOM. I look at him inquisitively and he shrugs
and rolls his eyes.

"You know Jimmie Lee—always with some bourgeois new
thing. This must be The Hot New Place."

When the elevator doors slide open, I expect a crush of people,
but we step into an open space that is devoid of anyone except a
female bartender behind a beautifully appointed bar lined with
candles all aglow. "Hello!" she welcomes us. There are closed
pocket doors to our left and right, but other than music, I don't
hear anything or sense any movement on either side.

Johnny helps me remove my coat, and when I turn, a set of
doors slides open and, "Surprise!!"

There are the women I love most in the world—Mommy and
my mother-in-law; my cousins Charlotte, Lucy, and Terri; my
sister-in-law Roberta; and my dearest friends—Cindei, Jeanne,
Allyson, Glenda, Valerie, and Charise, who has brought my children here, not to Radio City after all. Nica's eyes are shining, her
smile's a mile wide as she clutches Carter's hand, refusing to let
him break free no matter how hard he tries. Clearly, she has been
assigned the important task of containing her excited little brother.

They all look so beautiful, smiling and bathed in candlelight
in a gorgeous room filled with books, elegant, plush chairs,
and vases of every conceivable size and shape overflowing with
huge coral peonies. The peony is my favorite flower. I've never
seen them in winter or in this spectacular hue.

My fortieth birthday looms, and this, I quickly realize, is
my party.

I hug and thank each one of them as I take in every lovely
detail: My favorite music is playing in the background. My favorite books are scattered about. Johnny, Carter, Nica, and my
favorite women are here with me . . . all except one.

Roberta, the consummate planner, quickly takes charge, carrying out a meticulous plan in which nothing has been left to chance. I am seated by a crackling fire as my drink order is taken and I'm handed a beautifully wrapped box. Inside is a leather-bound book they had custom made. As I scan the Contents, I see they've each written a chapter for and about me. The final chapter is by Cookie. My heart races as I think, *yes!* She must be here . . . somewhere. *Just wait,* I silently chastise myself, echoing words she has used to gently admonish me in the past. *Let it all unfold. Do not miss what's happening in the moment because you're impatient for what's around the bend.*

Per her Aunt Roberta's instructions, Nica retrieves the book from me and reads her tribute aloud. Next comes Carter, then Johnny. Now, I'm told, it's time for the three of them to leave. Dinner, and the women-only phase of the evening, is about to begin.

The pocket doors at the opposite end of the bar slide open, and I'm ushered into a private dining room even more beautifully decorated than the first. A long table is blanketed with more coral peonies and shimmering silver-potted votives. A canvas runner silkscreened with the covers of books I love runs the length of the table. There is my own *Take a Lesson* alongside classics like *Beloved, The Color Purple, To Kill a Mockingbird, The Color of Water, A Tree Grows in Brooklyn,* and *The Secret Life of Bees.* A few actual books have been fashioned into vases by wrapping them around test tube–like vessels filled with yet more of those glorious flowers. I am certain it's all the handiwork of my friend Saundra Parks, from the Daily Blossom.

A three-course meal is served, and in between courses, each woman reads her "chapter" aloud. Mommy begins, and they proceed chronologically, ending with Charise, whom

I've known the least amount of time, but with whom I feel I've shared every moment of my life. The only person who's known me for a shorter time is Cookie. Hers is the only chapter left.

I hold my breath, certain she is going to appear, the icing on my fortieth-birthday cake. Roberta and Johnny would have arranged it; they would have insisted upon it. They would have not taken no for an answer.

I'm beginning to fret over how best to feign my surprise and how to act around Cookie with Mommy present when Roberta stands and begins to explain that Cookie wanted to be here, but wasn't able to make the trip.

I almost giggle. *It's a setup*, I think, scanning the space for dark corners in which I'm certain she must be hiding. But then Roberta starts to read Cookie's tribute and the truth is unavoidable: she's not coming.

Her chapter is long and winding and I barely hear a word.

"Notes for your fortieth year: I am You and You are Me ~ from C to Shining C . . . In the words of Emily Dickinson: 'We turn not older with the years, but newer every day.' So, here you are: newer and as beautiful and soulful as you were at the dawning of your birth. Here you are in a new season: lighting up the galaxies with sunlight dancing in your big brown eyes. You are here: a living, breathing song of Christmas."

I struggle to keep my facial expression neutral, even though just beneath the surface I am starting to shatter. I usually love her writing and the way she expresses herself, but galaxies full of dancing eyes? *What?*

If I had the power of mental telepathy, my thoughts would cause the earth to swallow me whole right now. What a fool I was—yet again—for believing that she'd come to me, that she'd put aside her mountain of fears and hang-ups to be here, just for me.

"Author Jill Churchill confessed, the most important thing she'd learned over the years was that there was no one way to be a perfect mother and a million ways to be a good one."

There are a million ways to screw up being a mother too, and not showing up tonight is right up there at the top. Although I desperately want to get up and run down the stairs, out of the building, and into the cold dark night, I stay seated and soundlessly carve my thoughts into the tablecloth with my fingernail. Avoiding all eyes around me, I fix my own on the glow of a single candle and allow them to fill with tears.

Mommy, seated beside me, squeezes my hand and whispers, "It was so nice of Cookie to be a part of this."

Finally nearing the end, Roberta recites a poem by Sappho that I recognize. Cookie sent it to me some time back, on a postcard.

> Thank you, my dear
> You came, and you did
> well to come: I needed
> you. You have made
> love blaze up in
> my breast—bless you!
> Bless you as often
> as the hours have
> been endless to me
> while you were gone.

Happy New Fortieth Year, my Caroline! Don't Forget to Remember. . . .

I never would.

CHAPTER 23

LET IT BE

I never told Cookie—or anyone—how I missed her at my birthday party. It had been an otherwise perfect night, so I just let it be.

At the same time, I make no effort to see her the following year—2005. I never travel to her or invite her to meet me. This is not meant as a punishment; it's my attempt at acceptance.

We are each busy with work and the never-ending demands of our separate lives. We're no longer each other's first thought every morning or top priority each day. With Nica starting junior high and Carter in third grade, Johnny and I have transitioned from having little kids to big ones. Meanwhile, my parents are beginning to tire easily. Although they remain more than willing, I can't rely on Mommy, who is now seventy-four, and Daddy, eighty-one, to take on the kids as much. They would never admit it, but it has become taxing.

Cookie is feeling a lot of pressure to keep filling the coffers at King Cole Productions, no easy task when your star hasn't recorded a new song in more than forty years. It's nothing short of amazing that they have been able to keep Nat's music so prominent for so long. His big hits are nearly as central to American culture in 2005 as they'd been in 1955; in fact, he is still beloved by multiple generations throughout the world. But the family's expectation seems to be that it will go on forever, and dramatic changes in the music industry are making that more difficult every day. Cookie is doing her part, but I wonder if the bar is set impossibly high.

It's a given that, at the outside, Cookie and I will see each other Labor Day weekend 2006 because the BE Golf & Tennis Challenge is set to return out west. The plan is for my family to make a pit stop in Los Angeles to visit, as we did in 2004 when the event was in Palm Springs. This time, though, we'll be heading to Carlsbad, just outside San Diego, to the La Costa Resort and Spa. In early March, when I mention the new location to Cookie in an e-mail, she writes back, "Maybe we'll come."

Not wanting to get my hopes up, I don't take it that seriously; nor do I raise the idea again. But in the midst of our fourth-anniversary call in March, she brings it up. "We have to start planning for your BE event in San Diego. I know we have time, but send me all the details so I can start looking at dates and possibilities. I'm going to see who else wants to go, but John and I will definitely come. We could use a vacation."

I can't believe it and don't want to jinx it, but I decide to throw caution to the wind.

"What would you think if my parents came too?"

Cookie's gasp is followed by a heart-stopping pause. Then she bursts out laughing. "Well, as long as I don't have a nervous breakdown, that would be fine . . . I guess . . . I mean, it'll take me more than a New York minute to process the idea, but I think that would be . . . amazing."

My parents always attend the BE Challenge when it's on the East Coast. Less excited about the trek out west, they have generally skipped those years. But when I raise the possibility of their traveling to San Diego and meeting Cookie there, Mommy jumps at it.

"Great!" she says. "We'll go." Daddy doesn't share even a shred of her enthusiasm.

"Come on, Vera, you really want to go all the way to California?" he whines. "What for? We don't play golf, we don't play tennis. That's a long way to go to just be in a hotel. We have lots of hotels right here in New York. I can book us a room at that hotel right down on Baychester Avenue. Lumps, what's that place—" I picture the truck stop he's talking about and stifle a laugh as Mommy cuts him off.

"I want to meet Carole," she says, that resolute tone of hers that Daddy and I both know so well making itself clear. "I'm going, Robert, and so are you." *Robert? Uh-oh.* Looking distressed, but not yet defeated, Daddy gives it one more go.

"But why?" he pleads. "Why now? We can go some other time." Daddy screws up his face to emphasize his point, but Mommy doesn't even look his way. She just goes about her business, gathering up some papers from the dining room table and walking out of the room, already intent on other things.

"Vera Clarke? Did you hear me?" he calls after her.

"I heard you," she says casually, neither slowing down nor glancing back at either of us. She is on a mission, in the moment and in regard to Cookie. There is no point in trying to dissuade her.

He turns to me, beaten. "Well, Lumps, you heard your mother. Book the tickets. I guess we're going."

Daddy has indicated many times before that he feels no need or desire to meet Cookie. He has been his über-charming self the few times they've spoken on the phone. Cookie called once to wish them happy holidays; another time, Mommy called Cookie to thank her for a Mother's Day gift and Daddy also got on the phone to say hello. But he stays squarely on the sidelines, never reaching out to Cookie directly or inquiring about her, as Mommy frequently does. If I bring her up to them uninvited—which is rare—he listens politely but offers little in the way of a response. He is happy for me—he's said so many times—but he craves no relationship with her of his own, and although it worried me at first, I'm fine with it.

I am nervous in the extreme about the forthcoming trip, but Cookie still has me beat. For the first time in two decades, she is going to leave her precious Tarzana home and the city of Los Angeles, driving about 120 miles (with John, of course, at the wheel) for this occasion. It's no small undertaking for her, and although she seems excited, she also struggles to control as much of the plan as she can. Toward that end, she reserves a hotel room for herself and John in Laguna Beach, about halfway between her home and San Diego, a full hour's drive north of La Costa, where the rest of us (including Sage, Jen, Harleigh, and Pam) will be staying. I'm not thrilled. But in four years with Cookie in my life, I've learned the futility of trying to change her mind once it's set.

My family and I arrive at La Costa and are struck by the ideal weather, acres of lush property, southwestern architecture, and expansive views that extend in every direction, making it impossible not to feel as if all is right in the world. The fact that Deepak Chopra has an eponymous spiritual enlightenment center at the resort is a bonus (Cookie is a huge fan). It's a money machine, where every prayer bead and meditation has a price tag attached, and Deepak himself is probably nowhere to be found. Still, I take it as a sign that this is the perfect place for this meeting to happen.

It's been two years since any of us has seen Cookie. Two years is a long time in the life of a child, and my children—Nica's twelve now and Carter's nine—have changed tremendously since our last visit. Although they speak to Cookie on the phone now and then, and she's great about writing to them and sending little gifts for every occasion (or for no reason at all), their recollections of her are finite and growing distant.

I've changed too, in less obvious ways. Two more years of marriage and motherhood have made me more settled and confident, if not wise. With the kids' extracurricular demands intensifying alongside my parents' needs, I've downshifted my career, working from home full-time and only on specific projects, such as the Women of Power Summit, which I love. Ironically it's been a long time since I wrote down a list of my own dreams or goals. It feels most days as if I'm all about the kids and Johnny, and my parents.

My giddy elation over Cookie's presence in my life has ripened into a calmer but still intense devotion. We continue to talk a few times a month and to write to each other almost daily via snail mail—still mostly postcards—and e-mail.

But we increasingly get on each other's nerves. She bristles at my impatience and my incessant need to know things. She views me as pushy and presumptuous (although she goes to great lengths to use nicer terms like *driven* and *assertive*), aggressive attributes that she often attaches to my "fast-paced New Yawkuh" sensibilities and boogie-down Bronx upbringing.

I'm irked by her deeply entrenched phobias and her inability—or her unwillingness—to address them. Despite her great admiration for Dr. Rowe and his particular brand of therapeutic genius, I've seen little evidence of it. I wonder about the deep roots of her internal struggles, many of which seem to trace back to Maria, or beyond.

When I describe all this to Charise, who has neither met nor spoken with Cookie, the clinician in her surfaces right away: "She's been traumatized," she says, rock sure. "It sounds like she has PTSD." Since 9/11, I knew the acronym all too well: post-traumatic stress disorder.

I never mention this to Cookie. She thinks there's nothing I don't pursue, but she's wrong. She'd be stunned to realize how frequently I hold my tongue and control my desire to charge full speed ahead in pursuit of answers to the many questions that linger between us. I don't because it upsets her. I don't out of respect. I don't because what we have together far outweighs what we lack. I don't because I know there'll be plenty of time for all that. The days before we met were finite and are done; our postreunion days stretch out before us like La Costa's breathtaking vistas.

When Cookie and John arrive, with Harleigh and Pam in tow, I'm surprised by her appearance. Her hair is big and bouncy—a very different and more artificial style than any I've seen on her before. She also looks older.

She seems equally surprised by my appearance. "You've lost weight," she says, and I know by her tone that it's not a compliment. She simply can't get over the changes in Nica and Carter, all of which she deems "divine," but I can tell she is also a bit unsettled to see what happens when two years go by between visits with her grandchildren. "I just cannot believe how much taller you are," she tells Carter repeatedly. "My God, Nica, you've become such a young lady!"

The kids hang back slightly at first, but when Cookie springs her big surprise on them, all hints of shyness disappear: She has gotten tickets for them to go to the American Idol concert in San Diego that very night. Carter's happy, but Nica is beside herself, nearly passing out when she hears the news. She's been riveted by the television show and is especially enthralled with Lisa Tucker, one of the season's runners-up. My attempts to snag tickets closer to home came up short, and when Cookie found out, she called every contact she had, determined to make this dream of her granddaughter's come true.

The concert doesn't disappoint, and the next day Sage and Jen arrive and we attack San Diego's kiddie tourist attractions in a pack that includes Cookie and John, Sage and Jen, Pam, Harleigh, Carter, Nica, and me. The long hours of walking prove a struggle for Cookie. She moves slowly, mostly on John's arm, and has to sit often, catching her breath (and a smoke) while the rest of us keep pace with the kids. I'm taken aback by her lack of energy; she is so much younger than my parents, but in terms of her physical energy, she doesn't seem it.

Harleigh stays practically glued to my side all week, and I like it. My easy closeness with him is unlike anything I've experienced with anyone. We don't have much contact when we're apart. He's sent a few letters. I call and leave messages on his cell phone that he generally returns days later, if at all. But once we are together, we can talk about anything, and do, for hours. We often reflect on the probabilities if we'd grown up together. He's sure he would've wanted to hang around me all the time, given that he sort of does that as an adult. I routinely pretend to be horrified by the idea of him as a pint-size side-kick.

"There's no question that you would have been a pain-in-the-ass little brother," I carp. "Look at you now! The difference is, I would have had no patience for it back then. I'd have given you holy hell every day and made you cry—for sport."

"Really?" he asks, cracking up. "You'd have done me like that? Did I mention that I was pretty cute?"

"Who told you that lie? I've seen the pictures."

"Nice . . . very nice. So, now you're giving me a taste of what it would've been like? You really would've been low-down and cruel to your devoted little bro?"

"I would have kicked your ass on the regular."

"The sad thing is I probably would've liked it, as long as you let me hang out."

"That's pathetic," I say.

"I know," he answers. "What's even more pathetic is that it's true."

I sometimes worry about Sage feeling left out and self-consciously attempt to create some distance with Harleigh when Sage is around. I express my concerns to Harleigh, and he doesn't say much other than, "I hear you, but I wouldn't worry about it." The two were close in high school, according to Harleigh, but are much less so now that Sage's life is totally intertwined with Jen's. The couple is virtually inseparable, sharing one home, one cell phone, one e-mail, one car—it's sweet, if a little extreme. Harleigh doesn't begrudge them that, but being a third wheel holds no appeal.

If Sage felt miffed by Harleigh's and my Siamese twins routine in the early days, he seemed to get over it quickly. He's admitted to me that he often worries about Harleigh, who can be very insular, sometimes disappearing for weeks at a time. Sage wants to rebuild his closeness with Harleigh but he is respectful of our younger brother's perceived need for space. He's glad we've become close and is relieved that Harleigh confides in me. He says Harleigh is different when I'm around, lighter and more engaged in the family.

There's an appreciable ease to our hanging out together in San Diego. We've found comfortable niches with each other and we have a great time in the days leading up to the main event, which before we know it is upon us.

At ten in the morning, Cookie calls and asks to move her meeting with my folks, who had only arrived the night before, back an hour, to one o'clock. The plan is for us all to gather in Johnny's and my suite, on private, neutral ground, before going out to lunch. I agree.

An hour later, I use my own key to enter my parents' hotel room. Mommy is up, fully dressed, and on the phone with room service, ordering oatmeal (for Daddy) and sunny-side up eggs with extra-crisp bacon (for her). Daddy is still under the covers, watching the news. He has always been thin, but seeing him in bed in just his underwear, I realize how shrunken he's become.

"Up and at 'em, Daddy!" I say, trumpeting the words he used for years to rouse me. I then draw the curtains to allow light to pour into the room. "Just look at that big fat sun!" I exclaim, as if they've never seen it before.

Daddy pulls the covers over his head. "Wow, that's a sun all right. Thank you very much, that's enough."

"Oh, Bob, come on," Mommy scolds. "It's time to get up. Room service will be here soon."

"Get up for what? What's the point of going to a nice hotel if you're not going to lounge and have breakfast in bed? Come join me, my darling. There's plenty of room!" He pushes back the sheets on Mommy's side of the bed and pats the mattress suggestively. She giggles and rolls her eyes.

"Bob, come on. You have to get up now. It's almost eleven o'clock. I don't even know how you can still be in bed. It's two o'clock in New York! We don't have a lot of time. Come on now, don't do this. You know it's a big day."

"It is?" he teases. "What's so big about it?"

I grab a pillow off a chair and swat at him, missing on purpose.

*N*early two and a half hours later, Cookie walks into the living room of my suite, where my parents sit waiting. Daddy's been getting irritable and is threatening to go take a nap when she finally arrives, about thirty minutes late even after having pushed the meeting back.

She rushes in apologizing, perspiring, and laughing a nervous laugh. John is right behind her, also looking a bit stressed.

"Please forgive us for being so late," Cookie says. "You must've been thinking, 'Where *are* these people? Will they ever get here?'"

"No problem, not at all," Daddy responds, his cranky demeanor making an abrupt U-turn. "Welcome, welcome. Glad you made it." Mommy and I are relieved to see him turning on the charm.

Tossing her pocketbook onto a table without breaking stride, Cookie walks straight toward them, locking eyes with me as she passes, smiling a smile that is tight with nervousness, eagerness, hope, and self-doubt, all of which I am feeling too. John hangs back, giving her a wide lead. Mommy smiles broadly and struggles to rise from the couch.

"Oh, please, don't stand up," Cookie says, rushing to try to reach her in time.

Mommy, with that trademark conviction in her voice, insists, "Oh, I'm getting up for this!" And, with Cookie's assistance, she rises. They embrace warmly and kiss each other on the cheek. "It's *so nice* to meet you," Mommy says, and anyone could tell she means it.

Cookie laughs and blushes. I nearly melt into the floor.

"Oh, Vera, it is *so nice* to finally meet you—oh! And you too!" She bends to hug Daddy, who remains, grinning, in his seat. "Should I call you Bob?"

"Bob'll do," says Daddy. "Robbie too. Call me anything but late for dinner!" I cringe at his tired one-liners, but everyone laughs and seems to exhale a bit. Cookie introduces John, and they sit on the couch beside Mommy and Daddy, with Harleigh and me at a bit of a distance, watching, as if they're on television.

Listening to them exchange pleasantries, I feel oddly detached, as if I am hovering outside it all. The moment is like this entire four years has been: fantastic, complicated, and surreal.

The six of us spend the rest of the day together. We eat lunch outdoors, at a restaurant on the property, under a big umbrella that shades us from the late afternoon sun. We talk education and politics, all of us marveling over the emergence of Barack Obama and speculating about the chances of our ever ending up with a black or woman president. The children and Johnny pop in at different times to say hi, and we keep things light and fairly impersonal, but as the day winds down, Cookie leans in close to my folks and says, "Can you believe this is actually happening? It took more than a minute and a deep breath or two for all of us I suspect, but our extraordinary daughter finally brought us all together."

My head snaps up: *our* daughter? I look anxiously from Daddy to Mommy, in search of some reaction—shock or offense or resistance to the idea of sharing me in that way. But they don't resist; they open wide and let her in.

Forty-one years, eight months, and one sunny San Diego afternoon since our journey began, our circle is closed.

As we wait with Cookie and John for the valet to bring their car around, who appears a few steps from us but Deepak Chopra himself. Cookie is ecstatic as she rushes over to shake his hand. If that's not a blessing, what is?

After a warm send-off, Cookie and John drive toward home and Daddy returns to his room to take a nap. Mommy and I sit at a café table facing the setting sun, and she opens a card Cookie handed to her as she left.

Dearest Vera and Bob,

Just a note to tell you what a joy it was to finally meet you. Your love for Caroline is enormous, obvious and beyond description. You are entirely her parents and I thank God for you both.

My love for you remains eternal. We look forward to seeing you again.

Always,
Cookie

"That's lovely," Mommy says, running her finger over Cookie's distinctive all-caps print. "*She's* lovely, just like you."

"Thank you," I say and hug her tight.

For the next three days, Mommy and I are together quite a bit while Daddy stays mostly in bed. He watches television, sleeps, and takes nearly all of his meals there. He goes to none of the receptions, parties, or other events, frustrating Mommy no end. He doesn't get up for any extended period of time until the hour arrives for their flight back home, where it soon becomes clear that something is terribly wrong.

CHAPTER 24

BREATHE

$\mathcal{F}$rom the moment we return from San Diego Daddy seems
to grow thinner, weaker, and more resigned to his worsening
condition day by day while my fears about the possible causes
for his declining health mount.

September flies, as it always does, with us struggling to shift
from carefree summer mode to the take-no-prisoners back-to-
school routine. Daddy makes appointments to see his internist,
his cardiologist, and his urologist but he indicates no urgency
when he schedules them, so they are spread out over the course
of several weeks. I pass the time anxiously but with plenty to
distract me at home. Meanwhile Daddy does lots of nothing
and is seemingly unperturbed, except by Mommy, who is
spending increasing amounts of time at the gym.

At least three times a week, he calls my house, aggravated. "Where is my wife? Is she with you?"

"No, Daddy. It's Tuesday. Mommy meets her trainer on Tuesdays, remember?"

"Her trainer? Give me a break." More and more, he is grumpy and frustrated, and he suddenly seems to want Mommy near him all the time. Meanwhile, she is flourishing, seemingly oblivious to—or in denial about—how he is feeling.

Trying to cheer him by changing the subject, I say, "I think I'm finally getting that dog you never got me!"

"Are you kidding?" he asks. "What, you don't already have enough to do?"

After years of mulling it over, Johnny and I have finally decided to expand our family. The kids picked out a breed—a Cavalier King Charles spaniel—from a book Johnny bought them. They are excited, and Cavaliers are said to be ideal for families with young children. Johnny, who is the most excited of us all, takes the lead by finding a breeder about an hour away, in Beacon, New York, who has a litter on the way.

September also marks Mommy's birthday. She hasn't been into celebrating her September 11 birthday since 2001. Despite my nudging and my offer to do all the planning, she refused to even do much to commemorate her turning seventy-five the year before. So I opt to throw her a surprise party in our backyard, and at the appointed moment, she is not only astonished, she is thrilled.

I'm struck that day by how great Mommy looks. She's lost weight and gained energy and muscle tone, thanks to her two new best friends, Jenny Craig and Giovanni, her trainer at Bally's Health & Fitness. She looks better than ever, and she is more vibrant than she's been since her strokes ten years before.

Everyone comments and fusses over her, to her absolute delight, as Daddy mostly sits, too thin and far more quiet than usual. But the minute "Isn't She Lovely" begins piping through our backyard speakers, he pops out of his seat, grabs me around the waist, and says, "Come on, Lumps!"

Off we go, dancing our Lindy Hop on the bluestone patio as Nica, a budding filmmaker, captures us on video. For a minute, it's like old times.

When Daddy's eighty-third birthday rolls around one month later, we have a joint celebration, as always, for him and his big brother, Buster, who turned eighty-five exactly a week earlier. On a bright, breezy Saturday, the extended family gathers in my backyard once again. We keep the mood, food, and music going strong for hours, but there is no escaping the fact that Daddy is not himself. With the weather turning cooler, he is wearing clothing he hasn't worn in a year. His shirt collar gapes and a favorite old sport jacket hangs from the sharpened angles of his frame as if he borrowed it from a man twice his size. When "Isn't She Lovely" begins to play, he jumps up and takes me in his arms as always, but after just a few turns, he lets me go and drops into a chair, winded and spent, his eyelids heavy above sunken cheeks.

Earlier that day, we'd picked up our new puppy, a tiny ten-week-old that the kids named Bailey on the ride home. She is brown and white, with huge, soulful eyes and long floppy ears; Carter is completely smitten. When he excitedly pulls his Poppie aside to meet her, Daddy eyes the little dog with ambivalence at first, peering into her crate through his glasses.

"Look at that little thing," he says, almost to himself. "Ridiculous," he mutters, shaking his head. But Bailey, who is as cuddly and affectionate as she is energetic and new, quickly wins him over. So while Daddy catches his breath, I place the pup in his lap and watch him stroke her downy fur as she licks his hand. That hand, I notice, is trembling.

Daddy had only cared about one dog in his life. King was, in Daddy's estimation, the world's most beautiful, loyal, and obedient creature on four legs. He reluctantly left his prized Doberman with Mommy's brother, Phil, when we moved to Liberia, and when word arrived via telex that King had died, Daddy was inconsolable. Although I begged for a dog for years, he refused, admitting he didn't want to risk the pain of losing another pet. It was the only thing I ever really wanted that Daddy denied me.

Whenever I raise my concerns about Daddy's weight and diminished energy to Cookie, she warns me about the dangers of negative thinking. And in response to my speculations about cancer, she snaps, "I can't see how it's in any way helpful to go all the way *there*."

She is equally put off by my opinion that Daddy's lack of urgency about scheduling doctor-ordered tests is a problem. "Has it ever occurred to you, Little C, that Daddy knows best? I can appreciate where you're coming from, but really, this is *his* show, isn't it?" She urges me to simply "blanket Daddy in positive energy and healing light," and assures me that she will do the same.

Since I'm already tense with worry, such conversations don't help. They reinforce our differences, push us a bit apart. I'm all for positive, healing energy but I am for medical intervention and tangible remedies too. Cookie, who hasn't been to a conventional doctor in dozens of years, feels differently. I know enough from our exchanges over far less potent health scares through the years—one of the children having a fever, say, or Natalie's catching a bug on the road—that this is one of her most complicated trouble zones.

She is highly critical of traditional treatments, terrified of hospitals, distrustful of the entire medical establishment, and thus loath to see a doctor for any reason. As with most else, despite her many hours logged with her shrink, Dr. Rowe, she can't explain why except to say that perhaps she was traumatized by her parents—first her birth mother, Caro, then her father Nat—dying in hospitals. Her dismal experience giving birth to me in Lenox Hill had certainly not helped. I'm not sure about Sage, but she mentioned once that Harleigh wasn't born in a hospital.

At sixty-two, she's never had a Pap smear or a mammogram or a colonoscopy. She doesn't get her sight or hearing examined or even get her teeth cleaned by a conventional dentist, as far as I know. She drinks a slimy green liquid from her personal thermos each day—some sort of health tonic she believes keeps her well. Once when she twisted her ankle badly enough for it to swell and keep aching, she iced it, slathered it in arnica (a holistic version of Ben-Gay), wrapped it in an Ace bandage, and limped around until it felt better, refusing even to get it checked by a doctor no matter how fervently the rest of us urged her to do so. We never saw eye to eye over her approach then; we certainly wouldn't about Daddy's health now, so I stop discussing it. I withdraw slightly, immersing myself in all there is to think about and do. Whether or not she wants to hear about or believe it, my family is facing a real crisis for which I must take charge. Neither Daddy, who is too ill, nor Mommy, who is near paralyzed by her fear of losing him, is capable.

A few weeks after Daddy's birthday, when a biopsy of his only remaining lung shows Stage IV cancer, it isn't a surprise.

Already a cancer survivor, he's been living on borrowed time since his right lung was removed thirteen years earlier, just three weeks after Nica was born. He hadn't required chemotherapy or radiation back then; he'd recovered fully and swiftly, no small feat given that he was seventy at the time. Now no doctor or further test results are needed for me to know this time will be different.

Daddy's diagnosis is made in early December, just as it was for Cookie's father four decades ago. He is eighty-three years old, the same age Nat would have been on the day I first called her. He has only one lung, as Nat did at his end, and it is consumed with disease.

I don't know if these parallels occur to Cookie as they do to me. I'm not sure if the mere fact that my dad is ill brings her long-buried pain over her dad's loss rushing to the surface, causing her to retract in an effort to protect herself. What I do know is that I am losing my first best friend and my one and only father, and it becomes clear very quickly that Cookie can't handle it.

Mommy can't either. Refusing to concede defeat, she begs my father to take the experimental drug his doctor mentions, even though it has no proven track record and its thousand-dollar-a-month cost isn't covered by their health insurance. Asked to venture a guess on the medication's chances of working, Daddy's oncologist just shrugs and says, "Minimal, at best. But you never know."

Daddy catches my eye, winks, and mouths, "Snake oil." To appease Mommy, he agrees to consider it, but once he's back home he reverses himself, causing her to corner me in my car one day. Normally strong and stoic, Mommy does little to hide the fact that she is wild with worry.

"Daddy has to tell his doctor he wants this," she says, her eyes pained and pleading. "You have to make him call so we can get the prescription, TODAY."

"I understand how you feel," I make my voice as soothing as I can, as Cookie's sentiments about respecting Daddy's right to do things his own way come to mind. "But how can I make him? Isn't this his choice? I mean, if he really doesn't want to take it . . ."

"This is NOT his choice," she snaps. Her eyes now bulging, her tone frantic, she is near hysterics. "This is MY choice. *I* need him to take it. *I* need him to get well."

"Okay," I say, shaken. I've never seen her like this. "I'll talk to him." But talking to him isn't easy. I'm not in the habit of telling my father what to do or being a go-between for my parents. Accustomed to their being in sync and in control, I'm unnerved by the realization that suddenly they're neither.

Daddy takes the drug and Mommy begins watching for hopeful signs, but by mid-January 2007, he is bedridden and receiving hospice care at home. He only ventures out to see doctors and—in a show of Herculean effort and love—to attend Nica's confirmation at our church in early February, and the luncheon we host afterward, even though he doesn't eat.

Daddy willingly gives himself over to the aides who come each day to bathe him and change his bed linens. But I know we've reached the point of no return when he agrees to wear diapers—one of the few concessions to his illness he'd steadfastly refused to make.

My life takes on the dull, tiring pattern every caregiver knows so well. Most days, after getting the kids off to school and running only those errands that can't wait, I drive to my childhood home on Wilson Avenue, where I anxiously escort my parents to and from doctors' appointments, fetch groceries and medicine from the pharmacy, or pass the time simply lying in bed beside my dad, with Bailey snuggled between us, as we listen to music or talk. If I dare show up without Bailey, Daddy fusses, only half-teasing; thankfully, his spirits are generally good.

Mommy's sister Joy purchases an electric razor that Johnny or I use to shave the white stubble from Daddy's face. I punctuate these grooming sessions by lavishly patting him down with Grey Flannel cologne or Calvin Klein's Eternity. Mommy always makes a big to-do over how he looks and smells afterward. From his bed, he preens and flirts with her in response. As his oxygen tank hisses in the background, she climbs into bed beside him and they cuddle, as if they don't have a care.

Most evenings I try to get home in time for dinner with Johnny and the kids, but I usually fall into bed soon after, spent. A few times a week, either Johnny or I bring the children to the Bronx for a visit. This routine becomes my new normal, as does the fact that Cookie and I rarely speak.

She continues to send a steady stream of mail, at times expressing concern and best wishes for Daddy, but I rarely respond, because I lack the time, energy, or inclination. I am consumed by my father's ebbing days.

If Daddy feels pain or fear of what is coming, he doesn't allow me to see it. Increasingly weak and short of breath, he's no longer his usual chatty self, but he is as quick to smile or crack wise as ever. They are difficult days, but they are intensely beautiful and precious as well.

One day, as Bailey and I lie beside him, Frank Sinatra croons "My Way" in the background and the mood seems right, so I ask Daddy what the happiest part of his life was. He grins and points at me.

The best day of them all? He points at me again.

"Come on, Daddy," I object, "that's not an answer."

"The truth," he says, "is simple." He smiles and I puff up inside, thrilled to have gotten the response I secretly wanted.

Saddest day of his life? The day he lost his mother and, thirty years later, his sister Iris.

"Really?" I press. "Those were harder than losing your dad," the black nationalist Marcus Garvey devotee whose dreams Daddy adopted as his own; "or Uncle Marcus," the oldest brother he idolized; "or Aunt Beryl," who cleaned her apartment, planned her funeral down to choosing the caterer and menu for the repast, and then hurled herself out of her bedroom window, snapping tree limbs in her way, and leaving him shredded by grief?

"Yup," he says, tears pooling in his eyes before spilling across his temples and into his ears.

Over the years, Daddy has always been hard to pin down. As a professor, he was a great talker, teacher, and mentor, ever ready with a proposed solution or bit of well-churned advice. But at home, when the questions got too hard or the topic too uncomfortable, he always bolted. I know that the time to ask any questions I may have about his life is now. There may not be another chance.

"Your proudest moment?"

"That's easy: your Smith College graduation," he says.

"What about Columbia?" I ask, jokingly competing with my own self.

"A close second," he says, stroking Bailey's puppy-soft head. I laugh.

"Most stunned?"

"When I crossed the George Washington Bridge into New Jersey and your mother agreed to elope with me."

I giggle again. "You didn't think she would?"

"I wasn't sure," he says, surprising me. I'd always assumed he was certain she'd agree. If he wasn't, it was a gutsy move. "That lady has always had a bad case of the goat, and she really was resistant to getting married. Hard to believe, I know, given how thoroughly irresistible I am." I laugh even harder and he joins me.

"Most frightened?" I continue. He thinks for a moment, then his eyes grow wide as he recalls his trip home from serving as a radio operator in the Signal Corps during the Korean War. When the engines of the navy vessel he was on failed, the troops were ordered on deck, handed their life vests, and told to prepare to abandon ship. While the mechanics struggled to get the ship running again, they were sitting ducks for any enemy vessels in the area, and all Daddy could think about was his mother and the fact that he could not swim.

"Oh Lord! I didn't know if I'd ever see my dear sweet mother again. On that big boat, broken down in the middle of the Pacific, somewhere between New York and New Guinea, we just kept on praying and singing that navy hymn. It's the only hymn I still know all the words to: *Eternal Father, strong to save, whose arm doth bind the restless wave . . .*" Out of breath, he abruptly stops.

"Most angry?"

Daddy frowns but doesn't speak. He looks as if he has an answer but is unsure if he wants to share it. Then he says quietly, his eyes narrowing with the memory: "What those Brooklyn Jews did to me."

"Who? What did they do?" What is he talking about?

"They took her from me."

Her: I understand. "Your first wife? You mean her family?"

He nods. We have never discussed this. Ever.

"What was her name, Daddy?"

"Naomi." His throat catches as he says it, and new tears come, for us both.

"You never saw her again?"

He shakes his head, his face twisted with a sorrow I have never seen.

"I didn't think I could stand it, didn't think I would make it," he says. "I thought about dying."

Does he mean suicide? I don't have the courage to ask. "Your heart was that broken, Daddy? You really thought you might die?"

He nods, and a few anguished minutes drift by, in silence.

"Are you afraid to die, Daddy?"

He has been staring at the ceiling, seemingly lost in thought while stroking Bailey's hair, but he looks right at me now and begins stroking mine. Time seems to peel back; I feel like a little girl again when he says, "No, Lumpty. What's there to be afraid of? I know everybody there." He smiles.

Bailey wakes up as Mommy enters the room.

Our last long and lovely talk is over. It is March 9, 2007. Four days later, Daddy chokes on his morning cereal and Mommy calls 911 instead of the hospice as we had discussed. He is taken by ambulance to Montefiore Hospital, where he lingers for a full week, as the kind and solemn palliative care staff gently counsels us to accept the fact that he is near the end.

I pass each day in his hospital room, leaving to eat dinner with my family and sleep at home each night, before returning early with Mommy the next day. I am there when he is unconscious and connected to a respirator and there when he wakes up and has to be restrained so he can't yank out his breathing tubes.

I have just arrived home one night when I receive a call from the hospital. Daddy had freed himself from his restraints and ripped those tubes out in one fell swoop. I don't even stop to call Mommy; I just run to my car and race back to the Bronx, cutting the fifteen-minute drive nearly in half. I walk into his room, braced for the worst.

"Hey there, Boop-boop," he says, laying eyes on me. "What are you doing back here?" Freed of the breathing tube, for the first time in five days, Daddy talks to me. His voice is weak and a little gravelly, but he is grinning like a Cheshire cat.

The next day, Johnny and I are scheduled to head to sunny Boca Raton for the weekend. Cookie's sister Casey is getting married for the second time, in a formal wedding that I've been looking forward to attending. Casey chose to marry on March seventeenth, what would have been her father's eighty-eighth birthday. Of course, Cookie won't be there, but Timmie, Uncle Dinky, Sweetie, and Maria will, and I am relishing the chance to look Maria in the eye at long last and say, "Remember me?"

I bought an expensive strapless green silk gown for the occasion, and I have just the necklace to set it off: a luminous strand of gorgeous coin pearls in the inky blue-green shades of a deep, dark sea, a gift from Cookie for my thirty-ninth birthday. I'd never seen anything like them. As she would say, I planned to "dress to the ninety-nines." But when the hour of our departure arrives, there is no way we can leave Daddy's side. After his sudden burst of vigor the night before, he's taken a steep turn for the worse.

The day after Casey takes her wedding vows, I plow through a bag of unopened mail while Mommy reads and Daddy sleeps. Among the bills and catalogs and several stray postcards is a package from Cookie containing a gift to mark our fifth anniversary, a delicate pair of earrings made of silver, turquoise, and freshwater pearls. Our Day had nearly slipped by me unnoticed.

The next day, on Mommy's instructions, Johnny brings Carter and Nica to the hospital to say good-bye to their Poppie. He isn't expected to make it through the night, but if he does, he'll be moved to Calvary, a nearby hospice. Knowing that the transfer will take a while, I spend the following morning in meetings at *Black Enterprise,* then go to a luncheon where my friend Glenda is being honored.

Midafternoon, when I walk into Daddy's new hospice room, Mommy is there with some of her family. I'm the only person in the room under seventy.

I kiss everyone hello, approaching Daddy last. He appears to be sleeping, but when he feels my touch he instantly opens his eyes and looks surprised, perhaps by my arriving so late. Used to my almost constant presence, he must have been wondering all day where I was.

He slowly scans me from head to toe, taking in my gray pin-striped pantsuit and hair, which is freshly washed and styled for the first time in days. He lifts his left hand slightly off the bed, curling his thumb and index finger into a small circle, and smiles. For the umpteenth time in my life, my appearance meets with his approval, and I stand a little bit taller to know it.

As I scoot myself up onto the window ledge to sit, Mommy's sister Joy suggests that we sing, and the others join her, casting about for the words to "Let Me Call You Sweetheart." I nudge them closer to Daddy's personal hit list, and we scroll through a few of his favorites with the lead falling to whoever can best recall the lyrics. TiJoy mimics Sinatra on "My Way." Mommy and I sing "Isn't She Lovely," their cousin Fiori leads on "I'll Be Seeing You," and I belt out James Moody's "Moody's Blues" and Nat King Cole's "L.O.V.E.," the only one in the room who knows every word to both songs.

Before we finish, Uncle Buster arrives and pulls up a chair beside his baby brother, adding his voice to the impromptu choir.

Johnny stops in on his way home from a business trip. With his gregarious personality and tendency to joke around even more in sensitive situations, Johnny can sometimes be like a bull in a china shop. But he enters the room with quiet, deliberate care, gently kissing Mommy hello and remarking how pleasant Calvary and its staff are. He gives Uncle Buster a warm handshake and pulls in close for a slight hug, then he places his large hand on top of Daddy's and says, tenderly, "Hey, Pop, how are you feeling?"

Watching the whole scene, I choke up and have to look away. After talking quietly with Daddy for a few minutes, Johnny comes over and wraps me in his arms.

"How are you?" he whispers as I sink my face into his broad shoulder, more grateful for his presence than I can ever remember being. I shake my head, knowing that if I attempt to speak, I'll lose it. He just keeps holding me, the perfect answer to my unspoken need. "I'm going to get the kids and bring them," he says after a while. I nod, still secure in his arms, not wanting to let him go.

After Johnny and the others leave, I join Mommy at the foot of the bed, and she, Uncle Buster, and I chat softly as Daddy listens. Suddenly Daddy's breathing becomes ragged. We continue to talk as small beads of perspiration appear on his brow. Mommy dabs them with a tissue and strokes his forehead gently as she begins to hum a familiar tune. Uncle Buster is holding his hand as Daddy strains to breathe; each agonizing gasp appears shallower and slower than the last.

Breathe, Daddy, breathe! I urge him in my mind. As I imagine the words, I hear Cookie's voice: "Breathe, my darling," she'd say to me whenever I was stressed. "Just breathe."

Do they realize what's happening? I wonder as I push hard against the panic that is rising in my chest. *This is it.*

Time seems to slow as it does in the midst of a catastrophe like a car crash or an earthquake. I manage to race from the room to retrieve a nurse, stammering anxiously, "It's my father. . . I'm not sure . . . I think . . . he's expiring."

I know the nurse can't stop what is happening, and wouldn't, even if he could. People go to hospices to die, not to be saved.

So I sit at the foot of my father's bed and watch helplessly as his brow relaxes and he takes his final breath, his jaw locking in an open position when he can breathe no more. Despite the months and weeks of decline and preparation, of time together and hugs good-bye, I'm not ready.

The nurse takes his blood pressure, which has been high all my life. "Oh no . . ." I hear Mommy moan. "No . . ." she cries, still wiping his face with her tissue. Uncle Buster's chin drops to his chest; his shoulders slump and begin to shake. Unable to bear their grief, I turn to glance out the window, to make sure the world is still there and not splitting apart. What I see is the last pale glow of a pink and saffron sunset as I realize the next day will be the first of spring.

CHAPTER 25

THE HOLE

*M*y parents planned for this inevitability. They had wills and beneficiaries, a cemetery plot, and multiple insurance policies. My mother owns her home and car; she has friends and family who love her; she has her gym memberships and bridge club, good neighbors and cable television. What she lacks is a basic understanding of how to go on without her husband, and I am at a loss for how to help her.

In the days after Daddy dies, she suddenly appears smaller, moves more slowly, and often seems vacant and lost. Watching her, I find it hard to believe how carefree and vibrant she was on her last birthday. In the few months since, she seems to have aged by years.

It is three weeks before their fiftieth wedding anniversary, and she suddenly finds herself waking alone, eating alone, existing day and night, alone. I come by, others visit, but she now lives by herself in the house they shared for nearly all those years. There is no one to cook for, shop for, or share an interesting article with; no one to fuss over, laugh with, or hug. There is no one to take out the garbage or screw in the lightbulbs or call out to when the doorbell rings and she's in the bathroom. Mommy is suddenly contemplating each moment, each day, and the vast, open-ended future alone for the first time in her entire life. How does one do that? I have no clue.

Unsure how to go on without him myself, I just keep moving, scratching items off an endless to-do list. Each day I reserve a few hours to spend organizing his den, a small room off the living room that's a mess, overrun with books, old mail, and boxes destined for the Salvation Army that never found their way out the door. It's not as if this is out of the ordinary; Daddy's den was always a wreck. He would chide Mommy about the entropy in the rest of the house, as if that were all her doing. Meanwhile, his "study," as he called it, was also his dumping ground—a personal storage facility for stuff he kept hidden behind an always closed door.

I want to transform the room into a haven for Mommy, a place of comfort and good memories on display, attractive and inviting enough for her to enjoy, with the doors opened wide. But first I have to clean it.

Daddy was a pack rat. Both my parents were. The clutter of our house had always embarrassed me to the point where I rarely invited friends over. But now I'm grateful that he never threw anything away; I finger coins and stamps he saved from his travels throughout Africa and Europe and I read what appears to be every letter he received from family members while living overseas. I find a tin box full of journals written during his boyhood on Dawson Street in the South Bronx, a large scrapbook of my published articles, and seemingly every greeting card and handmade note I ever gave him. Each hour spent in his den, which still smells of his cigarettes and old books, offers me solace and joy as I thrill to each newly discovered artifact of his long life.

One afternoon I dislodge a small worn manila packet from the back corner of his deepest desk drawer. Inside are old photographs, handwritten letters, and an ancient black leather billfold with faded gold initials embossed in the lower right hand corner: *N.C.* I open it to find the photo of a young woman posing on a swing, looking straight into the camera with a broad smile. I extract the photo from its sleeve and flip it over. In a neat, scrolling script, it says, "Sept. 1, 1947, at Camp Boiberik." According to the yellowed identification card, filled out in the same hand, it's Naomi Schwartz, 1415 Forty-eighth St., Brooklyn. I close the wallet and stare at its monogram: N.C. is Naomi Clarke, Daddy's first wife.

Along with the billfold, the packet contains photos from their small wedding, three-by-five-inch black-and-white images of Naomi with orchids pinned to the shoulder of her shiny white dress; of her with my grandmother Drusilla, smiling; of Daddy laughing with Uncle Buster and his buddy Al Hampton, my godfather; and of Daddy and Naomi waving good-bye through the rear windshield of a car. They all look so happy.

It appears as if the party took place at my grandparents' apartment on Dawson Street. Everyone in attendance is recognizable as family or a close friend; only the bride and another woman, also white, are unknown to me.

There are two letters. Crudely written in pencil on scraps

of paper, one is an emotional appeal to Naomi from her father, Louis ("I write this letter to you not only with pails of tears running down my face, but blood . . ."), begging her not to detach herself from him and the rest of her family. The other is an old-fashioned air mailer addressed not to my dad, but to Esmerelda Powlis, his best friend Joey's wife. Dated March 1, 1952, it was sent from Tel Aviv, Israel:

> Have you seen much of Bob? How is he getting along? I'm sure that by now he has become accustomed to the way things are, and can only remember me as the Naomi who caused him so much pain and suffering, and not as the Naomi whom he loved so much, and who loved and still loves him terribly. Soon the parties, dances, bridge sessions, boat rides, etc. will cause him to forget all this unhappiness, and I'm sure that he will soon find another girl and will fall in love with her, and then I will just be an unpleasant dream that he once had. As for me, I just exist from day to day. It's amazing how a person goes on living, even after they decide that there is nothing left to live for.

Daddy was forced to relinquish Naomi against his will, just as Cookie had been made to do with me. The thought of Daddy's tears as he spoke of wanting to die without Naomi and the anguish in Cookie's account of giving me up wash over me as in my own raw and crushing grief I come to understand: the agony of certain losses never ends.

*C*ookie e-mails each day. I respond sporadically and briefly. She leaves messages and I call her back at times when I know she won't answer. Postcards keep coming in pairs, in packs, incessantly, as they have for years. The deep double-wide file drawer in my home office is nearly out of space. For the first time, I begin to toss cards into the drawer unread. I have so many postcards and so little *her*.

In five years I've seen her five times—and always on her terms and in her neck of the woods. I'm tired of it and she knows it. That much is clear when I receive this e-mail just before Mother's Day:

There must be reasons for why things are the way they currently are and why each of us feels the things we feel. These are interesting obstacles to overcome. It's a grand opportunity for us all. What do we need to do to make it better?

Everything seems to get so convoluted at times. Do we have the skills, the compassion, the wisdom to gracefully, intelligently handle it?

I'm down to "take a lesson" or two or ten thousand. I'm down to pick myself up and start all over again, every second or every minute of each day. We need to remember this: no matter how many false starts or missteps, it's all a profound learning experience and the Creator is in every detail. . . .

I read about a man who described himself as a pessimist and his wife as such an eternal optimist that she eventually rubbed off on him. He said she could walk into the house, discover a pile of shit in the middle of the living room, and joyously say, "Wow! Who got us a pony?"

Hopefully our love will see us through and we will joyously prevail. I am ever the optimist.

Keep the faith,
C.

"Who got us a pony?" I can't stop laughing (and this time it's not to keep from crying). Part of me wants to keep my heels dug deep and my misery and frustration at full tilt. But the truth is I am sick of myself, and I know that none of it is going to do any of us any good. It's not going to bring Daddy back, or fill the hole that he left, or make Cookie fly to my side and burst through my front door.

CHAPTER 26

FRAYING

$\mathcal{T}$here is a new ease between me and Cookie—and all of
us—when I spend about a week in Tarzana in February 2008,
slipping away to Palm Springs for a few days to attend my company's Women of Power Summit, then returning to Cookie's
house. We finally know each other. We get each other. We no
longer tiptoe around, second-guess, or overanalyze each other.

Tooling around Los Angeles behind the wheel of my
rental car, for the first time I have the honor of driving Miss
Cookie. In a caravan with our usual traveling team of Sage and
Jen, Harleigh and Pam, we hit our favorite haunts, catching
a movie, hanging at Venice Beach, and strolling arm in arm
through the lush meditation gardens at the Self-Realization
Fellowship Center in Glendale. In a crazy shift, we head from

there to a little outdoor spot in Santa Monica called Cha Cha Chicken where we devour spicy Caribbean fare and yell above the traffic and thumping reggae.

Heading home from the restaurant, giddy and sun kissed, Cookie rides shotgun as we peel around Topanga Canyon's hairpin curves. The radio's blasting, and with the windows and sunroof all open, it's the next best thing to being in a convertible. With one arm hanging out the window, I'm snapping my fingers and belting out a tune with Whitney Houston when Cookie turns to look squarely at me over the top of her round, wire-rimmed sunglasses, her mouth agape.

"What?" I demand, knowing full well what she's thinking. I drive fast; her dad was known for being a speed demon too.

"Day-um!" she shouts, stretching the word *damn* into two fully enunciated syllables. "Isn't this your first time driving on this crazy-ass road?"

I nod, grin, and gun it. She throws her head back, laughing hard. "Well, you sure don't act like it," she yells above the noise. "I'm impressed."

"Hey, we got places to go," I say. "We can't be messing around, taking our time. Life is short."

"My funny, fearless daughter," she says, shaking her head and reaching to gather my flying tresses from in front of my face. "You are too much for words."

The angle of the setting sun, the pull of the wind whipping through our hair as we race through the scenic canyon, Cookie's full-throttle laugh, and that sweet, carefree feeling that comes with knowing you are absolutely loved for exactly who you are . . . the whole trip felt like that, effortless and blessed.

As I pack for the journey home, she surprises me with a parting gift: a tiny amber pearl on a golden chain, wrapped in clear cellophane tied with a pale yellow bow made of tulle. It's the latest in a collection of pearls she's given me over time; their touching symbolism is never lost on me. Her note, written on a postcard, says, "For my little C, with a million thanks for these amazing days and with all my love, your CCma."

I leave with a deep sense of peace and promise. All the honeymoon-is-over angst is behind us. We have ripened, individually and as a pair. We are a natural. We are good.

What we share has become central to us both. We cherish and desire it, protect and cling to it, but we no longer try to dissect, label, or explain it. There's no need. Anyway, we agree that if we tried, no one else would understand. Yet it's not lost on me that although I've accepted what we didn't have— and can never have—I'm not sure Cookie does, or ever will. She continues to feel she was robbed. The vantage points of a mother and child are never the same.

Days after I return to New York, Cookie calls, upset. Sweetie is in New York too, and she's been hospitalized. In town to promote her new album, after a few brief appearances, she took ill. I offer to go to her—she's in Lenox Hill, where I was born—but Cookie discourages it.

"I'm not sure she wants visitors," she says. "She needs rest. They're running tests, still trying to figure out what's happening." She sounds more anxious than I have ever heard her. While she is vague about Sweetie's symptoms, without question she is terrified. "I told Sweetie not to make this trip," she says. "She's been running around too much and too fast, like she always does. I begged her to stop."

Cookie had been fretting about Sweetie on and off for a while, but Sweetie was always on the move, and fretting was Cookie's way, so I'd thought little of it. Until now.

I feel close enough to Sweetie to visit her regardless of what Cookie says. In fact, it occurs to me that if she is that ill, it would be odd if I *don't* go. I can sit in for Cookie and report back to her. In that way, I can help comfort them both; it's so obvious to me that this is what I should do. But Cookie is insistent that Sweetie's close circle of local friends has her in hand. She is almost frantic in her assertion that I *not* go. She also mentions a concern about "protecting Sweetie's privacy" and says something akin to "the fewer people around the better." I know it isn't her intention, but Cookie's choice of words and her insistence that I stand down make me feel like an outsider. It stings a little. Still, not wanting to overstep my bounds, I honor her wish that I not go see her ailing sister.

Cookie gives me daily updates on Sweetie's condition, which grows worse. I learn she had recently been diagnosed with hepatitis C and was receiving chemotherapy to treat it. The chemo damaged her kidneys so badly they are failing. It looks as if she will now need dialysis and might ultimately require a kidney transplant. The news is shocking, and until now Cookie has kept it from me.

Cookie is at her wit's end, but during the weeks that Sweetie convalesces in New York—first in the hospital and then at the home of close friends in Brooklyn—Cookie never once suggests that she might fly to New York, and she never changes her mind about my going to see Sweetie. Her reaction is beyond my ability to grasp entirely, but it affirms what I have come to see as an enormous difficulty in dealing with illness.

Cookie often quotes Don Miguel Ruiz's *The Four Agreements*, which she'd been introduced to by Sage. She reads and rereads it, studies it, and tries hard to embody its principles, convinced they are the key to the contentment and serenity she is after.

The Agreements are so simple: be impeccable with your words; don't take anything personally; don't make assumptions; always do your best. We discuss them often. They make so much sense. The second is the most challenging for me. From our very first conversation, I personalized everything. Now it is finally clear that Cookie's inability to fly has nothing to do with me. In fact, that phobia remains impassable for her *in spite* of my existence. Now, it is keeping her from Sweetie despite what I know for sure: Cookie wants nothing more than to be by her sister's side.

Maybe that's why she doesn't want me to visit her; perhaps my being with Sweetie at such a critical moment will only compound the anguish Cookie feels because of her inability to do the same.

After several weeks, Sweetie is finally well enough to go home to Los Angeles. She remains sick but unstoppable. Picking up where her tour left off, she is the personification of the old entertainment industry credo: *the show must go on.* I observe from my safe home base, flabbergasted, as Sweetie gets dialysis in parts of the globe where most people wouldn't get a pedicure. Cookie wrings her hands and chews her little sister out regularly, begging her to slow down, take a break, seek alternative treatments. Sweetie waves Cookie off and keeps doing her thing; apparently she trusts the universe in a way that Cookie often touts, but has not actually mastered.

Months go by and Cookie's mounting stress becomes increasingly apparent. It's not just Sweetie she's fretful about; it's everything. She admits facing steep, maybe insurmountable, challenges on multiple fronts. The business, her personal finances, and her relationship with John are all fraying, and she confides her fear that she may be unable to repair any of them in a way that truly satisfies. She begins to talk about retiring and the need to take time off. I listen and encourage her to make the changes that will give her some much-needed relief, but I know it's just talk, as every bit of time and energy she has is expended trying to make it all right. I know too that, over and above the rest, what she wants most is for Sweetie to be well, and whatever the range of her powers may be in the other areas plaguing her confidence, that's one thing that she just can't fix.

CHAPTER 27

TOO FAST

*L*ate afternoon on the day before Mother's Day 2009, the phone rings in my car. I am zipping north on the New Jersey Turnpike, heading home from a girls' night out in Atlantic City.

I smile when the caller's name appears on my phone: Harleigh. It's been weeks since I called him, but what else is new?

"I don't believe it," I declare into the open air of my Volvo. "Look who finally decided to call me back!"

"I know," he says, in his deep, lush voice. "I'm sorry. I only wish I were calling you back just to shoot the breeze. I'm actually calling with some difficult news." My grin vanishes. "Mom is quite ill."

I know before he says it: cancer.

"It isn't clear what type or, I guess, where it originated,"

Harleigh says, proceeding to explain that it has already invaded several of her organs—lungs, colon, liver, pancreas. Fighting to contain my reflexive terror, I instantly confront what Harleigh and the others are still hoping isn't the case: this is as bad as bad can be.

Cookie was feeling poorly the entire week, he says, growing worse each day: pain in her back, in her stomach, her head, pain that made her finally take to her bed, her legs swollen and aching so badly that she moved from her own room to the one I slept in whenever I visited, to the bed with the bright orange sheets, its mattress the only one she could bear.

She'd applied all of her arnica and other natural salves and balms. She'd called in her homeopath, Sharon; she religiously drank her organic green gook and other naturalistic tonics. She read her *Daily Word* and *Science of the Mind* devotionals, and her uplifting daily e-mails from Reverend Angela. She got still and meditated and prayed to God, Goddess, and All That's Divine in the universe. For all I knew she prayed to her long-lost Babe and Nat, her birth father Kenny Lane, and her brother Kelly too. But nothing is easing her pain.

That she was finally persuaded to see a flesh-and-blood physician is evidence enough that she's frightened, out of ideas, and very nearly if not actually desperate—a lot like I am feeling now. But she's still young, I remind myself; she'll get through this. She isn't Daddy—mine or hers.

"How is she?" I ask, attempting to sound big-sister-steady.

"She seems to be handling it okay, probably better than I am," Harleigh replies. "But she's not saying much. We're trying to make her comfortable. She just can't seem to get comfortable."

"Should I come? Do you think she wants me to come?" I ask, hoping that he'll say no. I would go in a heartbeat if he said yes, but the truth is I don't want to have to go. I don't want there to be a need to go. I don't want any of this to be happening.

I want her to be fine. I want to fly out there with the children in the summertime so we can all go together to the beach and the Getty, Cha Cha Chicken, and the Self-Realization Fellowship Center. I want to rent a convertible and fly through Topanga Canyon with her beside me and the sun at our backs. I want to sleep in the bed with the tangerine sheets, walk the labyrinth in the early morning while she sleeps, and sit, cracking each other up, as we sip iced tea in her mismatched Adirondack chairs after dark, just as we have too few precious times before. I want to pull off the highway into a parking lot and call her right now, talk for hours like we did in the early days when every little thing we shared—favorite songs, poems, words, colors, meals—gave new shape and character to our impressions of each other and new life to our otherwise predictable days.

"I'm sure she'd love to see you, Sea,"—short for Sea Star, Harleigh's play on the word *sister*. Initially he only used it when he wrote to me, but at some point it took over. He is like Cookie in so many ways. "I want you to come, we all do. But I know you have stuff going on there and maybe we should get some more information first."

He's right, I always have "stuff." Mother's Day tomorrow coincides with Johnny's birthday, and Carter turns twelve in exactly one week. After that, I'll go. There's no rush, anyway. This could be a long haul.

"We should know more in a few days," I hear Harleigh say. "They need to figure out what the treatment will be and whether she'll need to stay in the hospital for it. Of course, we're hoping she can be home. You know how she is. So, hold tight and don't make any plans just yet. I promise I'll call to let you know what's happening."

"Every day?"

"Absolutely," he says, sounding more like a big brother than a younger one. "Every day."

"Okay. Thanks, Har." I so want to hug him.

"Don't thank me. My motives are completely selfish. I needed to hear your voice. I can't tell you how helpless I feel. It's hard to see her like this."

"Does Sweetie know? Isn't she away?"

"No, it turns out she didn't go to Korea, or wherever she was headed. I think she's coming to the house tomorrow."

Tomorrow, I think, ruefully: Mother's Day.

My mind travels backward as we sign off and I drive toward home. It has been a tumultuous year since our last visit. Cookie and I are both going through rough patches in our relationships. She has been talking about ending hers once and for all. She'd mentioned this many times over the years, but this phase has gone on longer than any before it.

There are also business-related stresses. Producing her father's latest release, a thoroughly modern album of collaborations called *ReGenerations*, took an enormous amount of time, tenacity, and stamina. Hopeful that it would be both an artistic and a commercial success, Cookie threw herself into it, weathering every challenge to get it made her way. Her vision was to sort of pick up where Natalie's hit *Unforgettable*, a duet with one of their dad's master recordings, left off. Matching standouts from a new generation of great talent—folks like Will. i.am, Michaelangelo L'Acqua, The Roots, and CeeLo Green (before he became a household name)—with some of Nat's other hits—"Nature Boy," "Walkin' My Baby Back Home," and "Lush Life"—the latest digital technology was used to give these classics an entirely new sound and feel. It was a bold project, and she had to fight for it every step of the way.

Capitol, still known as "the house that Nat built," was all but gone, morphed into a new music company, EMI. The new folks didn't seem to care that Nat King Cole had his own postage stamp and a branch of the United States post office named for him. They appeared unmoved by the fact that "When I Fall in Love" and "Unforgettable" were still among the most popular wedding songs of all time. What they cared about was new record sales, and they were less and less interested in creating or promoting new music using the voice of a man who'd been dead for forty-five years, even if staggering numbers of fans still loved him.

While Cookie battled EMI for the *ReGenerations* she envisioned, she also got into it with the family, a fight far more devastating than anything on the professional front. Displeased by KCP's declining profits, which the siblings shared with Maria, Tim and Casey began questioning Cookie's leadership. They campaigned to replace her with a non–family member as CEO even as Cookie went about producing *ReGen*. Maria backed the twins, Natalie stood with Cookie, who hung on but was crushed by the fallout. In an act of what she called "emotional self-preservation," she cut off communication with the twins and began talking more and more about stepping down from KCP. It wasn't fun anymore, she said. The business was so different.

She didn't care for the politics of it or the constant game playing; she despised the subjugation of artistry, creativity, and experimentation in favor of money, money, and more money; and she certainly wasn't up for a fight, especially with her own sisters, girls she had helped to mother when she was still in desperate need of some tender mothering of her own. She'd had enough of family infighting with Maria over the years. It had taken an enormous amount out of her and from her; she didn't have enough left to lose even more. But she faced a financial impediment to retiring. Her beautiful home and unfailing generosity camouflaged the bitter truth. She was deeply in debt, and her list of dependents—to one degree or another—was too long.

Her stress over these matters was intensifying. Although she rarely addressed it all directly and tried not to dwell there when she did, she had sounded downright grim in our last conversation. I tried but failed to lift her spirits, avoiding the all-too-obvious questions I knew better than to ask.

I couldn't help but wonder if I'd missed some signs with Cookie. She had to have been feeling poorly for a while; had she mentioned it? Johnny's mother was in the throes of battling a gallbladder cancer that we were told was incurable. Did Cookie stay mum about her own health so as not to compound my worries? Or had she attempted to confide in me and I'd been too wrapped up in my own life to notice? Or maybe, like so many of us women, she was overly consumed by everything other than herself.

In January she had sent an early cut of the new album and was eager for my feedback. She also requested that Nica and Carter listen to it and render their opinions too. She wanted to know if it resonated with the younger set, and at thirteen and ten they were definitely beginning to have their own strong musical tastes.

I loved everything about the album; in my opinion, it was brilliant. She'd worked so hard and it showed in every de-

tail. The cover art by Sage, called *Presence*, was a mesmeriz-
ing collage of Nat singing into a standing mike, suspended in
a night sky full of stars. Cookie fought to have eco-friendly
packaging—none of those hard-to-open-quick-to-crack plastic cases for this CD—just a tri-fold cardboard sleeve featuring
graffiti art and poetry by Escaped Crusader. The music itself
was fantastic and she was delighted to learn that her grandchildren thought so too.

Through the winter, Cookie poured her energy into planning a release party. It was to be held in March, the week of
Sage's fortieth birthday. I considered flying out to surprise her.
I would show up at the party and stay a few days, through
Sage's more low-key celebration. I wanted to support her—she
sounded like she needed it—and to be there for Sage on his
momentous day. But she sounded so exhausted and stressed
that I second-guessed myself. When I called Jen to get her in-
put, she confirmed my doubts, saying Cookie was so fried that
a surprise of any kind probably wasn't a great idea.

"She would want to be in a good frame of mind so she
could spend time with you and enjoy you, and right now she's
just not," Jen explained. "There's been so much going on. At
this point, I think she's just trying to get through all this so she
can get some rest."

"I understand," I said. "I'll wait and come this summer,
with the kids."

"That'll be great," said Jen. "She'll love that."

But when I saw the photos Cookie e-mailed me of the party,
I wished I'd gone. It was held at a gallery; all the artwork she'd
commissioned for the album was on display. Harleigh supplied
live music, Sweetie and a few of the artists who worked on
the album attended, and the turnout was great. It was a night

of celebration, of hard-earned victory. But Cookie looked drained, unhappy, and unwell.

Now here it is, weeks later, and the reasons for her appearance are coming to light. Forget waiting, I tell myself. I arrive home and immediately book a flight for the next week. I will get through Johnny's and Carter's birthdays and then go to Tarzana, prepared to stay for as long as she needs me.

Less than twenty-four hours later, when I call to speak to Cookie on Mother's Day, John tells me she's with Sweetie, and I choose not to interrupt. When I call again later, she's sleeping. The next day Sweetie calls me with the intention of telling me what I already know. She says she and Cookie had a good time together the evening before and that she's going to accompany her to the hospital for tests the next day.

"It might be lung cancer, but they're still not one hundred percent sure," Sweetie says. "We just have to pray and wait until all the tests come back." Neither of us says it but their father's fate is in our minds, and as much as I fight it, I can't help thinking of my dad as well.

The doctors spend the week poking, prognosticating and hoping, hypothesizing and examining, explaining and guessing, gauging and assuaging, and doing all the things doctors do when cancer is caught terribly late. They want to hospitalize her. She refuses. They want to start administering medications. She declines them. They tell her she is beyond a surgical solution, which is just as well, because she would have probably said no to that too.

I receive daily updates from Sage or Harleigh or Jen, John, or Sweetie, but never from Cookie, and she is never available to talk when I call. I know she is suffering and don't want her to have to muster more strength or cheer or anything for me.

So I wait—for once, I don't push—satisfied that I'll be with her in a matter of days.

Cookie is told that she needs to begin chemo. Aggressively. Immediately. She vows to consider it. Her doctors want to admit her while she thinks it over, so they can keep an eye on her and help manage her pain. She insists on doing all of her mulling in her own house, her dream home, her oasis, where she now spends most of her time in the bed with the tangerine sheets. On the nightstand beside her is a bowl molded from a Nat King Cole *Ramblin' Rose* LP and a clock made from a reproduction of the *Mona Lisa*—gifts from me, sent on special occasions during the seven years since we met. She had delighted in those quirky presents when they arrived in the mail, and I take solace in knowing that she has pieces of us nearby, even if I'm not yet physically there with her.

By Carter's birthday, there's good news—it's not lung cancer—but we still don't know the source of her disease, and the optimal course of treatment can't be identified until we do. Carter turns twelve with no call or special delivery from the West Coast, but he has too much fun to notice. Meanwhile my anxiety is mounting. I haven't spoken to Cookie or received anything from her—e-mail, snail mail, smoke signal, call—in weeks. It's the longest period of silence we've endured since we met. I can't wait to get to her; just thirty-six more hours.

But by the next day Cookie's breathing is labored and her pain so acute that she's rushed to the hospital. Sage calls to tell me they're being asked to put her on a ventilator. If they do, I know she won't be able to speak. I hear him say what I most dread: "Caroline, you need to come now." I explain to the kids that Cookie is ill and move up my flight.

As I stand in line waiting to board, it occurs to me that I no longer fear flying, nor do I cautiously wade into oceans and pools; now I dive in headfirst, unafraid.

My cell phone rings. It's Sweetie, with amazing news: she has just learned she has a kidney donor and the transplant surgery must take place right away.

"That's incredible," I say, buoyed by the good news, but Sweetie is actually conflicted; she doesn't want to leave Cookie's side. Of course she has no choice. Everyone, including Robbie and Timmie, has told her to go. I add my voice to the chorus of encouragement, invoking Cookie's as well.

"You know she'd want you to do this, Sweetie," I say. "It's okay. I'm on my way."

"She's waiting for you, honey," she says. "Get here."

I've heard other people say they knew the moment someone close to them passed away. I had never been one of those people. But about three hours into my flight, I look out the plane's window. It is clear and bright and the ride is so smooth it feels as if we are standing still, suspended out there in the sun-soaked heavens without a care. I've been silently chanting, "Wait for me, wait for me, Cookie, please wait for me." But I stop suddenly as an ache I've been carrying in the pit of my stomach all morning gives way. That gnawing mix of near-panicked-eagerness, steely hope, and dread is suddenly just . . . gone.

It's over, I think, glancing at my watch so I will remember the exact time. I know.

Cookie dies while I sit in an aisle seat on a Jet Blue flight from New York that is destined to touch down at Burbank airport two hours too late. It is May 19, 2009, ten days since Harleigh's call.

As I helplessly sink into my seat, her own sentiments, written on a postcard sitting in that file drawer back in my office at home, drift to my mind. Sent years earlier, the words stayed with me because they had the texture and beauty of poetry as she described her feelings at Spence-Chapin on the day she had to let me go:

> I ached to see you just one more time
> To kiss, to touch, to bless you
> To reluctantly say good-bye for now or . . .
> good-bye, but I won't forget you.

I cover my face with my hands and break apart.

$\mathcal{W}$e are an improbable bunch gathered in this spare white marble alcove to say a final good-bye. I have been here only once before. Three years ago, Harleigh and Sage brought me to see Nat's final resting place days after Cookie died. Looking up at his elegant crypt, marked simply with a golden replica of his autograph and the years of his birth and death, I couldn't help but marvel that he lived to be only forty-six years young. That many years plus one have passed and now Maria is being laid to rest here too.

Thoughts of Cookie wash over me and I long to hook my arm through hers as I take in the images of Sweetie, Tim, and Casey sitting side by side, my brothers locked in thoughts all their own, cousins and friends, now cherished and familiar, and my children, here to mourn a woman they never knew but whose impact they nonetheless felt.

"Cookie," I wanted to call to her in a whisper and hear her answer. But Cookie is gone. Like her adored father, she left too soon.

The years have done little to soften our searing sense of loss. And yet, so much has happened.

Cookie's beloved house was sold. I imagine it's very different now, but the truth is its spell was broken the moment she died. Turns out it wasn't her eclectic collections of art and music or her enchanted gardens or intoxicating incense that made the place so magical; it was Cookie.

Sweetie recovered and stepped into the gulf Cookie's absence created. Harleigh spent most of a year living with my family in New York before returning home to Los Angeles to move on with his life. Together, Sage and Jen managed to weather one crisis after another until things finally settled down and we all rejoiced in the arrival of Teo, their longed-for first child. Still at BE, I was now hosting a television show—a career turn that would have tickled Cookie no end. Nica would be leaving for college in a few weeks, and Carter, done with his first year in high school, was now taller than us all. It bears repeating as there's no truer truth: life goes on . . . but so does grief.

My mother-in-law died, having lived more than three years with her cancer. One month later Maria died, shortly after learning of hers. By then, she and I had long since had our face-to-face meeting at Aunt Baba's house the week that Cookie passed.

There was no emotional moment of reconciliation, no embrace or contrition or meeting of the minds. Our encounter was tense and accomplished little, except that we spoke honestly and directly, with me asking most of the questions this time. What had Cookie been like growing up? I wanted to know. What was Maria's favorite memory of the niece who came to be her first child? Did Cookie remind her of her late sister, Babe? Was Maria proud of Cookie in the end?

Her answers were clipped and mostly unsatisfying. She claimed an inability to remember much, which came as no surprise. However, with no prompting from me, she clearly recalled our first encounter when I was in college and was insistent that she had her suspicions but no way of knowing for certain that I was Cookie's child.

"I'm glad you found her, and that you two had some time to get to know one another," she told me. "It's too bad that it has ended this way, so soon."

We exchanged Christmas cards after that, with her once mentioning in a note that she expected to come to New York the following spring, and might welcome a chance to meet my children—her first great-grandchildren. A few months later, Sweetie called with her mother's grim diagnosis. Maria never made that trip and we never spoke again.

In the days after she passed, Timmie and I let go of the quiet strain that had simmered between us for so long. She was there for her mother in the end, as I had been for my dad. Our relationships with them were quite different but the unfathomable depth of our distress as they faded away was the same; there is nothing like losing a parent. Hugging each other on the evening of Maria's wake, we couldn't help but laugh at the irony: Maria lived unapologetically by a divide-and-conquer creed, but in death—"whether she wanted to or not," Casey quipped—she united us.

Now as we step from the hushed coolness of the mausoleum into the shimmering heat of a bright July afternoon, I begin to weep. Just as they were three years before, my tears are for Cookie, and all that wasn't meant to be.

Cookie died without knowing how the world would receive *ReGenerations* or that her beloved Sweetie would receive a new chance at life on the very day she passed away. She died without seeing Nica and Carter bond effortlessly with Timmie's and Casey's sweet, striking sons and without meeting Teo Lane Cole, who bears his grandmother's original surname and a familiar glint in his eye.

She died too suddenly and too soon. She left without a final glance or laugh or sigh. She left without saying good-bye to me—just as she had the first time.

How I wish we'd had more time. I don't claim we deserved more, or that life is cruel or unfair. I just wanted more . . . of her and with her, and I make no apologies for that. But what a time we had in just seven visits spread out over seven years. And what memories we made, stringing postcards across the yawning distance between us like ropes of Christmas lights.

Weeks before her house was sold, on June 7, 2009, we buried a small box of Cookie's ashes in a hole at the center of the labyrinth in her backyard and held a memorial. Friends traveled from near and far to share their memories and stroll through her beautiful garden one more time. Jen and Harleigh greeted them and accepted condolences as Sage took refuge behind his deejay equipment, enveloping us all in music Cookie loved: Sade, John Lennon, Ray LaMontagne, Amos Lee, St. Germain, Sting, and of course her ex Stevie Wonder, and her dad. Their words and melodies offered bittersweet comfort as I moved awkwardly among Cookie's loved ones, most of whom I'd never met.

It was a casual gathering with no somber black attire worn or standard Psalms solemnly read. Instead, standing in front of the deep green M-velope, as her collection of wind chimes tinkled and moaned and a scattering of hummingbirds hovered among us as if to listen in, Cookie's dear friends, the actors Beverly Todd and Dick Anthony Williams, read some of her original poetry. Carter talked extemporaneously about the grandmother who he said left a huge impression, even though he'd seen her so rarely and over so short a time. Nica, too distraught to speak, clung to her Aunt Sweetie, who, still fragile from her transplant, clung right back. Seth shared his gratitude for the woman who helped raise him; Harleigh read a letter he'd written, found among Cookie's meticulously saved treasures; Sage and Jen paid tribute to her eloquently and in tandem, as they did most everything.

When I began to speak, it was with an awareness that many of those gathered had no idea who I was:

Cookie, as we all know, loved games and she revered the power of an open mind and vivid imagination. So please play along with me as we travel back in time to 1964 in New York City on a stormy Christmas eve. Try to imagine her, wide-eyed and lovely, newly twenty years old, very pregnant, and far from home, trudging through the snow in labor to get to a hospital.

Picture her, a frightened young woman—still a girl, really—struggling throughout the night and fully into the next afternoon to deliver a child among strangers on Christmas day. No one was there to come rushing in afterward with open arms and hearts bursting with joy. No one arrived bearing kisses or congratulations. There were no flowers or flashing cameras, no stuffed animals or blessings for a long and happy life. There was no anything except a shattered young mother and the child that she wished she didn't have to give away. I was that child.

Cookie should have been home with her family, tearing presents open beside a towering tree, not alone in a city three thousand miles away, giving birth to an eight-pound baby she would be forced to relinquish and told to forget. But she didn't forget. . . .

Fast-forward thirty-seven long years and picture her again, sitting in her office overlooking this garden. In the midst of an otherwise ordinary day on the verge of spring, the phone rings, she answers, and it's me—the daughter she lost and still longed to know. Cookie was awesome; she rose to the occasion as if she'd been expecting it all along.

In just seven years and seven visits, we created memories more powerful than our losses and a bond strong enough to withstand life's most crushing blows, even this one. Seven is a lucky number—it was Cookie's favorite—and I'm the luckiest girl in the world because I had amazing parents who loved me enough to share me, and God made Carole Cole my mother not just once, but twice.

The sun set and her friends and family headed home. As they said good-bye, each was given a memento: a postcard with an arresting image of Cookie taken not long after I was born. We inscribed it with the last words she left us, written in her unique all-caps print on a small chalkboard two days before she died. As a nod to a biblical verse, she wrote: BE STILL AND KNOW THAT I AM. Barely visible, around her wrist, is a bracelet strung with pearls.

Be still
and know that
I am

PHOTO CREDITS

$\mathcal{T}$he images at the start of the chapters are all self-explanatory and courtesy of the author unless specifically noted below.

The Gift: Spence-Chapin's original location, postcard courtesy of Spence-Chapin Family Services

Lucky Me: Daddy, Mommy, and Caroline, first day home, January 29, 1965

Telling: Caroline on her parents' phone in the Bronx circa 1986

The Call: Mark Your Calendars! postcard, courtesy of Spence-Chapin

Mixed-Up: Mommy, Daddy, and Caroline in Yvonne Jean Jacques's (Aunt Vonnie's) kitchen, summer 1977

Planted: Baby cactuses beside Cookie's pool, fall 2002

Royalty: Ink portrait of Charlotte Hawkins Brown by Carole Cole

Far Away: Cookie (second from left) at Cazenovia College, May 1964

Mamaria: Maria Cole and Cookie on a yacht in Saint-Tropez, circa 1960

Careful: The first picture Cookie ever sent, taken in October 1965

Believe: Cookie's house, Tarzana, June 2002

Fret Not: Johnny, Caroline, Carter, and Veronica in Cookie's house, August 2002

Blessed: Caroline and Mommy shortly after her strokes, October 1997

What Now?: Natalie (Sweetie), Cookie, Caroline, Freddy Cole (Uncle Dinky), in Cookie's kitchen, August 2002

Party On: Table setting at my fortieth-birthday celebration, December 2004

Let It Be: Postcard illustration of La Costa Resort and Spa

Breathe: Bailey Cuddles Graves, circa 2008

The Hole: Daddy behind the waving hand of Naomi Schwartz

Fraying: Cookie and Sweetie

Too Fast: "Dog on Route 66," postcard, courtesy of photographer Shellee Graham

Epilogue: Cookie's labyrinth, June 2009

ACKNOWLEDGMENTS

$\mathscr{B}$oth of my mothers impressed upon me the importance of writing detailed thank-you notes. This book is essentially that: an expression of undying gratitude for my parents Carole Cole and Vera and Robert Clarke. I must also thank Janet Hill Tolbert and DeWayne Reed, who championed this project for years before there was ever a word on a page. Their safety nets of steadfast cheer, care, and prayer caught me in free fall many a time.

Without Ruth Mills, there would have never been a proposal, let alone a finished book. Generous, genuine, and skillful, Ruthie connected me to my fierce and fabulous agent, Jane Dystel. Jane, in turn, led me to the deft and dedicated Dawn Davis, who purchased this book on behalf of HarperCollins and massaged it into being, and Maya Ziv, who gamely shepherded it across the finish line.

Heartfelt thanks to the wonderful Jill Krementz for a photo shoot I'll never forget, proofreader extraordinaire Aimery Dunlap-Smith, and my trusty computer guru Scott Chen, who responded with swift cheer to every frazzled SOS.

My fairy godmother Ann Douglas was ever present, ever wise, willing, and compassionate. Also always in my corner with whatever was needed—a nudge, a hug, some grub—were Ndela Edwards, Angelique Frances, Roberta Graves, Jeanne Howell, Charise Littlejohn, Allyson Moore, and Anthony Toran. Natalie Cole, Jennifer Vylasek, Barbara Mummers, Gini Booth, Beverly Todd, and Oz Scott opened their treasure troves of memories wide and gave unconditionally and without hesitation. My mother-in-law, Barbara Graves, read early copy in her ebbing days; her unwavering belief in me sustains me still.

To my cheering section at *Black Enterprise*, thank you for the support and flexibility that enabled me to complete this. Deepest gratitude to my Clarke, Cole, and Graves families and to every person named in this book for being a part of Cookie's and my journey.

Finally, to Veronica, Carter, Johnny, Sage, and Harleigh, for selflessly and bravely embracing this story as it unfolded and encouraging me to share it, I offer my gratitude with all the awe and humility a heart can hold. As Cookie would say, *Love reigns.*

ABOUT THE AUTHOR

𝒜n award-winning journalist, CAROLINE CLARKE has spent most of her career at *Black Enterprise,* where she has held a series of key positions. Previously, she was a staff writer at *The American Lawyer* and several newspapers. She holds a bachelor's degree from Smith College and a master's degree with honors from Columbia University Graduate School of Journalism. A passionate adoption advocate, she lives in New York with her family.